JAPANESE EXPORTS AND FOREIGN DIRECT INVESTMENT

This book addresses the question of how competition takes place in international manufacturing industries. There is a large catalog of literature about how large firms, *oligopolists*, compete in domestic markets and about how broadly competitive processes determine international trade. However, the intersection between these two areas is missing, and we know little about how oligopolists interact with each other across international boundaries. This book examines patterns of rivalry among firms from different countries across national boundaries and their influences on international trade and investment. Using various data on Japanese firms in manufacturing industries from the late 1950s through the early 2000s, the first part of this book presents a series of empirical analyses that examines effects of market structure on export pricing, linkages of domestic and foreign market structures on trade performance, and patterns of oligopolistic interactions among firms from different countries involved in exporting. The second part of this book deals with the impact of strategic interactions on foreign direct investment. In particular, this book examines bunching in foreign direct investment and strategic interactions in intra-industry cross-market foreign direct investment, and the effects of these actions and interactions on entry patterns and postentry performance.

Hideki Yamawaki is Professor of Management in the Peter F. Drucker and Masatoshi Ito Graduate School of Management at Claremont Graduate University. From 1990 to 1997, he was Professor of Economics at the Université catholique de Louvain in Belgium. From 1982 to 1990, he was Research Fellow at the Wissenschaftszentrum Berlin für Sozialforschung in Germany. In the past 20 years, he has published many articles in professional journals and volumes in the fields of industrial organization, international trade and investment, and international business strategy. His research has focused on examining the behavior and performance of U.S., European, and Japanese corporations in international markets. Professor Yamawaki has served as a consultant to the European Commission, the World Bank, and the OECD. In 1995, he was appointed a member of the Economic Advisory Group at the European Commission. He has served as an associate editor of the *Review of Economics and Statistics* and as Managing Editor of the *International Journal of Industrial Organization*.

Japanese Exports and Foreign Direct Investment

Imperfect Competition in International Markets

HIDEKI YAMAWAKI

Claremont Graduate University, California

CAMBRIDGE
UNIVERSITY PRESS

CAMBRIDGE
UNIVERSITY PRESS

32 Avenue of the Americas, New York NY 10013-2473, USA

Cambridge University Press is part of the University of Cambridge.

It furthers the University's mission by disseminating knowledge in the pursuit of education, learning and research at the highest international levels of excellence.

www.cambridge.org
Information on this title: www.cambridge.org/9780521871921

First published 2007
First paperback edition 2012

A catalogue record for this publication is available from the British Library

Library of Congress Cataloguing in Publication data

Yamawaki, Hideki.
Japanese exports and foreign direct investment : imperfect competition in international markets / Hideki Yamawaki.
p.   cm.
Includes bibliographical references and index.
ISBN-13: 978-0-521-87192-1 (hardback)
ISBN-10: 0-521-87192-1 (hardback)
1. Japan–Commerce.   2. Exports–Japan.   3. Competition, Imperfect–Japan.   I. Title.
HF3826.5.Y345   2007
382.095′2 – dc22   2006039234

ISBN 978-0-521-87192-1 Hardback
ISBN 978-1-107-41052-7 Paperback

To my mother
for many reasons

Contents

Tables

Figures

Preface

I owe many people debts of gratitude for their help in the development of this book. Certain parts of this book were written and published in various forms while I was at the Wissenschaftszentrum Berlin from 1982 to 1990 and Université catholique de Louvain from 1990 to 1997. I benefited greatly from the research opportunities and the intellectual environments that these institutions provided. I am particularly indebted to Paul Geroski, Alexis Jacquemin, Dennis Mueller, Hiroyuki Odagiri, F. M. Scherer, and Leonard Weiss for their criticisms and suggestions on various papers that are now integrated in this book. I thank David Audretsch, Manfred Fleischer, Elizabeth de Ghellinck, Christian Huveneers, Joachim Schwalbach, and Leo Sleuwaegen for their advice and encouragement.

José de la Torre, Marvin Lieberman, and Mariko Sakakibara at UCLA's Anderson Graduate School of Management offered many insights and useful comments on certain parts of this book. I thank my colleagues at the Peter Drucker and Masatoshi Ito Graduate School of Management at Claremont Graduate University for their moral support and encouragement.

Over the years, I have had many opportunities to present the material in this book in various forms at seminars and conferences. I extend my thanks to Nicola Acocella, Luca Barbarito, Jean-François Hennart, Fukunari Kimura, Bruce Kogut, Franco Malerba, Jean-Louis Mucchielli, Yoko Sazanami, and Klaus Zimmermann for such opportunities and their valuable comments.

I would like to thank my coauthors of various papers for allowing me to use certain parts of the results of our joint research in this book: parts of Chapter 1 are the result of joint research with David Audretsch and Leo Sleuwaegen; parts of Chapter 5 are the result of joint research with David Audretsch; and parts of Chapter 9 are the result of joint research with Shigeru Asaba. I also want to thank the *Review of Economics and Statistics*, the *International Journal of Industrial Organization*, and the *Journal of Industry, Competition, and Trade* for granting me permission to include parts of my articles in Chapters 4, 5, 7, and 8 in this book. I would like to thank the three Cambridge University Press referees for their insights and useful suggestions on an earlier draft of this book.

I was fortunate to receive stimulation and direction from many great teachers in my student days many years ago. I owe a special debt to Masu Uekusa, whose undergraduate seminars at Keio University in the mid-1970s exposed me to the field of industrial organization for the first time and gave me a lasting impression of the importance of empirical research in industrial organization. Fumimasa Hamada showed me the importance of time-dependent factors in industry and firm analysis. Robert Fogel inspired me to introduce historical perspectives into the empirical analysis of market structure and behavior. Michael Spence showed me the importance of the industry case approach in empirical research of strategic behavior in markets.

My greatest intellectual debt is to Richard Caves, whose help and encouragement extend back to my first days in graduate school in the United States. He read almost all of the major articles I wrote from graduate school through the 1990s, shared his numerous insights and invaluable suggestions, and showed me numerous research avenues at the intersection of the fields of industrial organization and international economics.

The idea of writing this book first came when I encountered a book, *Japan in the Beginning of the 20th Century* (published by the Department of Agriculture and Commerce, Japan, in 1904) in the main library of the Claremont Colleges few years ago. In its preface, Haruki Yamawaki wrote, " the knowledge which the world possesses about things Japanese is at best superficial, . . . chiefly because reliable publications . . . giving a succinct account of the economic and other affairs of Japan have not existed." In the past 60 years, a vast amount of research on Japan's economy, industry, and business has been conducted by many researchers and has created a large body of knowledge about Japanese industry. This book is intended to make a small contribution to this end.

Hideki Yamawaki
Claremont, California

1

Introduction

How do firms compete in international markets? This question is a central concern of modern corporations that operate across national boundaries. Despite its importance, it is only in the past 25 years that economists have addressed this question and offered new theoretical approaches. The field of international economics was the likely candidate to address such a question. Central to the concerns of conventional trade theory, however, was explaining trade patterns by differences among countries in their relative endowments of factors of production. The theory of international trade has depended on the assumption of purely competitive markets. The questions of how firms compete and the effects of interfirm rivalry in international markets were only infrequently addressed within a conventional framework of international economics.

The study of industrial organization, by contrast, addresses explicitly the question of how firms are organized and how they compete in imperfect markets. It does not depend on the premise of a perfectly competitive model but, instead, takes into account real-world frictions such as imperfect information, barriers to entry of new firms into a market, transaction costs, and government policies. Central to the concerns of the study of industrial organization is thus the effect of market structure on behavior and performance, and their interactions. The models of industrial organization proved to be useful, particularly in the economic analysis of multinational corporations, in the analyses of the effects of oligopolistic sellers on international trade, and in determining the effects of international trade on market structure and performance long before a new theory of international trade emerged (Caves, 1971, 1974).

The study of international trade underwent a significant change when this new trade theory, which incorporates the models of industrial organization, flourished in the 1980s. The central aspect of this new trade theory is the introduction of *scale economies, product differentiation,* and *imperfect competition* to the trade model. This new approach grew out of a frustration over the conventional trade theory, which often lacked the power sufficient to explain the emerging pattern of intraindustry trade, intrafirm trade, and foreign direct investment in the real world (Helpman and Krugman, 1985). Here, the new approach finally showed ways in which firms from different countries compete in international markets in the form of a formal model, suggesting the possibility that sellers in national markets interact with sellers from foreign markets across national boundaries.

1.1. Objectives

The purpose of this study is to present empirical evidence on how firms compete in international markets. In particular, this book deals with rivalry among firms in national markets and among firms originating from different national markets across national boundaries, and their influences on international trade and international investment. The first part of this book presents a series of empirical models in which firms choose price and quantity for exports under the assumption of international oligopoly. Chapters 2–5 and 8 examine the effects of market structure on export pricing, oligopolistic interdependence among firms in export pricing, the systematic linkage of competition across national boundaries, and the oligopolistic influence on international trade. The second part of the book mainly deals with the impact of market structure on foreign direct investment. Its focus is again on interfirm rivalry. Chapters 6 and 9 examine the impact of oligopolistic rivalry among sellers in a national market on foreign direct investment, especially on their choices of entry mode and postentry performance. Chapter 7 looks at the issue of strategic interactions in foreign direct investment among firms from different countries.

Because the purpose of this book is to present empirical analysis of firm behavior in the international context rather than in a theoretical model, it depends heavily on empirical data. In this study, we use several sets of historical data on Japanese firms and industries and their foreign counterparts over the period from the late 1950s through the 1990s. Using Japanese data to test hypotheses on international oligopoly is justified for several reasons.

First, the pattern of Japanese competitiveness evolved over time in the period between the late 1950s and the late 1990s. The unprecedented success of Japanese firms in industries such as electrical machinery, non-electrical machinery, office machines, instruments, and automobiles in penetrating the world markets was perhaps the most startling record in international industrial competition from the late 1970s through the early 1990s. Japanese exports in textiles, pottery products, iron and steel, metal products, and general machinery were the key industrial products that contributed to Japan's high growth rate between 1955 and 1970. This historical pattern of Japan's industrial competitiveness provides us with a rich opportunity to examine if the behavior of Japanese firms changed as their international competitiveness evolved over time.

Second, Japan's major exporting industries improved their competitive positions and grew to be a major competitive force in international markets by the early 1980s. During the period of 1975–1984, Japanese products, such as TV and radio receivers, hi-fi equipment, motorcycles, motor vehicles, watches, cameras, office machines, and optical equipment were well accepted by the consumers worldwide, and thus attained the largest shares in the total exports from the European Community (E.C.), United States, and Japan. The growth of Japanese firms and industries in the world market during the late 1970s and the 1980s provides us with empirical evidence to test the hypothesis that oligoplistic rivalry across national boundaries influences international trade.

Third, Japanese firms were involved intensively in foreign direct investment (FDI) in the United States and Europe beginning in the mid-1980s. Indeed, the flow of Japanese manufacturing FDI in North America surged from US$1.2 billion in 1985 to US$4.6 billion in 1987, and peaked in 1989 at US$9.6 billion. Japanese firms entered into a cross section of U.S. and European industries through new-plant investments and acquisitions of local firms. This record of foreign direct investment by Japanese firms will provide us another opportunity to investigate the impact of market structure and oligopolistic rivalry among sellers in a national market on foreign direct investment.

Finally, the business environment surrounding Japanese firms changed markedly since the early 1990s when Japan's so-called bubble economy collapsed. Japan's distinctive institutions and business practices that contributed to the competitiveness of Japan's industrial firms in the past decades have adapted to the new environments. Although they are often reluctant, Japanese firms have found it necessary to overhaul and revamp their business strategies and operations worldwide. Many of their foreign subsidiaries were shut down and sold, and many firms exited from the new business lines they entered hastily in the late 1980s and early 1990s. This provides us a rare opportunity to investigate the relationship between oligopolistic behavior, in particular bunching behavior, in foreign direct investment and in the postentry performance.

As noted above, although this study relies on data on Japanese firms and industries and examines their behavior in international trade and investment, it does not intend to provide a thorough explanation for the international competitiveness of Japanese firms and industries, nor does it intend to be an exhaustive list of Japan's distinctive features in its institutions, industrial organization, and business practices that underlie its competitiveness. Because there is a large catalog of literature on the sources of Japanese competitiveness, those interested in these subjects should refer to this literature.[1] This book also does not deal with the subject of Japanese foreign direct investment in a comprehensive manner. Again, my focus in this book is to examine an oligopolistic influence on foreign direct investment and its impact on performance. Thus, the reader will not find much analysis of the incidence and development of Japanese multinational firms and the financial factors of Japanese foreign direct investment.[2]

---

[1] The most recent study on Japanese competitiveness is Porter, Takeuchi, and Sakakibara (2000). See Chapter 10 of this book for the literature that explains the source of Japanese firms' competitive advantages.

[2] See Caves (1993, 1996) for an extensive survey on these subjects.

1.2. Conceptual Framework for Empirical Analysis

The central aspect of the theoretical framework used in this study is the premise that most of trade and foreign direct investment is in the industries that are characterized as oligopolies. The new trade theory departed from the traditional premise at least in two aspects (Krugman, 1989). One is the introduction of economies of scale and product differentiation into the model. The second aspect is the introduction of imperfect competition in the model. Here the old assumption of pure competition is replaced by the assumption that domestic and foreign firms are oligopolies and form oligopolistic interdependences. Although their specific aims were different, the models developed by Brander (1981), Brander and Krugman (1983), Spencer and Brander (1983), Krugman (1984), and Helpman and Krugman (1985) were fundamentally concerned with modeling the role of imperfect competition in international trade. Chapters 2, 3, 4, and 8 of this book examine the export pricing behavior in imperfect markets, and Chapter 5 is concerned with the impact of international oligopoly on trade performance. In all these chapters, the theoretical models are essentially inspired by this line of literature and use the assumption that domestic and foreign firms engage in oligopoly games.[3]

Although the statistical model in Chapters 2 and 3 is derived directly from the profit-maximization problem of an exporting oligopoly, the models developed in Chapters 4 and 5 incorporate a new aspect into the theory of international oligopoly. Figure 1.1 is provided to illustrate this point. As noted earlier, the central aspect of the international oligopoly approach is the introduction of imperfect competition and hence market structures of both home and foreign countries into the model. Suppose there are two countries, A and B, each with one firm in industry X. The firms in both countries engage in international trade. Assume that the firms in both countries maximize profits while behaving as oligopolists. For the firm in country A, its profit-maximizing level of output for export

---

[3] This approach that assumes that domestic and foreign firms interact in oligopolies deviates also from the early literature in industrial organization that examined the impact of market structure on trade performance (e.g., Hufbauer, 1970; Pugel, 1978; Caves, Porter, and Spence, 1980; Marvel, 1980) and the impact of international trade on industry performance (e.g., Khalizadeh-Shirazi, 1974; Pugel, 1978, 1980). See Caves (1989) for a survey on the early literature.

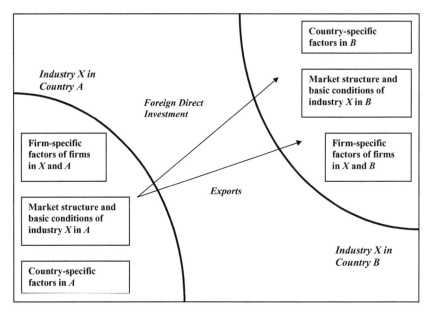

Figure 1.1. Determinants of international trade and investment.

and the export price are determined by the elements of market structure and basic conditions in the home market as well as foreign market. This model differs significantly from the model used in the early empirical literature in industrial organization that regards only the home country's market structure in explaining the trade behavior and performance. It also deviates from the traditional trade literature that takes into account primarily country-specific conditions.

In general, the empirical analysis of this book considers seller concentration, barriers to entry, product differentiation, and barriers to exit as key elements of market structure. In addition, it takes into account several factors as determinants of basic conditions for a particular industry. They include technology, cost structures, scale economies, learning, location, demand elasticity, cyclical character of demand, rate of growth, and consumer's purchase method. Chapter 3 demonstrates the systematic linkage of competition between U.S. and Japanese firms in a given industry. The statistical analysis finds that the profits on exports of Japanese firms increase with Japanese market structures as well as U.S. market structures.

Chapter 4 then confirms this finding by using a model that is a corollary to the model of Chapter 3, showing that the Japanese import share in the U.S. market increases with the competitive advantages of the Japanese industry relative to the U.S. advantages. Competitive advantages are measured here by a number of market-structure and cost-related variables.

Although industry-specific market structure plays an important role as a determinant of export behavior and performance, it is, in fact, the firms that engage in exporting activities in an industry. This point reminds us that firm-specific factors also play a role as a cause of trade and determinant of performance. The analysis in Chapter 8 investigates this issue specifically by using firm-specific data and provides evidence on export pricing behavior in international oligopoly in the luxury car market in the United States. Here the firm-specific factors are introduced in addition to market-structure variables as determinants of export pricing.

To investigate an oligopolistic influence on foreign direct investment requires that the role of firm-specific factors be taken into account. The previous research on the presence of multinational enterprises (MNEs) found that FDI is industry-specific as well as firm-specific.[4] When the investment behavior of multinational firms is investigated in Chapters 6, 7, and 9, the firm-specific factors are explicitly taken into account in the empirical analysis. Firm-specific factors here refer to a number of variables such as tangible assets; intangible assets such as technological skills, know-how, reputation, and brands; financial resources; and capabilities in distribution, sales, marketing, and service. The statistical analysis in Chapters 6 and 9 finds that Japanese foreign direct investment in the United States in the late 1980s was influenced by oligopolistic interactions among Japanese firms after controlling for a number of firm-specific characteristics. And, Chapters 7 and 9 find that the postentry performance of foreign affiliates in Japan and the postentry performance of Japanese affiliates in the United States were both determined by their corporate strategies.

In addition to industry- and firm-specific factors, country-specific factors have been proven to determine trade and investment patterns, and national competitive advantage of an industry. Conventional trade

---

[4] See Caves (1996) for a survey.

theory has suggested that differences among countries in their endowments of factors of production cause international trade. The study of multinational corporations suggests the importance of country-specific factors in its location decision (Dunning, 1977; Markusen, 2002). A study of national competitive advantage has proposed that a set of country-specific factors determine a country's international competitiveness in a particular industry (Porter, 1990).[5] And, a country's regions may play a significant role in international trade (Fujita, Krugman, and Venables, 1999). As noted earlier, the principal focus of the book is on examining the pattern of oligopolistic interactions among firms in national markets and across national boundaries, and their influence on trade and investment. Therefore, in this study, the impact of country-specific factors is incorporated generally as controlling factors in the statistical specification. As a consequence, there is only a minimal amount of analysis of country-specific factors in the book, except the analysis of foreign exit from Japan in Chapter 7.

1.3. Japanese Exports and Foreign Direct Investment: Overview

Although the main theme of this book is to examine the pattern of international competition engaged in by Japanese firms and their foreign rivals, individual chapters address different questions on their exporting and FDI behaviors that pertain to specific time periods. Table 1.1 provides an overview on the principal focus of each chapter and the time period for which data are constructed for empirical analysis. Chapters 2–5 and 8 examine export competition, and Chapters 6–7 and 9 are concerned with foreign direct investment. To put the empirical analysis of each chapter into perspective, this section provides a brief overview of the historical trends of Japanese exports and outward FDI in the post–World War II era and highlights their key features at an aggregate level.

---

[5] These are factor conditions; demand conditions; the existence of related and supporting industries; the national environment in which firms are organized, managed, and compete; and the role of government. Porter (1990). See Yamawaki (2002b) for the importance of industrial clusters in Japan.

Table 1.1. *Overview of the book*

Chapter	Analysis	Period
2	Market structure and export pricing behavior.	1970–1984
3	Technology, demand, and export pricing behavior.	1970–1984
3	Domestic and export pricing behaviors in the steel industry.	1957–1975
4	Foreign market structure and profitability.	Late 1960s–early 1970s
5	Oligopolistic interactions in U.S. imports.	Late 1970s
5	FDI in distribution and exports.	Mid-1980s
6	FDI in the United States and Europe.	The 1970s–the 1990s
6	FDI and entry mode.	The 1980s
7	Strategic interactions between Japanese and foreign firms, and exit of foreign firms in Japan.	1973–1994
8	Foreign rivals' responses in the U.S. luxury car market.	1986–2001
9	Exit in the United States.	1985–2000

Exports

The upper panel of Figure 1.2 presents Japanese exports measured in the value of the Japanese yen between 1950 and 2004. Although the general pattern that emerges is an upward trend, there are at least several distinctive periods between 1950 and 2004 that differ markedly in their growth patterns. Japan's exports grew steadily during the 1950s, but it was during the 1960s that Japanese industries rapidly expanded their international market presence and experienced unprecedented high growth. Although the shift to the floating exchange-rate system in the beginning of 1973 and the first oil crisis in the autumn of 1973 changed the international environment in which Japanese firms operate, Japan's exports surged strongly after 1973 and continued to grow remarkably through 1985. Japan's exporting industries faced another challenge when the U.S. dollar depreciated against the Japanese yen after the Plaza Accord in 1985. Japanese exporters whose main production facilities were located in Japan found their international competitiveness significantly eroded as the high value of the yen diminished their cost advantages measured in the U.S. dollar. Consequently, Japan's exports declined sharply in 1986. The Japanese economy grew slowly and remained sluggish through

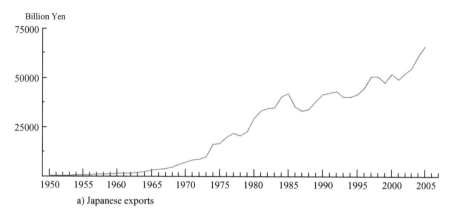

a) Japanese exports

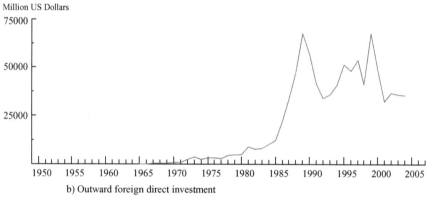

b) Outward foreign direct investment

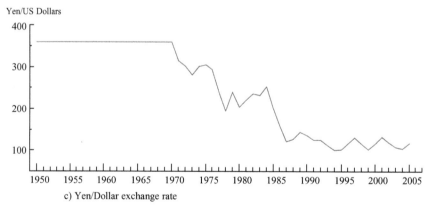

c) Yen/Dollar exchange rate

Figure 1.2. a) Japanese exports, b) Outward foreign direct investment, and c) Yen/Dollar. Exchange rate, 1950–2005.
Source: Ministry of Finance, Japan.

the 1990s. Japan's exports grew, on average, at a much slower pace during the 1990s than in its high-growth era of the 1970s and 1980s. Finally, Figure 1.2 shows that Japan's exports started growing again after 2002.

The composition of Japan's exports changed markedly during the 1960s and through the 1970s as Japan's comparative advantage shifted from cheap unskilled-labor intensive goods such as textiles, apparel, and light industry products to capital-intensive goods such as iron and steel machinery, electrical equipment, and automobiles (Komiya and Itoh, 1988; Nakamura, 1995).[6] Table 1.2 presents a comparison of the shift in mean export shares between the European Community (E.C.),[7] Japan, and the United States over the period of 1962–1984 for twenty-two aggregated industrial sectors. The three regions were chosen here to focus on competition between major industrialized regions in the export market during the 1960s through the mid-1980s. The export share measure is used to reflect the relative competitiveness of each of the three regions vis-à-vis the other two (Audretsch, Sleuwaegen, and Yamawaki, 1989). Japan showed a smaller share of exports throughout the entire period in industries in food, beverages and tobacco, petroleum products, chemicals, animal and vegetable oils, and pharmaceuticals. By contrast, Japan's mean export share was higher in electrical machinery, metal products, and iron and steel than the other two regions. Between the 1962–1974 and the 1975–1984 periods, Japan's mean export share declined in industries such as leather, cork and wood, textiles, stone, clay and pottery, apparel, and footwear. However, Japan gained its export share markedly in industries intensive in R&D and/or engineering such as nonelectrical machinery, electrical machinery, office machines and computers, transportation equipment, and photographic equipment.

To examine further if the export shares for the E.C., Japan, and the United States in a given industry move systematically over time, the author performed elsewhere (Audretsch, Sleuwaegen, and Yamawaki,

---

[6] For evidence on the influence of factor endowments on trade for Japanese industries, see Leamer (1984), Urata (1983), and Balassa and Noland (1989).

[7] We use the E.C. as the term to identify the original member countries within the European Community.

1989) a nonparametric rank-correlation test between market shares and time trend for the 1963–1974 period and the 1975–1984 period. Each of 165 SITC (the Standard International Trade Classification) three-digit industries in the sample was classified then as systematically gaining, losing, or showing no trend in its share of exports based on the rank correlation coefficient. Using a 10 percent statistical significance level criterion, approximately 80 percent of Japanese exports in this period were characterized by a trend in gaining market share, but for the E.C. and United States, export-share losing industries outweighed export-share gaining industries in 1974 and 1985 trade values.

The majority of these patterns occurred in SITC sectors 7 and 8, which are mainly comprised of the machinery, electric apparatus, and transportation equipment industries. The sources of gain in exports for the SITC three-digit industries within these 3 one-digit sectors are listed in Tables 1.3 and 1.4. The most striking result that emerges from these two tables is that the gain in Japanese export shares was achieved particularly at the expense of market shares of their U.S. rivals during both the 1963–1974 and 1974–1984 periods.

This trend, however, did not carry over to the 1990s. By examining the pattern of the changes in world export share for all Japanese goods-producing industries between 1990 and 1996, Porter, Takeuchi, and Sakakibara (2000) found that of the 1,618 industries in which Japan participates, its world export share has declined in 1,250 industries and risen in only 166. Their study identified declining shares even in Japan's most successful exporting industries in the 1970s and 1980s such as copiers, cameras, video tape recorders, and line telephone equipment.

The geographic composition of Japan's exports also changed over time. Table 1.5 shows that Asia was the key export market for Japanese exporters during the 1950s. This pattern, however, changed during the 1960s when Japanese firms shifted their focus from Asia to North America. This trend continued through the mid-1990s, with some exceptions during the late 1970s through early 1980s. Most recently, the importance of North America as Japan's key export market declined as the importance of Asian markets resurged during the mid-1990s.

Table 1.2. *Mean export shares between the E.C., Japan, and the United States, 1962–1974 and 1975–1984*[a]

Sector	E.C.[b]		Japan		United States	
	1962–1974	1975–1984	1962–1974	1975–1984	1962–1974	1975–1984
Food, beverages, and tobacco	0.348	0.351	0.099	0.069	0.534	0.616
Crude materials	0.394	0.364	0.221	0.180	0.769	0.456
Petroleum products	0.392	0.523	0.025	0.016	0.583	0.461
Animal and vegetable oil	0.224	0.160	0.086	0.096	0.681	0.744
Chemicals	0.441	0.414	0.152	0.141	0.529	0.481
Pharmaceuticals	0.391	0.261	0.078	0.092	0.529	0.647
Leather	0.461	0.481	0.228	0.147	0.311	0.373
Rubber	0.543	0.471	0.195	0.352	0.261	0.177
Cork and wood	0.327	0.410	0.401	0.191	0.272	0.399
Paper	0.152	0.210	0.203	0.189	0.645	0.601
Textiles	0.420	0.447	0.405	0.290	0.175	0.207
Stone, clay, and pottery	0.483	0.540	0.747	0.262	0.144	0.148
Iron and steel	0.448	0.426	0.375	0.503	0.177	0.071
Metal products	0.361	0.260	0.402	0.516	0.237	0.224
Nonelectrical machinery	0.332	0.359	0.096	0.485	0.578	0.399
Electrical machinery	0.137	0.137	0.383	0.607	0.230	0.300
Office machines and computers	0.227	0.136	0.100	0.381	0.673	0.498
Transportation equipment	0.441	0.285	0.271	0.538	0.287	0.281
Apparel	0.416	0.527	0.460	0.224	0.125	0.298
Footwear	0.684	0.928	0.311	0.035	0.005	0.037
Instruments	0.331	0.269	0.306	0.379	0.363	0.353
Photographic equipment	0.376	0.195	0.300	0.506	0.325	0.300

[a]Exports from each region/country are divided by the total exports from the E.C., Japan, and the United States. Data are obtained from the OECD Trade Statistics.
[b]Only the original six countries in the European Community, Belgium, France, (West) Germany, Italy, Luxembourg, and the Netherlands, are included in the sample.
Source: Audretsch, Sleuwaegen, and Yamawaki (1989, table 1).

13

Table 1.3. *Sources of gain in exports for Japan for the machinery, electrical equipment, and transportation equipment sectors, 1963–1974*

Japan + United States −	Japan + E.C. −
Vapor power engines	Office machines (not for data processing)
Combustion engines	Parts and accessories of office machines
Rotating electric plant	Radio receivers
Agricultural machinery	Telecommunications equipment
Tractors	Passenger motor cars
Civil engineering plant	Special purpose motor vehicles
Paper manufacturing machinery	Motorcycles
Printing machinery	
Machine-tools for working metal	
Metal working machinery	
Heating and cooling equipment	
Pumps for liquids	
Office machines (not for data processing)	
Parts and accessories of office machines	
Radio receivers	
Gramophones, sound recorders, etc.	
Telecommunications equipment	
Electrical switches, relays, etc.	
Electrical household equipment	
Passenger motor cars	
Trailers	
Parts and accessories of motor vehicles	

Notes: The definitions of industries used in this table are based on three-digit SITC codes. Thirty-eight 3-digit industries are in the sample. Japan + US − indicates the Japanese industries gaining market shares and the U.S. industries losing market shares. Similarly, Japan + E.C.− indicates the Japanese industries gaining market shares and the E.C. industries losing market shares in the 1963–1974 period. Classification of industries to these two categories is based on the result of rank correlation test between market shares and trend between 1963 and 1974.
Source: Audretch, Sleuwaegen, and Yamawaki (1989, table 3-A, appendix A, and appendix B).

Outward Foreign Direct Investment[8]

The second panel of Figure 1.2 presents Japan's outward FDI between 1965 and 2004. Concurrent to the trend in exports shown in the upper

[8] There exists an extensive literature on Japanese foreign direct investment that examines its patterns for different periods. These include Tsurumi (1976), Kojima (1978), Ozawa (1979), Franko (1983), Kujawa (1986), Yoshida (1987), Wilkins (1990), and Yonekura and McKinney (2005).

Table 1.4. *Sources of gain in exports for Japan for the machinery, electrical equipment, and transportation equipment sectors, 1975–1985*

Japan + United States −	Japan + E.C. −
Combustion engines	Agricultural machinery
Rotating electric plant	Machine tools for working metal
Tractors	Office machines (not for data processing)
Printing machinery	Data processing machines
Machine-tools for working metal	Gramophones, sound recorders, etc.
Metal working machinery	Passenger motor cars
Heating and cooling equipment	Parts and accessories of motor vehicles
Pumps for liquids	Motorcycles
Air pumps and compressors	
Mechanical handling equipment	
Data processing machines	
Parts and accessories of office machines	
Gramophones, sound recorders, etc.	
Electrical power machinery	
Electric switches, relays, etc.	
Electrical household equipment	
Semiconductors	
Passenger motor cars	
Trailers	
Parts and accessories of motor vehicles	
Aircraft and parts thereof	

Notes: The definitions of industries used in this table are based on three-digit SITC codes. Thirty-eight 3-digit industries are in the sample. Japan + US − indicates the Japanese industries gaining market shares and the U.S. industries losing market shares. Similarly, Japan + E.C.− indicates the Japanese industries gaining market shares and the E.C. industries losing market shares in the 1975–1985 period. Classification of industries to these two categories is based on the result of rank correlation test between market shares and trend between 1975 and 1985.
Source: Audretch, Sleuwaegen, and Yamawaki (1989, table 3-A, appendix A and Appendix B).

panel of Figure 1.2, Japan's FDI evolved over time and showed distinctive patterns for different periods. During the late 1960s and early 1970s, Japan's FDI showed a relatively large weight in natural resources. Japanese firms sought supply sources of natural resources abroad in timber, pulp, mineral ore, and oil investing in a large number of resource-oriented development projects. This pattern of investment is consistent with Japan's need for raw materials to supply manufacturing activities in resource-poor Japan (Tsurumi, 1976; Wilkins, 1990).

Table 1.5. *Japanese exports by region, 1950–2005 (%)*

Year	Asia[1]	Europe[2]	North America[3]	South America	Africa	Oceania	Total
1950	46.15	12.04	25.42	3.68	9.03	3.68	100.0
1955	41.85	10.22	26.52	7.46	10.22	3.73	100.0
1960	35.82	13.36	33.15	4.45	8.70	4.45	100.0
1965	32.37	15.48	34.70	2.92	9.66	4.80	100.0
1970	31.23	17.41	36.73	3.09	7.36	4.16	100.0
1975	36.74	18.55	26.38	4.24	9.96	4.12	100.0
1980	38.09	19.41	29.30	3.63	6.14	3.42	100.0
1985	32.55	16.28	43.26	1.26	2.66	3.98	100.0
1990	34.11	23.36	36.34	1.08	1.98	3.13	100.0
1995	45.53	17.37	31.56	1.48	1.70	2.36	100.0
2000	43.21	17.92	34.48	1.20	1.05	2.15	100.0
2005	49.82	16.11	25.80	1.70	1.33	2.53	100.0

Notes: (1) Includes Middle East; (2) Includes Turkey; (3) Includes El Salvador, Cuba, Guatemala, Costa Rica, Dominican Republic, Nicaragua, Panama, Puerto Rico, Honduras, and Mexico. *Source:* Ministry of Finance, Japan.

Japanese firms started investing in manufacturing abroad during the 1960s. During the 1970s, Japanese manufacturers established factories for simple manufacturing activities by investing in the nearby Asian countries, while they set up sales and distribution subsidiaries to support their exports in North America and Europe (Tsurumi, 1976; Wilkins, 1990; Yamawaki, 1991a). Throughout the 1970s, Japanese firms invested heavily in the whole trade sector of the United States. By the end of 1986, total assets held by U.S. affiliates in wholesale trade of Japanese nonbank companies were US$38.8 billion and accounted for 45 percent of total foreign assets in the U.S. wholesale trade sector. This heavy investment in the U.S. distribution sector was driven by the need to support the marketing of goods exported from Japan.

During the early 1980s, Japanese companies started seeking to locate production in the United States. In part, this shift in the geographic focus of Japanese FDI toward North America was driven by the motives to circumvent trade frictions and to locate business activities close to customers. In particular, voluntary export restraint agreements in the early 1980s in the United States are considered a significant factor that

Table 1.6. *Japanese foreign direct investment in manufacturing, by sector, 1965–2004 (%)*

Sector	1965–1969	1970–1974	1975–1979	1980–1984	1985–1989	1990–1994	1995–2000	2000–2004
Food	4.98	6.46	4.26	4.39	3.67	6.36	6.38	15.76
Textiles	20.7	19.31	11.01	3.93	3.07	3.15	3.16	2.49
Lumber and wood	12.20	10.99	4.15	2.61	2.94	4.22	1.84	1.20
Chemicals	4.99	12.39	22.03	14.29	15.67	13.38	16.87	11.57
Metal	18.0	14.36	22.68	22.73	8.80	7.85	7.68	6.63
Machinery	6.73	9.23	6.59	9.11	11.08	9.23	9.78	5.43
Electrical machinery	10.97	11.09	13.87	16.91	24.29	24.13	25.20	34.29
Transportation equipment	11.97	6.88	8.36	17.94	19.62	15.73	19.63	14.10
Others	4.74	9.41	6.98	7.86	10.87	15.95	9.46	8.53
Total	100.0	100.0	100.0	100.0	100.0	100.0	100.0	100.0

Source: Ministry of Finance, Japan.

motivated Japanese assemblers to locate in the United States.[9] It was, however, in the mid-1980s that Japanese investors burst into the United States and Europe. Japan's foreign investment surged markedly after 1985 and peaked in 1989. It was concentrated in North America and in Europe in industries such as electrical machinery and automobiles (Table 1.6). This upward trend contrasts with the decline in exports in the 1985–1987 period (Figure 1.2).

Figures 1.3 and 1.4 show that Japan's investment increased again in 1992 but declined sharply in 1998 and then increased markedly in 1999. The surge of investment in 1999 was observed mainly in North America and Europe.[10] Japan's foreign investment in Asian countries follows a similar trend as in North America and Europe between 1985 and 1988, although it appears to deviate from the latter after 1999.

Although Japan's foreign direct investment grew over time since the 1960s, its growth was relatively gradual up until the mid-1980s. Why did Japanese firms rush to invest in the U.S. and European markets after 1985? At least two sets of factors can provide us with some explanations for this trend: (1) the development of firm-specific transactional factors by Japanese firms and (2) macroeconomic factors in Japan. As described earlier in this section, Japanese exporters of electrical machinery and automobiles, in particular, gained world market shares in the 1970s and through the early 1980s. The source of their success in international markets was in part due to Japan's comparative advantage (Leamer, 1984; Saxonhouse, 1983, 1988), which provided an effective platform for manufacturing activities for the firms that domiciled in Japan. Although Japan's source of comparative advantage was its relative abundance in capital (Leamer, 1984), Japan's technology base also showed a significant

---

[9] For evidence on the effects of government policy to restrict trade on FDI, see Blonigen (2001) for the U.S. experience. See also Belderbos (1997b), Belderbos and Sleuwaegen (1998), and Girma, Greenaway, and Wakelin (2002) for the E.U. experience on antidumping.

[10] This surge occurred mainly in the food and electrical equipment sectors and was presumably the result of major acquisitions by Japanese firms in these sectors in 1999 FY. The significant increase in Europe reflects an emerging pattern of FDI by Japanese firms to acquire foreign firms through their holding subsidiaries in Europe. Japan Tobacco acquired R.J. Reynolds International through its holding company in the Netherlands in May 1999.

Million US Dollar

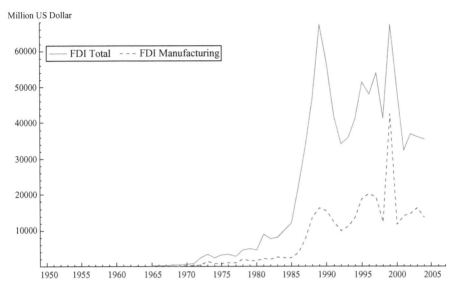

Figure 1.3. Japanese outward foreign direct investment (FDI), 1965–2004.
Note: Approval and notification base.
Source: Ministry of Finance, Japan.

relation to exports (e.g., Audresch and Yamawaki, 1988; Petri, 1991). Evidence on the rapid growth of R&D expenditures and personnel in Japan (Okimoto and Saxonhouse, 1987), the emergence and development of technology-intensive industries (Odagiri and Goto, 1996), and the impact of technology on firm growth (Odagiri, 1983, 1992) all suggest that Japan's R&D base played a key role in industrial development in Japan during the 1960 through the 1980s. Thus, Japanese firms accumulated intangible assets in R&D-intensive industries over time and took advantage of such proprietary assets. And they deployed their technological capabilities in the host country in the mid-1980s (Kogut and Chang, 1991; Hennart and Park, 1992; Drake and Caves, 1992; Caves, 1993).

Although the development of firm-specific factors provides an explanation for the increase in Japan's foreign investment, it does not provide a clear answer to the question of why it surged markedly in the mid-1980s. It is well known that the Japanese economy experienced a large increase in land prices and stock prices in the late 1980s. The increase

Million US Dollars

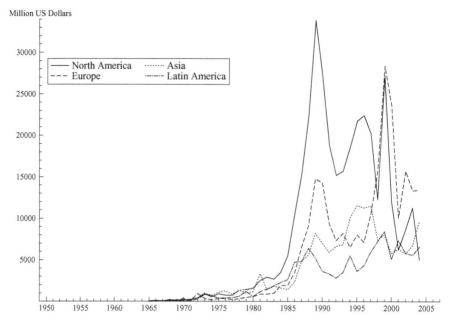

Figure 1.4. Japanese outward foreign direct investment by region, 1965–2004.
Note: Approval and notification base.
Source: Ministry of Finance, Japan.

in prices in the Japanese stock market and real estate markets may have
provided Japanese firms with opportunities to raise funds easily and
cheaply and created wealth gains.[11] Equally, exchange-rate movements
in the mid-1980s may have played a role as a determinant of Japanese foreign investment. When the U.S. dollar depreciated against the Japanese
yen, the purchasing power of corporate liquidity in the Japanese yen was
enhanced over corporate assets denominated in the U.S. dollar (Froot
and Stein, 1991). The impact of such wealth effects on foreign investment may be significant when capital markets are imperfect. Given a
premium for monitoring costs charged for external financing, Japanese
firms with larger assets denominated in the appreciating yen experienced

[11] For a more detailed account of the increase in land prices and stock prices, see Ito
(1992).

relative wealth gains and assigned a low opportunity cost to internally generated finds.[12]

Although these micro and macro explanations are consistent with the burst of Japan's foreign direct investment in the mid-1980s, their impacts are likely to be interwoven when we disaggregate Japan's foreign investment according to different modes of entry, at least in the United States. One of the main features of Japanese investment in the late 1980s was the increasing use of acquisitions to enter the U.S. market. With the U.S. dollar depreciated against the yen after 1985, Japanese firms made more acquisitions in U.S. industries as the firm-specific assets of U.S. firms became more valuable by generating returns in appreciated yen (Blonigen, 1997).

Although aggregate data of exports and foreign direct investment are useful to show general trends of these two international activities, they fail to show specifically how exports and foreign direct investment are interrelated. Generally speaking, they are interrelated in complex ways through a number of underlying factors such as comparative advantage, transportation and other trade costs, plant-level scale economies, corporate-level scale economies, market size, market potential, and the extent of vertical integration (Krugman, 1983; Brainard, 1997; Markusen, 2002).[13] Figure 1.5 is used to illustrate this issue. It shows domestic production, exports, and overseas production in the Japanese automobile industry in units between 1970 and 2005.[14] In general, before 1985, Japanese automakers' domestic production increased parallel to exports, suggesting that Japanese plants supplied automobiles for exports. This pattern, however, changed after 1985. Automobile exports from Japan peaked in 1985 in terms of units and declined gradually until 1996. On the contrary, Japanese automakers' overseas production units increased since 1985 and surpassed exports in 1994. In 1985, overseas production accounted for only 7 percent of total production in the Japanese automobile industry,

---

[12] In addition, the cost of capital measured by the accounting-earnings measure is lower in Japan than in the United States (Ando and Auerbach, 1988). This condition may have allowed Japanese firms to gain access to funds at a lower cost in Japan.

[13] For a survey on the relationship between export and FDI, see Head and Ries (2004).

[14] Includes passenger cars, trucks, and buses.

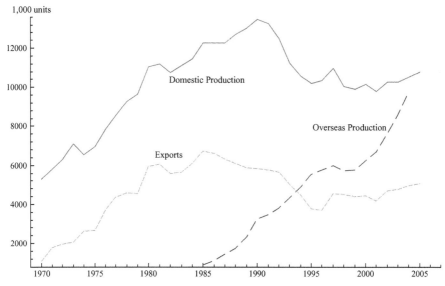

Figure 1.5. Japanese automobile industry, 1970–2005.
Note: Production and exports are based on the figures for passenger cars, buses, and trucks.
Source: JETRO and Japan automobile manufacturers Association.

while in 2004 the percentage of overseas production in total production increased to 48 percent. To address the question of whether overseas production is complementary to or substituting exports needs careful treatment.[15] The pattern presented in Figure 1.5 appears to suggest at least that exports and foreign direct investment are interrelated to each other in the case of Japanese automobile industry.

1.4. Japan's Corporate and Economic Organization

This book does not intend to examine the source of Japanese firms' competitive advantage in international markets. Its main focus is to examine the ways in which Japanese firms compete in international markets. Thus, this book leaves the more detailed assessment of their competitive advantage and disadvantage to the existing literature in economics

---

[15] See Belderbos and Sleuwaegen (1998), Blonigen (2001), and Head and Ries (2001, 2004).

and management dealing with various aspects of Japanese firms and their management practices. Some salient features of Japan's business and economic organization, however, significantly influence the pattern of international competition and performance for Japanese firms as they are important elements that affect industrial organization. We will examine this link in Chapter 10 fully after presenting the main empirical findings.

Among the main features of the Japanese corporate model are the corporate organization that facilitates quick introduction of new products and continuous improvements in quality; the lean production system in which a firm can make a greater variety of products at lower cost and make the same variety of products at lower cost and higher quality; and the human resource policies that lead to efficient skill formation and continuous improvements through learning in the long run. Japanese firms' success in process innovation, quality improvement, and quick introduction of new products during the 1970s and the 1980s are all accounted for by their focus on these areas in R&D. The Japanese corporate structure that facilitates horizontal flow of communication and horizontal coordination among different departments within the firm and the internal labor system in which the R&D personnel are rotated from the R&D department to other operating units and departments within the firm, proved to be very effective in the process of new product development and engineering (Aoki, 1990). Among other features of Japanese business and economic organization are the groupings of many enterprises known as *keiretsu*; the presence of large number of small enterprises that operate as subcontractors to large assemblers in regional clusters; the imperfection in capital market; and the government policy toward strategic industry.

One approach to examine these features of Japan's business and economic organization and their impacts on the pattern of international competition is to estimate their influences directly. Another approach is to infer their influences from the observed pattern of international competition. Although the first approach is more appealing, it is often not feasible to implement such research design because many of these features are unquantifiable and entangled in complex ways. In this book, therefore, I take primarily the second approach. I first examine the pattern of competition within the framework of economic models of imperfect competition and then interpret the statistical results in the light of special features of Japan's business and economic organization. As the importance and influence of these economic models differ between the different phases of development in Japanese industries, these features are examined in their relations to the patterns of exports and foreign direct investment over the 50-year period after World War II in Chapter 10.

1.5. Issues of Data

Although the theoretical literature of international oligopoly flourished in the 1980s, the empirical literature on international oligopoly has been very limited. I suspect that this paucity of empirical research is primarily due to the difficulty in obtaining data that are suitable for hypothesis testing, at least in two aspects. First, the international oligopoly model requires empirical researchers to collect data on market structures for different countries. In a case of reciprocal trade between two countries, data on both home and foreign countries are needed. Market-structure variables, by definition, are industry specific and hence vary across different industries. To construct a market-structure variable for both home and foreign countries requires that the industry definition in one country be matched with the definition used in the other country. Matching industry classifications of different countries is often not an easy task and is very tedious even for a single year.

Second, to investigate oligopolistic interactions among firms from different countries requires that variables in empirical analysis be defined as time-dependent and firm/industry-specific. Because interfirm rivalry occurs generally within an industry, the previous empirical research in industrial organization that examines competitive interactions among firms resorts to an industry analysis and/or a panel-data analysis. A cross-section time-series panel is more desirable to test hypotheses on international oligopoly, but it entails onerous efforts to collect data due to the unavailability of standardized data in different countries. The empirical models in Chapters 4–7 and 9 all had to deal with these issues and circumvent many problems that arise in data collection. Thus, the statistical specifications used in this study often deviated from the specifications derived from the theoretical model.

Because individual chapters of the book address different questions on international competition, the data required for empirical analysis are also different in the unit of observation and the time period. As Table 1.1 shows, the statistical analyses in Chapters 2–5 and 8 focus on export competition, and the analyses in Chapters 6, 7, and 9 are concerned with foreign direct investment. Chapters 2–5 use industry-level data, and Chapters 5–9 use firm-level data. The data for statistical analysis were collected on the basis of the availability, and their sources vary from one analysis to another. Thus, the data are not necessarily comparable among different analyses in the book. The Appendixes to this book describe the sources of individual data used in different chapters.

2

Export Pricing under Imperfect Competition

2.1. Introduction

This chapter and Chapter 3 are both concerned with the analysis of pricing behavior of firms that operate in international markets. Because the underlying aim of this book is to examine the relationship between market structure and firms' behaviors in international markets, I start this chapter by presenting a simple model of export pricing that incorporates elements of market structure and provides empirical evidence on the determinants of export price. As noted in Chapter 1, my focus is on testing hypotheses on export pricing behavior by using data on Japanese industries during the 1970s and the 1980s.

One of the most distinctive patterns of international trade involving Japanese firms during the 1960s and through the 1980s is the change in the relative importance of Japan's major exporting industries to her economy. When I compared export shares between the countries in the European Community (E.C.), Japan, and the United States for the periods of 1962–1974 and 1975–1984,[1] I found that Japan's export shares increased markedly in industries such as nonelectrical machinery, office machines and computers, transportation equipment, electrical machinery, and photographic equipment (Table 2.1). As it is well known, those were Japan's major exporting industries in the 1980s and through the 1990s. Japan's export shares declined markedly in stone, clay, and

---

[1] The 1962–1974 period marks Japan's high-growth years, and the later 1975–1984 period marks those years after the second oil crisis and before Japan's stock market boom and the appreciation of the yen against the U.S. dollar in 1985.

Table 2.1. *Mean export shares in Japan for 1962–1974 and 1975–1984*

Industry	1962–1974	1975–1984
Food, beverages, and tobacco	0.0989	0.0689
Crude materials	0.2213	0.1801
Petroleum products	0.0250	0.0158
Animal and vegetable oil	0.0861	0.0963
Chemicals	0.1516	0.1408
Pharmaceuticals	0.0780	0.0915
Leather	0.2277	0.1466
Rubber	0.1953	0.3517
Cork and wood	0.4012	0.1913
Paper	0.2030	0.1887
Textiles	0.4053	0.2899
Apparel	0.4549	0.2244
Footwear	0.3110	0.0348
Stone, clay, and pottery	0.7471	0.2623
Iron and steel	0.3751	0.5025
Metal products	0.4023	0.5162
Nonelectrical machinery	0.0955	0.4850
Electrical machinery	0.3826	0.6065
Office machines and computers	0.1002	0.3810
Transportation equipment	0.2713	0.5375
Instruments	0.3059	0.3790
Photographic equipment	0.2998	0.5058

Notes: The export share at the two-digit level is defined as Japan's exports to the original six members in the E.C. (Belgium, France, Germany, Italy, Luxembourg, and the Netherlands) and the United States, divided by the total amount of exports from Japan, the E.C. and the US. Data are obtained from the OECD Trade Statistics.

pottery, footwear, apparel, and cork and wood during the same period. It is clear that Japan's underlying industry structure changed, and the weights attached to exporting industries shifted from labor-intensive light industries to technology-intensive industries in this period. Japan had a small share of exports throughout the 1960s and the 1980s in industries such as food, petroleum products, chemicals, and pharmaceuticals, while its export share was persistently high in metal products, and iron and steel.

This observation suggests the importance of a cross section variance in competitive positions of Japanese firms in the world market during the 1970s and 1980s. Japanese exporters in industries such as electrical machinery and automobiles increased their market shares markedly in the world export market and, hence, may have behaved as oligopolists in the world market. However, those in stone, clay, and pottery may have behaved as pure competitors in the world market. This observation leads us to ask the following questions: do firms behave as pure competitors in the world market? Or, do firms behave as an oligopoly? Although this question is central to the study of export behavior of firms, it has not been addressed sufficiently in the existing empirical literature.

As noted in Chapter 1, the "new" theoretical research in international trade that started almost 25 years ago introduced the industrial organization approach and incorporated increasing returns to scale, imperfect competition, and product differentiation to the traditional trade theory (Brander, 1981; Brander and Krugman, 1983; Spencer and Brander, 1983; Helpman and Krugman, 1985). The traditional premise that treats exporting firms as pure competitors and price-takers in the world market is contested by the alternative one that assumes exporting firms as oligopolists and price-setters who interact with foreign rivals in the export market. This theoretical literature provides a framework to test hypotheses on export pricing behavior.

The industrial organization approach in international trade is well-established in the study of exchange pass-through, which uses the assumption of imperfect competition in modeling the export pricing behavior (Mann, 1986; Dornbush, 1987; Baldwin, 1988; Feenstra, 1989; Knetter, 1989, 1993; Goldberg and Knetter, 1997). Because the main focus of the previous research in that area is on the pattern of exchange pass-through, it often does not investigate empirically the question of how market structure affects the firms' export-pricing behavior. In fact, only a few empirical studies have examined the relationships between the elements of market structure, such as product differentiation, scale economies, learning, and concentration and market share, and the export pricing behavior (Caves and Williamson, 1985), with the determinants of interfirm differences in exchange pass-through (Yamawaki, 2002). The assumption of imperfect competition that is the essence of the "new" trade theory has been subjected to very little empirical scrutiny. The list of existing empirical studies that addresses this issue is short and includes early studies by Huveneers (1981) for Belgium industries and Hazledine (1980) for Canadian industries. The purpose of this chapter and

Chapter 3 is therefore to develop a simple model, investigate whether national firms behave as an international oligopoly in the export market, and identify the factors that determine such behavior.

2.2. Models of Export Pricing Behavior

International Oligopoly with Differentiated Products

Consider, first, the case of international oligopoly with differentiated goods that is motivated by the models developed by Brander (1981), Brander and Krugman (1983), and Helpman and Krugman (1985). Assume that there are two countries, one domestic and one foreign. Assume also that a monopolistic firm dominates each country market before trade takes place. Once trade between the two countries takes place, the domestic exporter forms oligopolistic conjectures with its foreign rival. Assume further that products produced in the domestic country are differentiated from products produced in the foreign country due to embodied national characteristics, making them imperfect substitutes for each other. With products differentiated internationally, the domestic monopolist is able to segregate the domestic market from the export market.

The inverse demand functions for the domestic firm in the domestic and market export market are given by

$$P_d = P_d\,(D,\,D^*) \qquad\qquad (2.1)$$
$$P_f = P_f\,(X,\,X^*) \qquad\qquad (2.2)$$

where prices of the domestic firm's product in the domestic and export markets are denoted by P_d and P_f, respectively, and P_d is expressed in terms of the home currency, but P_f is in terms of the foreign currency. The domestic firm produces output D for domestic consumption and output X for export. Similarly, the foreign form produces output D^* for export and output X^* for consumption in its own market. Prices are assumed to fall as a firm's own output and the rival firm's output increase. The domestic firm's short-run cost function is defined as

$$C = C\,(Q; w,\,m,\,F), \qquad\qquad (2.3)$$

where Q is total output, $Q = D + X$, w and m are the wage rate and the price of raw materials in the home currency, respectively. F denotes fixed costs.

The domestic firm maximizes its total profits originating from the domestic and export markets in terms of the home currency

$$\Pi = P_d\,(D,\,D^*)D + e\,P_f\,(X,\,X^*) - C\,(Q;\,w,\,m,\,F), \qquad (2.4)$$

where e is the home-currency price of foreign exchange. The first-order condition for the export market is

$$e\,P_f + e[(\partial P_f/\partial X)X + (\partial P_f/\partial X^*)(\partial X^*/\partial X)X] = C', \qquad (2.5)$$

where C' denotes marginal costs. Arranging the terms in the bracket of Eq. (2.5)

$$Pf = [\varepsilon/\varepsilon - 1 - \varepsilon\eta\sigma(P_f^*/P_f)(s/1 - s)]C'/e, \qquad (2.6)$$

where $\varepsilon = -(\partial X/\partial P_f)(P_f/X)$, $\eta = -(\partial P_f/\partial X^*)(X^*/P_f)$, $\sigma = \partial X^*/\partial X$, P_f^* is the price of the foreign firm's product in the foreign market, and s is the domestic firm's market share in the foreign market, $s = P_f X/(P_f X + P_f^* X^*)$. In Eq. (2.6), the mark-up in the export market is defined by the bracket term and is a function of the parameters of the demand function (ε and η), the conjectural variation (σ), market share (s), and relative prices (P_f^*/P_f).[2]

The partial effect of an increase in market share on the mark-up (λ) and, thus on export price, is positive, $\partial\lambda/\partial s > 0$, and $\partial P_f/\partial s > 0$, and the effect of an increase in foreign price is also positive, $\partial\lambda/\partial P_f^* > 0$ and $\partial P_f/\partial P_f^* > 0$. The influence of fluctuations of the exchange rate and other cost factors on export price will be realized through two routes: through changes in costs in terms of the foreign currency; and through changes in the mark-up.

---

[2] The conjectural variation approach is generally rejected from a theoretical point of view (e.g., Shapiro, 1989). However, Dockner (1992), Sabourian (1992), Lapham and Ware (1994), and Cabral (1995) have provided a formal justification for using the conjectural variation approach on practical grounds. These studies have shown that under certain conditions the outcome of a static conjectural model is consistent with the outcome of a dynamic model.

Eq. (6) yields the familiar price formula:

$$P_f = \lambda C'/e, \tag{2.7}$$

where λ is the mark-up term for the domestic firm. This export price equation for the domestic firm may be rewritten with only observable variables:

$$P_f = f(P_f^*, e, s, w/e, m/e, Q), \tag{2.8}$$

where P_f^*, e, and s are the factors that determine the mark-up term.

International Oligopoly with Homogeneous Product

Consider next the case of international oligopoly with homogeneous products. In this case the demand functions are defined by $P_d = P_d(D + D^*)$, and $P_f = P_f(X + X^*)$, and the price of the domestic firm's product in the foreign market, P_f, is assumed to be the same as the price of the foreign firm's product in the foreign market, P_f^*. The relative price term that was included in Eq. (2.8) for differentiated goods, therefore, is not included in the mark-up term for homogeneous goods. On the other hand, market share remains as its determinant. Thus, Eq. (2.8) will be defined for homogeneous goods as

$$P_f = g(e, sx, w/e, m/e, Q), \tag{2.9}$$

where $sx = (/X/(X + X^*)$.

Price-Takers in the World Market

Finally, consider the case where exporters behave as price-takers in the world export market. Assume that the exporting country is small in the world market and its domestic firms produce a homogeneous good. In this small country setting, the exporting industry will face a perfectly elastic export demand at the prevailing world price. Domestic firms will take the world price as given, producing for export at $P_f = eP_f^* = C'$, where e is the home-currency price of foreign exchange. In this case, domestic firms' export price then should be determined solely by and be proportional to the world price. Therefore, the export price equation for price-takers can be written as

$$P_f = h\,(P_f^*, e). \qquad (2.10)$$

2.3. Hypotheses and Empirical Specifications

To test the three models represented by Eqs. (2.8)–(2.10), a general empirical model that encompasses each of these models as a special case is specified as[3]

$$\ln XP_t = a_0 + a_1 \ln F\,P_t + a_2 \ln EXCH_t + a_3 \ln DEMAND_t$$
$$+ a_4 \ln SHARE_t + a_5 \ln(ULC/EXCH)_t$$
$$+ a_6 \ln(UMC/EXCH)_t + u_t, \qquad (2.11)$$

where XP is domestic firms' export price, FP is foreign rivals' price; $EXCH$ is the home-currency price of foreign exchange; $DEMAND$ is a variable that measures domestic demand fluctuations; $SHARE$ is domestic firms' share in the world market; ULC is unit labor costs in the home currency; UMC is unit material costs in the home currency, and u is the error term. $DEMAND$ is included in this specification to measure the effect of cyclical domestic demand conditions on firms' total output as included in Eq. (2.3).

Hypotheses

In the international oligopoly models, export price is determined by the mark-up formula (2.7), $P_f = \lambda C/e$. However, in the price-taker model, export price is determined by the world price, $P_f = eP_f^* = C$. This means that export price of international oligopolists should be determined by

---

[3] It is likely that this specification suffers from the problem of *endogeneity*. In particular, the estimated coefficient for market share variable may be biased. Increased production efficiency of Japanese industry causes both the increase of its market share and its declining price, and thus a negative correlation between the two. One method to alleviate this potential simultaneity is to use instruments. It was, however, difficult to obtain appropriate instruments that are not correlated with the residuals of the equations for individual industries. Alternatively, the lagged market-share variable was used instead of current market share. This specification, however, suffered from autocorrelations. Therefore, although it is not satisfactory, only the OLS estimate is reported in this section.

the elements that determine λ. Export price of price-takers should be proportional to the world price and should not be determined by market share. Therefore, under the oligopoly models,

$a_4 = 0$ (Hypothesis 1)

should be rejected.[4]

If international oligopolists determine export price as predicted from the model with differentiated products,

$a_1 = 0$ (Hypothesis 2)

should be rejected.

For the case of price-takers, we test the hypothesis of

$a_1 = 1$ (Hypothesis 3).

If export price is not determined proportionally to the foreign price, Hypothesis (3) should be rejected. To summarize, the following coefficients are expected:

In the case of price-takers,

$a_4 = 0$ and $a_1 = 1$.

In the case of international oligopolists with homogeneous goods,

$a_4 \neq 0$ and $a_1 = 1$.

In the case of international oligopolists with differentiated goods,

$a_4 \neq 0$ and $a_1 \neq 0$.

2.4. Empirical Estimates of Export Price

Data and Variables

The data sample covers thirty-four Japanese manufacturing industries at the SITC (Rev. 2) three- and four-digit level over the period 1970–1984,

---

[4]   In the classic oligopoly model, the effect of market share on price should be positive. We test $a_4 = 0$ here to take into account the possibility of negative correlation between price and market share caused by increasing production efficiency through learning.

for which the necessary data are available. The average industry export share, defined as total exports divided by total shipments over the 15-year period, is 17.4 percent in my sample, with a range from 3.5 to 63.2 percent. For each industry, annual data were collected for the variables included in Eq. (2.11). Because a significant change in the exchange rate occurred in 1985, I chose 1984 as the last observation year in the statistical analysis. As I examine later in Chapter 6, Japanese firms started investing directly in the U.S. and European markets after 1985. They established new plants and acquired local firms intensively after the Japanese yen was appreciated against the U.S. dollar in 1985. Sources of data used in the study and the list of industries are presented in the Appendix of this chapter.

The definitions of variables are presented in Appendix Table A.2.1. The dependent variable, *XP*, is an index of average unit export price for Japanese industries in U.S. dollars. This variable is obtained annually by dividing the total dollar volume of export sales to the world by the export sales measured in quantities. Foreign competitors' price, *FP*, is also an index of average unit export price in U.S. dollars constructed in the same manner as *XP*. The use of the average unit export price in empirical analyses has been criticized (Kravis and Lipsey, 1972, 1982). However, I had to use the average unit price in this analysis to obtain independent variables that are available at the same level of industry classification for a cross section of Japanese industries.

The major foreign exporters that compete with Japanese exporting firms in the world market were selected by measuring the significance of contacts made in Japan's major export markets and by the availability of data. For most of the industries in my sample, the OECD countries were identified as major foreign competitors of the Japanese industries (see Table A.2.4 in the Appendix).

Short-run domestic demand disturbances, *DEMAND*, were constructed as the annual percentage deviation of total production for domestic consumption (using the 1970 price) from the time trend in total industry production (production for domestic consumption and exports) (using the 1970 price). Four different functional forms of time trends were fitted to total production for each industry, and the best-fit trend was chosen on the basis of adjusted R^2 to construct *DEMAND*.

The four functional forms used are: $Q = a + bt$; $Q = a + bt + ct^2$; $Q = a + b \ln t$; and $\ln Q = a + bt$, where Q is total output and t is the time variable. Where necessary these regressions were adjusted for serial correlation. Thus, *DEMAND* is expected to represent the extent of unexpected short-run domestic demand pressure.[5]

Unit labor costs, *ULC*, are defined as total labor costs divided by total industry production (in the 1970 price), and unit material costs, *UMC*, are defined as total material costs divided by total industry production (in the 1970 price). Both variables were constructed annually from the census of manufacturers' data. Total industry production in a constant price was obtained by deflating the value of industry shipments at the SIC four-digit level by a unit-price index constructed from the quantity and value of shipments data at the constituent six-digit commodity level.

The Japanese exporters' share in the world market, *SHARE*, is constructed annually as total Japanese exports to the rest of the world divided by total world exports. In my sample of thirty-four Japanese industries, the average market share across industries over the period 1970–1984 is 16.2 percent, with a range from 2.8 to 58.7 percent.

Empirical Results

International Oligopoly versus Price-Takers

Using the time-series data over the 1970–1984 period for each of the thirty-four industries, Eq. (2.11) was estimated by the maximum likelihood method assuming the residual is first-order auto-regressive. After testing the hypothesis that the estimate of the auto-regressive coefficient is zero, the equation was reestimated assuming no serial correlation for those cases where the null hypothesis was accepted. The final estimation result of export price equations is presented in Table A.2.2 of the Appendix. Where serious multicollinearity was found between *ULC* and *UMC*, a combined variable, $UC = ULC + UMC$, was included in estimation.

---

[5] For previous empirical studies on the effect of domestic demand pressure, see Ball, Eaton, and Steuer (1966), Artus (1970), Dunlevy (1980), and Tarr (1982).

Table 2.2. *Results of hypothesis tests on export pricing behavior*

Hypothesis	Number of industries that reject the hypothesis	Sample size
Hypothesis 1(H_0: $a_4 = 0$)	10	32^a
Hypothesis 2(H_0: $a_1 = 0$)	8	10^b
Hypothesis 3(H_0: $a_1 = 1$)	7	22^c

Notes: The maintained hypotheses are described in the text. All the hypotheses are tested on a two-tailed test at the 10 percent level of significance.
[a] Two industries are omitted due to the unavailability of market share data.
[b] The test is conditional on the rejection of Hypothesis 1.
[c] The test is conditional on the acceptance of Hypothesis 1.

Table 2.2 summarizes the test results of the three hypotheses described in the previous section. The null hypothesis that market share does not determine the export price (Hypothesis 1) is accepted in twenty-two industries out of the thirty-two sample industries for which market share data are available. This result suggests that ten out of the thirty-two Japanese export industries, or 31 percent of the sample, exhibit the export pricing behavior that is consistent with the behavior under imperfect competition. These industries are textile yarn, steel plates and sheets, construction machinery, metalworking machinery, radio and TV receivers, telephone equipment, cameras, tape and video recorders (including audio equipment), and photographic films. These were indeed Japan's major exporting industries in the 1960s and the 1970s and through the mid-1980s.

The null hypothesis that foreign competitors' price does not affect Japanese exporters' price (Hypothesis 2) is rejected in eight industries among those ten industries where export pricing is consistent with models of imperfect competition. The null was accepted in the remaining two industries. This result suggests that in the eight industries, Japanese exporters set export price in response to changes in foreign price and its own market share.

The null hypothesis that export price is determined solely by and proportional to the world price (Hypothesis 3) is tested for the industries that have accepted Hypothesis 1. In fifteen industries out of the twenty-two industries, the null hypothesis was rejected. Thus, in the remaining seven

Table 2.3. *Classification of industry according to the hypothesis tests*

$a_4 = 0\ a_1 = 1$	$a_4 \neq 0$	$a_4 \neq 0\ a_1 \neq 0$
Synthetic Rubber**	Paper and Paperboard	Textile Yarn
Synthetic Fibers**	Textile Yarn	Steel Plates and Sheets
Fertilizers**	Steel Plates and Sheets	Construction Machinery
Cement**	Construction Machinery	Metalworking Machinery
Soap and Detergents	Metalworking Machinery	Radio and TV
Cotton Fabrics	Radio and TV	Telephone Equipment
Pumps for Liquids	Tape and Video Recorders*	Cameras
	Telephone Equipment	Photographic Films
	Cameras	
	Photographic Films	

$a_4 = 0\ a_1 \neq 0$
Tractors
Boilers
Steam Engines
Railway Vehicles

Notes: The test statistics are obtained from the estimation results of Eq. (2.11). The full estimation results are Table A.1 in the Appendix. All the hypotheses are tested on a two-tailed test at the 10 percent level of significance.
*The world price variable, *FP*, is not available for this industry and was omitted from the estimation
**The coefficient for *FP* is the only significant variable in regression for this industry.

industries, the Japanese export price responded proportionally to the changes in the world price. These seven industries are synthetic rubber, synthetic fibers, soap and detergents, fertilizers, cotton fabrics, cement, and pumps for liquids. Out of these seven industries, four industries, synthetic rubber, synthetic fibers, fertilizers, and cement, show that export price is not statistically determined by cost variables.

The four industries listed in the second row of Table 2.3 show that export price is not determined by unit costs and market share but is positively related to foreign price. The coefficient for *FP is different from one but has a positive sign and is statistically significant. In fact, FP is* the only variable that has a statistically significant coefficient for these industries. This finding seems to imply that the export price behavior in these four industries is generally consistent with the behavior of price-takers, given possible measurement errors present in unit-price data.

In summary, the result suggests that ten industries are classified as international oligopolies, and eleven industries are classified as price-takers. However, the remaining thirteen industries are not classified into either of the two cases.

The Effect of Market Share

In the model of international oligopoly, the effect of market share on export price is expected to be positive, $a_4 > 0$. In six industries, the mark-up enhancing effect of market share was found statistically significant. However, the coefficient for market share was significant but had a negative sign in four industries. The negative coefficients were found in steel plates and sheets, radio and TV receivers, cameras, and tape and video recorders, suggesting that high sales volume is likely to lower export prices. It is conceivable that lower prices led to higher market share in these industries where scale economies are very important.[6] All of these four Japanese industries have very large average shares in the world market over the 1970–1984 period, reaching 59 percent for tape and video recorders, 47 percent for both cameras, and radio and TV receivers, and 30 percent for steel plates and sheets. These industries were ranked among the top-five exporters in my sample on terms of world market share.

The Effect of Unit Costs

The effects of changes in material and labor costs on export price are estimated by a_5 and a_6 in the model. The hypothesis that $a_5 + a_6 = 0$ was tested and was rejected in 22 industries. Thus, Japanese exporters set export price in response to changes in unit costs in 65 percent of the sample examined in this study. To examine if export price moved proportionally to unit costs, the hypothesis, $a_5 + a_6 = 1$, was tested. Table 2.4 shows the sixteen industries where this hypothesis was accepted.

---

[6]   The negative correlation may indicate the possibility of simultaneity. The problem of simultaneity, however, is not corrected properly because of the difficulty of finding appropriate instruments that are not correlated with the residuals of the equation. See Footnote 18.

Table 2.4. *Classification of industry according to the estimated parameters in the export price equation*

$a_4 < 0$	$a_4 > 0$	$a_5 + a_6 = 1$
Steel plates and sheets	Paper and paperboard	Synthetic dyestuffs
Radio and TV	Textile yarn	Paints and ink
Cameras	Construction machinery	Paper and paperboard
Tape and video recorders	Metalworking machinery	Textile yarn
	Telephone equipment	Cotton fabrics
	Photographic films	Glassware
		Steel bars
		Machine tools
		Ball and roller bearings
		Radio and TV
		Telephone equipment
		Electric circuits apparatus
		Insured wire
		Passenger cars
		Sewing machines
		Semiconductors

$a_2 > 0$	$a_3 > 0$
Soap and detergents	Paint and ink
Textile yarn	Soap and detergents
Steel plates and sheets	Plastic materials
Steel bars	Paper and paperboard
Tractors	Textile yarn
Telephone equipment	Cotton fabrics
Semiconductors	Steel plates and sheets
Photographic film	Steel bars
	Telephone equipment
	Cameras
	Photographic films

Notes: The *t*-test statistics are obtained from the estimation results of Eq. (2.11). All the hypotheses are tested on a two-tailed test at the 10-percent level of significance. For the test of the costs variables, where applied, the coefficient on UC is examined if it equals one. The standard error to construct *t*-test statistics for $a_5 + a_6$ is obtained from $Var(a_5 + a_6) = Var(a_5) + Var(a_6) + 2Cov(a_5, a_6)$.

The Effect of Exchange Rate

In the model of international oligopoly developed in the previous section, the foreign exchange rate affects export price through the mark-up term and unit costs. A positive sign for the coefficient for the exchange rate suggests that changes in currency values are adjusted by changes in the mark-up, and a negative sign for the coefficient for the exchange rate suggests that changes in currency values are passed through on export price. In eight out of the twenty-nine industries for which the estimates of a_2 are available (Table 2.4), the coefficient for the exchange rate is statistically significant and has a positive sign, implying that Japanese exporters in these industries squeeze mark-ups to remain competitive in the export market when the Japanese yen appreciates against the U.S. dollar.

In seven out of these eight industries, the net effect of a change in the exchange rate on export price measured by $a_2 - (a_5 + a_6)$ was statistically not different from zero. This finding suggests that the effect of an appreciation (depreciation) of the Japanese yen that inflates (deflates) production costs in terms of U.S. dollar is fully compensated by the reduction (increase) in mark-ups. The net effect was positive and significantly different from zero in one industry, photographic films, implying that the Japanese firms in this industry squeeze the mark-ups more than required to offset the increase in production costs incurred by an appreciation of the Japanese yen.

The Effect of Domestic Demand Pressure

The remaining parameter in the export price equation is the elasticity of export price with respect to domestic demand pressure, a_3. In eleven out of the thirty-four industries (Table 2.4), the coefficient for *DEMAND* is statistically significant and has a positive sign, suggesting that Japanese exporters respond to unexpected short-run domestic demand disturbances by varying export price. In other words, Japanese exporters in these eleven industries tend to cut their export price to smooth out unexpected reduction in domestic demand.

However, Japanese industries that were successful in the world market during the period in question, such as tape and video recorders, radio and TV receivers, semiconductors, and passenger cars, have the estimated coefficients that are statistically not different from zero. This suggests that export price in these industries are insensitive to unexpected domestic disturbances. This issue will be examined further in Chapter 3.

Finally, the effect of domestic disturbances is not significant in the four industries that are identified as price-takers in the world market, which suggests that their export price is independent from domestic demand conditions.

2.5. Conclusions

In this chapter, I have presented a simple model of export pricing and applied it to the time-series data of thirty-four Japanese industries over the period of 1970–1984. The statistical analysis found that not all of the Japanese industries behave as oligopolists in the world market. Although in 30 percent of the sample industries their export pricing behavior is consistent with an international oligopoly, in 20 percent of the sample their behavior is consistent with that of price-taking competitors. I am unable to make any clear-cut conclusions for the remaining 50 percent of the sample because the statistical result was not robust enough to support the oligopoly and competition hypotheses.

Although the number of industries where their behaviors are consistent with an oligopoly is relatively small, the list of these industries indeed includes Japan's major exporting industries during the 1970s and 1980s. These industries are steel plates and sheets, construction machinery, metalworking machinery, radio and TV, cameras, telecommunication equipment, tape and video recorders (including audio equipment), and photographic films. Their strong competitive positions in the world export market presumably allowed them to behave as international oligopolists during the 1970s and 1980s.[7]

The major empirical result of this chapter, that Japan's major exporting industries display price-setting behaviors, provides evidence that

---

[7] One interesting question, then, is whether these industries are oligopolies in Japan. The unweighted average of largest four-firm concentration ratios for these industries was 66.6 percent in 1980, but the figure for the seven Japanese industries where the export pricing behavior was consistent with price-taking behavior is 43.1 percent in 1980. Apparently, this result suggests that there is a dichotomous relationship between the level of concentration at home and the pattern of competition in the international market. In the Japanese industries with lower concentrations, firms are more likely to behave as price-takers in the international markets. However, the firms in concentrated industries are more likely to be price-setters.

supports the theoretical development in trade theory that uses the industrial organization approach. However, it is important to note that not all the industries behave as international oligopolists. Indeed, exporters in many industries still behave as price-takers in the world market.

3

Export Price, Learning, and Domestic
Demand Disturbances

3.1. Introduction

As shown in Chapter 1, Japanese firms were remarkably successful in penetrating the world export market of manufactured goods such as machinery, electrical equipment, electronics, and automobiles during the 1970s and 1980s. Although such export performance of Japanese manufacturing firms is greatly attributed to Japan's comparative advantage in capital-intensive and skill-intensive manufacturing and the Japanese firms' competitive advantages in manufacturing practices and organizational capabilities (Chapter 10), the pricing behavior of Japanese firms was often criticized for allegations of dumping. Numerous cases of dumping were filed in the U.S. and European markets against Japanese products such as television sets, steel products, telephone equipment, electronic components, and office equipment throughout this period.[1] Such dumping allegations did not necessarily infer Japanese firms' engagements in dumping in the subsequent antidumping suits. They suggest that Japanese firms show a high propensity to cut export price occasionally in the foreign market. This chapter, therefore, asks a question of what motivates Japanese firms to lower prices frequently in the export market.

The classic theories of dumping argue that dumping occurs when a firm with monopoly power that can segregate the home from foreign markets maximizes profits by discriminating prices in the two markets (Viner, 1923; Yntema, 1928; Robinson, 1933; Haberler, 1937; Wares, 1977). In

---

[1] Belderbos and Sleuwagen (1998) for a list of Japanese electronic products under antidumping investigation by the E.C. in the 1980s.

this literature, dumping is regarded as monopolistic price discrimination between the home market and foreign market based on the underlying difference in the demand conditions of the two markets.

More recent theoretical research on dumping seeks factors that motivate firms to export at a price below the costs of production (Ethier, 1982; Davis and McGuiness, 1982; Eichengreen, 1982; Eichengreen and Van der Ven, 1984; Gruenspecht, 1988). Ethier (1982) and Eichengreen (1982) emphasize that exporting firms set prices below costs on a cyclical basis, and cyclical fluctuations in demand are the basic condition for such "short-run" dumping. Thus, their models predict that a domestic firm cuts export price to the level of marginal cost when it suffers a reduction in demand.

Another explanation for low levels of price in the foreign market set by firms that export is given by the presence of learning economies. Under the presence of learning economies, production costs are expected to decline as output cumulates over time (Spence, 1981). To the extent that domestic firms set price along the learning curve, their export price declines over time and is lower than levels of production costs incurred in the previous periods. In their studies that examine the semiconductor and jet aircraft industries, Baldwin and Krugman (1988a and 1988b) show that the existence of the learning curve affects the behavior of oligopolistic firms and plays an important role in determining the international competitiveness of firms in these industries. And Gruenspecht (1988) suggests that dumping is a possible pricing strategy in the presence of learning economies.

Despite the importance of this issue, there have been relatively few empirical studies that investigate the cause of the high tendency for the Japanese export price to move downward. The aim of this chapter is, therefore, to estimate the elasticity of export price with respect to short-run demand disturbance and the elasticity of export price with respect to the cumulative output for the Japanese industries to shed some light on this issue. As summarized earlier, the theory suggests that persistent dumping occurs when a firm with market power engages in price discrimination between domestic and foreign markets. The empirical analysis presented in this chapter, however, does not address intermarket price differentials directly. Instead, it examines how Japanese firms set export prices in response to domestic demand disturbances and cumulated output. After I present the estimates of the elasticity, their determinants will be explored later in this chapter.

3.2. Estimation of Elasticity

Statistical Model and Variables

The statistical model presented in Chapter 2 is used to estimate the response of export price to domestic demand pressure and cumulated output. The elasticity of export price with respect to short-run disturbances is measured by the coefficient for *DEMAND* in Eq. (2.11). *DEMAND* is constructed as the annual percentage deviation of total production for domestic consumption (at the 1970 price) from the time trend in total industry production (at the 1970 price). *DEMAND* measures the extent of unexpected short-run domestic demand pressure and hence, the extent of excess capacity over domestic production.

The learning elasticity is estimated by adding a new independent variable in the specification of Eq. (2.11). Suppose a firm's production costs have two components: the first component varies with input factor prices m_t and instantaneous output Q_t, and the second component is dependent upon cumulated output CMQ_t,

$$C_t = C_1(m_t, Q_t) + aC_2(CMQ_t)Q_t, \qquad (3.1)$$

where CMQ_t is defined as $CMQ_t = \sum^t Q_n$, $n = 0, \ldots, t$, and $C_2(CMQ_t)$ is assumed to decline as CMQ increases (Spence, 1981). The second component of the cost function represents the learning effect that reduces the cost of production as production cumulates over time.

A direct approach to estimate the learning curve elasticity is to regress production costs on cumulated output and obtain its regression coefficient. This approach requires information on production costs that is not easy to obtain. An alternative approach that uses price data is adopted in this chapter. This approach requires the condition that changes in the mark-up over costs are controlled for in the statistical analysis (Lieberman, 1984). The statistical model of the export price equation, Eq. (2.11) in Chapter 2, satisfies this condition and is therefore used to estimate the learning elasticity.

The accumulated output, *CMQ*, is constructed by cumulating the data on total industry production at a constant price through the end of each observation year. The identical measure has been used in the previous empirical literature on the learning curve (Lieberman, 1984; Ghemawat, 1984). The price equation was estimated over the 1970–1984 period for each of the thirty-four industries introduced in Chapter 2.

Statistical Results

Domestic Demand Disturbances

Table 3.1 presents the estimated coefficients for *DEMAND* and standard errors for the Japanese industries. In eleven out of the thirty-four industries in the sample, the coefficients for *DEMAND* are found to be significantly different from zero and have a positive sign. A positive coefficient suggests that Japanese firms responded to unexpected short-run decline in domestic demand and excess capacity by cutting export price. The industries that show large values for the elasticity are paper and paperboard, telephone equipment, photographic films, cement, cotton fabrics, steel bars, textile yarn, soap and detergents, paint and ink, synthetic dyestuff, plastic materials, and steel plates and sheets.

However, industries such as tape and video recorders (including audio equipment), radio and TV receivers, semiconductors, and passenger cars have the coefficients for *DEMAND* that are statistically not different from zero, suggesting that export prices in these industries do not respond to fluctuations in domestic demand and thus to the extent of excess capacity over domestic demand. These four industries were among Japan's most successful exporting industries during the period of this study. This finding is important in that the export pricing behavior of the dumping-alleged industries, such as steel products and chemical products, is different from the behavior of another dumping-alleged industries, such as TV receivers and semiconductors in Japan.

The Learning Curve

The coefficient for cumulated output (a_7) is found to be statistically significant only for a small number of industries in the sample. Indeed, it is significant and has a negative sign in only four industries. However,

Table 3.1. *Estimates of elasticity of export price with respect to domestic demand disturbances (a₃)*

Industry	Estimate of Elasticity	Standard Error
Paper and paperboard	1.066***	0.225
Telephone equipment	0.977**	0.364
Photographic films	0.957***	0.347
Cement	0.851	0.640
Cotton fabrics, woven	0.794***	0.146
Steel bars	0.752**	0.383
Textile yarn	0.640**	0.230
Soap and detergents	0.517***	0.134
Paints and ink	0.460**	0.228
Synthetic dyestuff	0.429*	0.291
Plastic materials	0.415**	0.176
Steel plates and sheets	0.413**	0.215
Integrated circuits	0.406	0.493
Synthetic rubber	0.397	0.375
Synthetic fibers	0.285	0.599
Construction machinery	0.265*	0.189
Insulated wire and cable	0.263	0.333
Electric circuit apparatus	0.211	0.236
Cameras	0.203**	0.099
Machine tools	0.203	0.166
Metalworking machinery	0.194	0.186
Steam engines	0.192*	0.113
Ball and roller bearings	0.152	0.167
Tractors	0.138	0.255
Tape and video recorders	0.120*	0.080
Radio and TV receivers	0.046	0.060
Semiconductors	0.043	0.089
Glassware	0.027	1.057
Sewing machines	−0.002	0.142
Passenger cars	−0.030	0.098
Boilers	−0.054	0.113
Pumps for liquids	−0.134	0.164
Railway vehicles	−0.163	0.223
Fertilizers	−0.210	0.435

Notes: The estimation method is described in Chapter 2. The levels of significance in a one-tailed *t*-test statistics are: *** = 1 percent, ** = 5 percent, and * = 10 percent.

Table 3.2. *Estimates of elasticity of export price with respect to accumulated output (a_7) and the estimated slopes of the learning curve*

	Integrated circuits	Semiconductors	Tape and video recorders	Cameras
Elasticity	−0.224	−0.193	−0.096	−0.052
Standard error	0.059	0.033	0.040	0.028
Percentage increase in cumulated output	The Level of Export Price as Percentage of its Previous Level			
0	100	100	100	100
100	86	87	94	96
200	78	81	90	94
300	73	77	88	93
400	70	73	86	93
500	67	71	84	91
600	65	69	83	90
700	63	67	82	90
800	61	65	81	89
900	60	64	80	89

Notes: The estimation method is described in the text. The entire sample consists of thirty-four industries. The coefficient for cumulated output, *CMQ*, is statistically significant at a 1 percent level for integrated circuits and semiconductors, and significant at a 5 percent level for tape and video recorders, and cameras. The calculation of the level of export price as percentage of its previous level is based on the estimate of elasticity presented in the first row of this table.

these four industries in which the learning elasticity is negative are the industries where Japan increased her export share markedly during the 1970s and through the 1980s. These are integrated circuits, semiconductors, tape and video recorders (including audio equipment) and photographic cameras. Table 3.2 shows the estimates of the elasticity of export price with respect to cumulated output for the four industries and the estimated slope of the learning curve.

The estimates of the learning elasticity are −0.22 for integrated circuits, −0.19 for semiconductors, −0.10 for tape and video recorders, and −0.05 for photographic cameras. These estimates are not inconsistent with the common estimates discussed in the existing literature. For example, the learning elasticity for semiconductors was assumed to be within the range of −0.2 and −0.3 (Baldwin and Krugman, 1988a).

Following the definition employed by Lieberman (1984), the estimated learning elasticity is translated into the learning curve slope in Table 3.2. The learning curve slope is defined as the level to which costs fall each time the cumulated output doubles. Thus, Table 3.2 shows that, in integrated circuits, export price falls to 86 percent of its previous level as the cumulated output doubles. Under this definition, the learning curve slopes are 87 percent for semiconductors, 94 percent for tape and video recorders, and 96 percent for photographic cameras. Table 3.2 also shows the extent to which the export price declines as cumulated output increases in the four industries. For example, in semiconductors, the export price falls to 87 percent of its previous level as output doubles, and drops further to 71 percent when output increases by 500 percent. The learning curve slopes for integrated circuits and semiconductors are comparable and much steeper than those for tape and video recorders and cameras.

The finding, for semiconductors, that export price does not respond to short-run fluctuation in domestic demand but responds to the learning curve, suggests that the export price behavior in this industry is motivated by long-term policy rather than short-term profit maximization. This result further implies the importance of distinguishing occasional price cutting in the short-run and a steady decline in price along the learning curve in the long-run.

3.3. Determinants of Elasticity

The analysis presented in the previous section suggests the difference in the estimated elasticity across industries. The questions that follow are: (1) why is export price sensitive to domestic demand fluctuations in some industries but not in other industries? and (2) what determines the slope of the learning effect? This section will examine these questions by using cross-sectional data for the thirty-four four-digit Japanese industries.

Domestic Demand Disturbances
The standard theory of production suggests that, in the neighborhood of standard capacity, the marginal cost curve of the industry with a high

ratio of fixed costs to variable costs is steeper than that for the industry with low fixed costs. The floor of marginal cost curves that is realized when firms operate with excess capacity is lower for the industry with high fixed costs than the industry with low fixed costs. This suggests that the interindustry difference in the response of price to demand disturbances is determined by the difference in the cost structure between industries. When firms in the industry with high fixed costs suffer a reduction in demand and thus have excess capacity, they will cut price more sharply than those with low fixed costs because of their steeper marginal cost curves. Thus, a decline in demand causes a price cut that is larger in industries with high fixed costs than in those with low fixed costs. This suggests that capital intensity of the industry has a positive relationship with the elasticity of export price with respect to change in demand.

Firms in the industry with high fixed costs may engage in a practice to slash export price occasionally for another reason. If the technology of the industry is such that the costs of adjusting the level of production are high and the continuous use of capacity is required (e.g., steel production), firms in such an industry will keep the level of production constant and sell output at a lower price when they face a reduction in demand (Eichengreen, 1982). This argument also predicts a positive relation between capital intensity and the export price elasticity.

Ethier (1982) suggests that firms that restrain from laying off workers in their long-run interests will sell output below their costs of production when demand is depressed. In the context of cross-section analysis within one country, this implies that the firms that rely on state-invariant employment arrangements are more likely to dump when demand conditions become unfavorable. In Japanese industries that undertake assembly or discrete processing operations, a significant proportion of small- and medium-sized firms are engaged in subcontracting. If subcontracting allows the parent firm to use its permanent labor force more fully while subcontractors absorb the risk of demand fluctuations (Caves and Uekusa, 1976), it is expected that parent firms in industries with substantial subcontracting arrangements are less likely to engage in price cutting in export markets than firms in industries with a low degree of subcontracting.

The basic conditions that allow domestic firms to engage in dumping in the export market are: (1) the ability to segregate the domestic from foreign markets; and (2) the existence of concentrated market structure. When domestic industries are small in the world market and open to trade, domestic producers are indifferent between the two markets in which they cut prices. On the other hand, if domestic firms are allowed to discriminate between the domestic and foreign markets, they are willing to maintain the level of domestic price in the protected monopolistic market while they charge a lower price in the foreign market if they face more competition and thus more elastic demand in the foreign market than they face in the domestic market. This implies that monopolistic firms respond more sharply to a reduction in demand by cutting export price if they can segregate the home market from the export market. Thus, the ability to segregate national markets is the necessary condition for such pricing behavior.

Based on these arguments, the estimated elasticity of export price with respect to short-run domestic demand pressure is explained by a set of independent variables listed in Appendix Table A.3.1. The industry's cost structure is measured by capital intensity, *KO*. The coefficient for *KO* is expected to have a positive sign. The hypothesis on subcontracting is tested by the variable that measures the industry propensity to use sub-contracting, *SUB*. The coefficient for *SUB* is expected to have a negative coefficient if parent firms use subcontractors as buffers against demand fluctuations.

The ability of the industry to segregate national markets is measured by the effective tariff protection, *EFT*, and the advertising/sales ratio, *AD*. *EFT* identifies industries that are protected from international trade and arbitrage. *AD* measures the importance of product differentiation based on advertising and branding. Industries with high advertising intensity are likely to use specialized know-how and skills that are not efficiently transferable from one country market to another. Both *EFT* and *AD* are expected to have positive coefficients as they measure the extent to which the domestic market is segregated from the foreign market.

Export share, *EXP*, and world market share, *SHARE*, are included in the specification to control for the extent of the industry's exporting activity. The industry that exports a large fraction of its total output will

Table 3.3. *Determinants of elasticity of export price*

Independent variable	Dependent Variable: Elasticity of Export Price with Respect to:	
	Domestic demand pressure	Accumulated output
Constant	−0.300 (0.308)	−0.149 (2.670)***
KO	1.168 (2.292)**	−0.192 (0.643)
RD		−0.149 (2.670)***
AD	0.131(2.292)**	
CONS		0.289(2.697)***
EFT	1.948 (2.378)**	−0.764 (1.444)*
EXP	−1.794 (1.815)**	−0.549 (1.450)*
HI	−0.035 (0.389)	0.057 (1.204)
SUB	2.028 (1.423)*	
SHARE	0.268 (0.321)	
Adj-R^2	0.224	0.286
N	34	34

Notes: *t*-test statistics are in parentheses. Both equations are estimated by the WLS method, using the inverse of the estimated standard error of the elasticity as weights. The levels of significance at a one-tailed *t*-test are: *** = 1 percent, ** = 5 percent, and * = 10 percent.

have production capacity that is well-matched to export production and, therefore, is less affected by short-run disturbances in domestic demand. Finally, the Herfindahl index of producer concentration, *HI*, is included to measure the extent of market competition.

Table 3.3 presents the estimation result of the equation that explains the elasticity of export price with respect to domestic demand pressure by cross-sectional data. Because the dependent variable is an estimated parameter, the weighted least squares (WLS) method was used for estimation, using the inverse of the estimated standard error for the dependent variable as weights.[2] In Table 3.3, capital intensity, *KO*, which identifies high fixed-costs industries, has a significant coefficient. Its sign is positive as expected, providing evidence to support the hypothesis that industries with high fixed costs respond more sharply to a decline in domestic demand by cutting export price.

Both of the variables, *AD* and *EFT*, which measure the extent to which national markets are segregated, have positive coefficients that are

[2] Saxonhouse (1976) for this method.

statistically significant. The positive signs on these coefficients suggest that domestic firms in the Japanese market, which is protected by tariff barriers and segregated from the foreign market by the difference in the consumer's taste and preference, cut export price more sharply when domestic demand declines than firms that are exposed to international trade.

The coefficient for export share, *EXP*, is significant and has a negative sign, suggesting that industries that face large export opportunities set up production capacity more independently from domestic demand conditions and adopt more autonomous pricing policies. And, the coefficient for *SUB* is significant and has an unexpected positive sign.

The Learning Curve

One of the most intuitive determinants of the slope of the learning curve is the level of R&D. Previous research on the learning curve shows that the level of R&D expenditures does not reduce costs directly, but R&D tends to reduce costs by accelerating the learning process (Lieberman, 1984). This finding suggests that R&D and cumulative output interactively reduces costs. The R&D expenditures to sales ratio, *RD*, is included as an explanatory variable in the regression equation that explains the learning elasticity. It is expected to have a negative relation with the learning elasticity because the elasticity of export price with respect to cumulated output is negative.

The extent to which the domestic market is protected from the forces of international competition may also determine the slope of the learning curve. Krugman (1984) argues that protecting the domestic market increases the cumulative output of the domestic firm and allows it to exploit learning economies more fully than it otherwise would. If excluding foreign competitors from the domestic market accelerates the learning process, the learning elasticity should become large as the degree of import protection increases. The effective rate of tariff protection, *EFT*, is included in the regression analysis to test this hypothesis.

In addition to these two variables, a set of independent variables is included in the specification to control for other industry-specific factors. These are capital intensity, *KO*, export share, *EXP*, the Herfindahl index of producer concentration, *HI*, and a dummy variable that identifies industries that produce consumer goods.

The equation that explains the elasticity of export price with respect to cumulated output was estimated by using the weighted least squares method. The estimation result is presented in Table 3.3. The coefficient for *RD* is statistically significant and has a negative sign as expected. This result may suggest that the level of R&D expenditures reduces costs through its interaction with the learning curve. R&D accelerated the learning process in Japanese manufacturing industries.[3]

The effective rate of tariff protection, *EFT*, has a significant coefficient and is negatively related to the learning elasticity as expected. This means that the slope of the learning curve becomes steeper as the tariff rate increases, implying that excluding foreign competitors from the domestic market helped to accelerate the learning process in Japanese manufacturing during the 1970s through the mid-1980s.

Among other independent variables included in the specification, the consumer-good dummy variable has a statistically significant coefficient with a positive sign, indicating that the learning effect is more likely to be present in the producer-good industries.

3.4. Domestic Price and Export Price

The statistical analysis of the previous sections assumed that export price is determined independently from domestic price. The classic theory of dumping argued that exporters are able to discriminate between the domestic market and the foreign market when they recognize oligopolistic interdependence fully or collude effectively in the domestic market (Viner, 1923; Robinson, 1933). When they can discriminate the two markets, the oligopolistic exporters maximize profits by charging a low price in the export market and a high price in the domestic market, given the difference in demand elasticity in the two markets. This implies that export price and domestic price are jointly determined and related to each other through underlying elements of market structure. In this

---

[3]   There is a possibility, however, that the positive correlation between cumulative output and price reduction at industry level reflects not only learning but also the cumulative advancement of product and process technology. In this case, the finding that learning curve is steeper for R&D intensive industry may simply suggest that it was caused by more cost reduction by R&D, not by the interaction between R&D and learning.

section, I will examine this issue by using data of Japanese steel industry in the period of 1957–1975. The Japanese steel industry from the late 1950s through the early 1970s is best described as an exporting industry where exports grew rapidly within 20 years. The average export share for this industry was 16.1 percent for 1955–1959, 18 percent for 1960–1964, 24.6 percent for 1965–1969, and 28.2 percent for 1970–1974.[4]

We assume that Japanese firms' products are distinguished from foreign competitors' products by physical traits and auxiliary services. The effect of product differentiation on price is assumed to be such that the firm cannot set price far distant from its rival's price without losing market share in the world market. Marginal cost in producing one additional unit of output is assumed to be the same for products sold in the export and domestic markets. Japanese firms are assumed to behave as if their perception on the short-run export demand elasticity changes as demand fluctuates. Based on Eq. (2.8), the mark-up for the export market, λ_x, is defined as

$$\lambda_x = f(P_f^*, CU, CR4), \qquad (3.2)$$

where P_f^* is the foreign rival's price in the export market, CU is capacity utilization, and $CR4$ is the largest four-firm concentration ratio. CU measures the extent of excess capacity over domestic demand and is a proxy to measure changes in firms' perception on the short-run demand elasticity. The elasticity of demand in the price equation derived in Chapter 2 is implicitly assumed as the elasticity of demand with respect to long-run price. However, individual firms may respond to short-run demand disturbances if it believes that the short-run demand elasticity fluctuates. When the current state of demand is unexpectedly weak and leaves the firm with excess capacity, the firm expects to increase sales by lowering price with a subjective conjecture that its demand curve is currently more elastic. Therefore, we expect a measure of demand condition to have a positive relationship with the mark-up.[5] $CR4$ is included to test

---

[4] See Yamawaki (1988) for a descriptive analysis of the development of the Japanese steel industry in the 1950s through the 1970s.

[5] Note that the elasticity of demand is negatively related to the mark-up term in the price equation.

the hypothesis that the extent of mutual dependence recognized among the domestic oligopolists influences their export pricing behavior.

For the domestic market, the mark-up, λ_d, is defined as

$$\lambda_d = f(CU, CR4). \tag{3.3}$$

CR4 is expected to have a positive effect on the mark-up, and hence domestic price, when the largest four-firm behaves as an oligopoly and recognizes mutual dependence fully (Yamawaki 1984).[6] And we expect a positive relationship between the mark-up and *CU* for the same reason as shown in Eq. (3.2). Our price equations for the export market and the domestic market are defined as $P_f = \lambda_x C'/e$ and $P_d = \lambda_d C'$, respectively, where P_f is the export price in terms of the foreign currency, P_d is the domestic price, C' is marginal cost, and e is the exchange rate. Taking the logarithm and substituting the mark-up terms into the price equations,

$$\ln XP_t = a_0 + a_1 \ln FP_t + a_2 \ln CU_t + a_3 \ln CR4_t + a_4 \ln UMC_t + u_t, \tag{3.4}$$

$$\ln DP_t = b_0 + b_1 \ln CU_t + b_2 \ln CR4_t + b_3 \ln UMC_t + v_t, \tag{3.5}$$

where *XP* is Japanese firms' export price in the home currency, *FP* is foreign rivals' price in the export market, *CU* is capacity utilization, *CR4* is the four-firm concentration ratio, and *UMC* is unit material cost in the home currency, *DP* is Japanese firms' domestic price, and u and v are the error terms.

Table 3.4 presents the estimation results of Eqs. (3.4) and (3.5). Both equations are estimated by two-stage least squares (2SLS) method to correct for simultaneous equations biases. In estimation, *CU* and *CR4* are assumed to be endogenous in the system. In the export price equation, the coefficient of capacity utilization is statistically significant and has a positive sign as expected. On the contrary, its coefficient is insignificant in the domestic price equation. The effect of producer concentration is also asymmetric between export price and domestic price. The coefficient for *CR4* is significant and has a negative sign in the export price equation, and it has a positive coefficient in the domestic price equation. What does this result tell us about the pricing behavior of Japanese steel manufacturers

---

[6] See Yamawaki (1984) for a formal derivation of domestic price equation.

Table 3.4. *2SLS estimates of domestic and export price, Japanese steel industry, 1957–1975*

Variable	Export price (ln *XP*)	Domestic price (ln *DP*)
Constant	2.128 (1.732)	−0.409 (0.531)
ln *FP*	0.856 (3.952)***	
ln *CU*	0.554 (1.705)*	−0.155 (0.590)
ln *CR4*	−0.645 (1.900)*	0.388 (1.771)*
ln *UMC*	0.320 (1.581)	0.736 (6.865)***
SEE	0.060	0.061
DW	2.257	1.838
N	19	19

Notes: t-test statistics are in parentheses. The levels of significance at a two-tailed *t*-test are: ***= 1 percent; ** = 5 percent; and *= 10 percent. The endogenous variables are *CU* and *CR4*. The variables used as instruments are *FP*, *UMC*, *MP*, *WPROD*, and *GNP*. See the Appendix for a detailed account on variable definitions.

during the period of 1957–1975? First, the effect of domestic demand disturbances on price is observed only in the export market. Japanese firms are likely to cut export prices when domestic demand is unexpectedly weak and excess capacity exists. They are less likely to cut domestic prices but are more likely to maintain level prices. Second, high concentration tends to motivate Japanese firms to raise price in the domestic market. On the contrary, they reduce prices in the export market. This asymmetric behavior in domestic and export pricing in the highly concentrated industry reflects the difference in the extent of monopoly power possessed by Japanese firms between the domestic market and the export market. Although the empirical result in Chapter 2 suggests that Japanese steelmakers behaved as oligopolists in the export market, it is likely that they faced more competition in the export market than in the domestic market. In the late 1950s and the late 1960s, the Japanese steel industry was protected from international trade by high tariffs, and import penetration was extremely low (Yamawaki, 1988). Under such a market structure, the opportunity for buyers in the domestic market to engage in arbitrage – buy the good abroad and import it cheaply – is restricted. Thus, this result is consistent with the hypothesis of international price discrimination. These findings suggest that, at least in the case of Japanese firms in the steel industry during the period of 1957–1975, export price was jointly determined with domestic price in conjunction with the state of domestic demand conditions and market structure.

3.5. Conclusions

This chapter examined the effects of domestic demand conditions and learning economies on export price with an aim to identify the underlying factors that determine Japanese firms' dumping behavior. The statistical results of the estimates of the elasticity of export price show that the Japanese firms' export price behaviors, and the underlying factors, differ significantly among different industries. One of the important findings of this chapter is that in Japan's most successful export industries during the period in question, such as tape and video recorders (including audio equipment), radio and TV receivers, semiconductors, and passenger cars, export prices did not respond to fluctuations in domestic demand or to the extent of excess capacity over domestic demand. This finding suggests that the export pricing behavior of the dumping-alleged industries, such as steel products and chemical products, is different from the behavior of other dumping-alleged industries, such as TV receivers and semiconductors, in Japan.

On the contrary, the statistical analysis found that export price declined steadily over time along the learning curve in Japan's most successful exporting industries during the 1970s and through the 1980s, such as integrated circuits, semiconductors, tape and video recorders (including audio equipment), and photographic cameras.

This cross-sectional analysis was used to identify the determinants of the elasticity of export price and showed that: (1) Japanese industries that use capital-intensive technology and are protected from import competition responded to declines in domestic demand by cutting export price; and (2) Japanese industries that are intensive in R&D and are protected from import competition reduced export price along the learning curve.

Finally, this chapter has examined the relationship between export price and domestic price by using time-series data on the Japanese steel industry. The statistical model shows that when weak domestic demand leaves Japanese firms with excess capacity, they tend to reduce price in the export market and expect to increase sales with a conjecture that the export demand curve is currently more elastic. It also finds highly concentrated market structure facilitates such pricing behavior. This finding is, at least, consistent with the pattern often observed in the late 1950s through the early 1970s in the Japanese steel industry where the oligopolistic Japanese firms tried to maintain domestic price stable at a high level while using the export market to absorb domestic demand disturbances.

4

Foreign Market Structure, Export Price, and Profitability

4.1. Introduction

The statistical analysis in the Chapter 2 showed that the export pricing behavior of Japanese firms was often affected by foreign rivals' pricing in the world export market. Although this finding is useful, it is still very general and does not tell us about specific mechanisms through which foreign rivals set prices and Japanese firms respond to these mechanisms. If a foreign price is determined by structural characteristics in the foreign market, export prices, and accordingly the profitability of Japanese firms, will be affected by those foreign structural characteristics as well. In other words, if an oligopoly in the foreign market elevates prices substantially above marginal costs, Japanese firms that are well-equipped to jump entry barriers will be attracted to enter and export to this market. This suggests that market structure in the foreign markets to which Japanese firms export should be taken into account in the analysis of their export pricing behavior. Figure 1.1 illustrates this point.

The aim of this chapter is to present a simple model that is an extension of the model presented in Chapter 2. If the incumbents elevate prices substantially above marginal costs in the foreign market, Japanese exporters to this market should earn positive profits, given their cost conditions. In the first part of this chapter, I will first identify the determinants of Japanese profits in the foreign market and estimate their values. The second part of this chapter examines the same question in detail by presenting some descriptive analysis on the entry, and the pricing behaviors, of Japanese auto manufacturers in the U.S. luxury car market during the late 1980s and early 1990s.

4.2. Model[1]

This section develops a model of a domestic monopolist that exports to a foreign market. To make the model simple, I assume that the domestic firm sells in both domestic and foreign markets, whereas a foreign firm sells only in its home market. The domestic monopolist's marginal cost of producing one additional unit of output is assumed to be the same for the products sold in the domestic market and those sold in the foreign market. The domestic firm's product is assumed to be differentiated from the foreign firm's product in the foreign market due to national characters embedded in these products, which are considered to be imperfect substitutes in the foreign market. In this section, I assume the domestic firm to be a Japanese firm.

The assumptions of the one-way trade flow and product differentiation suggest that the domestic monopolist faces the following foreign demand function, which depends on a foreign rival's price, the monopolist's own export price, and the domestic demand function, which depends on domestic price:

$$X = X(P_f(1+t), P_f{}^*); \quad X_f < 0; \quad X_f{}^* > 0; \quad X_t < 0, \quad (4.1)$$

$$D = D(P_d); D_d < 0, \quad (4.2)$$

$$Q = X + D, \quad (4.3)$$

where X is foreign demand for goods produced in the domestic market, P_f is export price, P_f^* is price of foreign goods, t is the tariff rate levied in the foreign market, D is domestic demand for goods produced in the domestic market, P_d is domestic price, and Q is total output produced by the domestic firm. Subscripts on the functions denote partial derivatives.

The foreign producer faces:

$$X^* = X^*(P_f^*, P_f(1+t)); \quad X_{f^*}^* < 0; \quad X_f^* > 0; \quad X_t^* > 0, \quad (4.4)$$

where X^* is foreign demand for goods produced by the foreign firm.

---

[1] The model presented in this section is explained fully in Yamawaki (1986).

The domestic firm's problem is to maximize its profits:

$$\Pi = R^d\,(P_d) + R^x\,(P_f,\,P_f{}^*,\,t) - C^d\,(c;\,P_d) - C^x(c;\,P_f,\,P_f^*,\,t),$$
$$(4.5)$$

And, similarly, the foreign firm maximizes its profits, assuming no exports:

$$\Pi^* = R^*(P_f{}^*,\,P_f,\,t) - C^*(c^*;\,P_f{}^*,\,P_f,\,t),\qquad(4.6)$$

where R is the revenue function, C is the cost function, and c is constant marginal cost. We assume that Π is concave in prices of the monopolist's country, and that the total profit and the marginal profit with respect to the monopolist's price increase with the price of the other country. This implies that $\Pi_{ij} > 0$. This profit maximization determines domestic and export prices as

$$P_d = P_d\,(c),\qquad(4.7)$$
$$P_f = P_f\,(c;\,P_f{}^*,\,t);\qquad(4.8)$$

and foreign price as

$$P_f{}^* = P_f{}^*\,(c^*;\,P_f,\,t).\qquad(4.9)$$

Total differentiation of the first-order condition with respect to P_f and P_f^* implies $dP_f/dP_f^* = -\Pi^x{}_{ff^*}/\Pi^x{}_{ff}$, and by assumption $dP_f/dP_f^* > 0$, so that the reaction functions are upward sloping. Thus far, the model has assumed that a monopolist controls production in each market. Empirically, however, the degree of market imperfection varies from one industry to another. Therefore, it is more empirically relevant to incorporate various elements of market structure explicitly in the model. Barriers to entry have been theorized to be significant factors to elevate price above marginal costs without attracting entry since Bain's (1956) seminal work. Seller concentration has a positive relation to price and profits in formal models of price determination (Cowling and Waterson, 1976; Yamawaki, 1984). Such consideration of market structure, therefore, suggests that P_d, P_f, and P_f^* should be determined by the following functions:

$$P_d = P_d\,(c: BE,\,CR),\qquad(4.10)$$
$$P_f = P_f\,(c;\,P_f{}^*,\,t,\,CR),\qquad(4.11)$$
$$P_f{}^* = P_f{}^*\,(c^*;\,P_f,\,t,\,BE^*,\,CR^*),\qquad(4.12)$$

where *BE* is a vector of entry barriers, and *CR* is producer concentration. Thus, BE^* and CR^* denote barriers to entry and concentration in the foreign market, respectively. Assuming that the domestic firm does not recognize mutual dependence with the foreign firm, Eqs. (4.11) and (4.12) yield the Cournot equilibrium solutions in prices in the foreign market:

$$P_f = P_f(c; c^*, t, CR, BE^*, CR^*), \tag{4.13}$$

$$P_f^* = P_f^*(c^*; c, t, CR, BE^*, CR^*). \tag{4.14}$$

Equations (4.13) and (4.14) show that the degree of barriers to entry and concentration in the foreign market positively affect export price through their effects on foreign price. Because $dP_f/dP_f^* > 0$, the domestic firm sets export price at a high level in the foreign market where foreign price is elevated above marginal costs given the high entry barriers and the high concentration.

Equations (4.13) and (4.14) can be defined in terms of price–cost margins by supposing that price in each market is expressed as the product of the mark-up factor and marginal cost, $P = \lambda c$, where λ is the mark-up factor. Assuming that the mark-up factor is determined by the ingredients in the price function, and using Eqs. (4.10) and (4.13),

$$PCM^d = PCM^d(BE, CR), \tag{4.15}$$

$$PCM^x = PCM^x(CR, c^*, t, BE^*, CR^*). \tag{4.16}$$

Equation (4.16) indicates that, given segregated national markets, the price–cost margin on export sales depends on foreign price and accordingly on foreign production cost, foreign entry barriers, and foreign concentration. Thus, the price–cost margin on export sales is expected to be high in industries where entry barriers and concentration are high in the foreign market.

4.3. Determinants of Price–Cost Margins on Exports

Specification and Variables

The theoretical model in the previous section suggests that both foreign and domestic market structures affect the price–cost margins on domestic sales and exports. Although this provides a useful framework for empirical analysis, one critical empirical problem that researchers face is that price–cost margins on export sales and domestic sales are often unobservable separately. We therefore assume that the observed price–cost margin is a weighted average of the price–cost margins in domestic and foreign markets that are unobservable (Pugel, 1980):

$$PCM = (1-XS)*PCM^d + XS*PCM^x, \qquad (4.17)$$

where *XS* is the share of exports in total industry shipments. Because the U.S. market was the most important destination for Japanese exports during the 1960s and the early 1970s, Eq. (4.17) is estimated for the Japanese industries exporting to the U.S. market.

From Eqs. (4.15), (4.16), and (4.17), the specification for regression is given by

$$
\begin{aligned}
JPCM = a_0 &+ a_1 DS * JMESCDR * JC4M + a_2 DS * JKREQ*JC4M \\
&+ a_3 DS*JADSL*JC4M + a_4 XS*USMESCDR*USC4M \\
&+ a_5 XS*USKREQ*USC4M + a_6 XS*USADSL*USC4M \\
&+ a_7 JKSL + a_8 JGR + \varepsilon,
\end{aligned} \qquad (4.18)
$$

where ε is random disturbance, and the prefixes *J* and *US* stand for Japan and the United States, respectively. In Eq. (4.18), the dependent variable is the price–cost margin and is determined by elements of market structure in both domestic (Japanese) and foreign (U.S.) markets. All the independent variables, except the capital–sales ratio (*JKSL*) and the rate of demand growth (*JGR*), are weighted by the domestic sales share (*DS = 1 − XS*) and the export share (*XS*).

The height of entry barriers is measured by the three traditional variables that have been used in the existing empirical literature on the determinants of profits and entry in industrial organization.[2] Minimum efficient plant scale relative to the market (*MES*) measures the barrier to entry due to scale economies. The efficient size of the plant is defined as the average size of the largest plants producing half of total shipments

---

[2] See Bain (1956), and Masson and Shaanan (1982, 1987). See also studies in Geroski and Schwalbach (1991).

in the industry.[3] Because the maximum limit price set by incumbents depends on not only the minimum efficient plant, but also on the extent of the cost disadvantage of suboptimal-plant scale plants (*CDR*), a variable constructed by the interaction between these two variables is used in regression analysis to capture the effect of entry barriers due to scale economies (*MESCDR*).[4] The second variable used to measure entry barriers is the capital requirement at minimum efficient plant scale (*KREQ*). The capital requirement at *MES* is obtained by multiplying *MESCDR* by the total assets of the industry. The need for large-scale investments that involve large sunk costs may discourage a potential entrant because the entrant's losses are large if entry is unsuccessful. To measure the effect of a barrier based on product differentiation through advertising and marketing costs, the advertising-to-sales ratio (*ADSL*) is included in the specification.

The four-firm producer concentration interacts with each measure of entry barriers because a relationship between price–cost margins and concentration should be present only when entry barriers exist. As Bain (1956) points out, without barriers to entry, there is no reason for market power to arise.[5] All of the independent variables included in Eq. (4.18) are expected to have positive relationships with the price–cost margin. Yamawaki (1986) provides a detailed account on additional variables tested in this model specification. The definitions of the variables and data sources are given in the Appendix to this chapter.

Regression Analysis[6]

The estimation result of Eq. (4.18) is presented in Table 4.1. Model (1) in Table 4.1 includes only the Japanese variables, but Model (2) includes both U.S. and Japanese structural variables. The U.S. minimum efficient scale variables and U.S. advertising variables, both interacted with concentration, have positive relations with the Japanese price–cost margin after controlling for the effects of market structure in the Japanese

---

[3] See Comanor and Wilson (1974) for this definition.
[4] Caves, Khalizadeg-Shirazi, and Porter (1975) provide a detailed account of this variable.
[5] See Salinger (1984) for a similar specification on barriers to entry and concentration.
[6] Yamawaki (1986) describes the statistical results fully.

Table 4.1. *Regression equations explaining Japanese price–cost margins (JPCM), 1970*

Independent variables	(1)	(2)	(3)
JKSL	0.202 (2.62)***	0.182 (2.46)***	0.200 (2.66)***
JGR	0.101 (1.83)**	0.103 (1.95)**	0.109 (2.02)**
DS*JMESCDR*JC4M	1.613 (3.41)***	1.012 (1.83)**	1.550 (3.37)***
DS*JKREQ*J4CM	−0.0005 (0.60)	0.007 (0.77)	−0.0004 (0.56)
DS*JADSL*JC4M	3.649 (1.98)**	2.814 (1.54)*	3.850 (2.15)**
XS*USMESCDR*USC4M		23.355 (1.68)**	
XS*USKREQ*USC4M		−0.027 (1.80)**	
XS*USADSL*USC4M		26.013 (1.84)**	
XS*USPCMFIT			1.189 (2.21)**
Constant	0.132 (4.67)***	0.126 (4.68)***	0.111 (3.81)***
Adj-R^2	0.247	0.321	0.290
F	5.46 (5,63)	5.03 (8,60)	5.64 (6,62)

Notes: *t*-test statistics are in parentheses. All the equations are estimated by the OLS method. The definitions of variables are in the Appendix of this chapter. Yamawaki (1986) provides detailed accounts on various test results on model specification. The levels of significance are *** = significant at the 1% level; ** = significant at the 5% level; and * = significant at the 10% level.

market. The negative coefficient for the U.S. capital requirements is caused by its high simple correlation with the U.S. *MES* variable ($r = 0.66$). Because all the U.S. variables are multiplied by export share, the partial effect of each U.S. variable on the price–cost margin varies with export share.[7] The *F*-test on the significance of the U.S. variables rejects the null hypothesis that the coefficients on the U.S. variables are jointly equal to zero at the 5 percent level of significance. Thus, the effect of an U.S. variable becomes larger as the export share of Japanese firms become larger. The result in Table 4.1 implies that the pricing decision of Japanese firms is affected by foreign market structure and that the extent to which foreign market structure affects the firm's pricing depends on the size of export opportunities it faces in the foreign market.

[7] The large difference of coefficients for domestic and export markets reflects the difference in values of domestic and export shares. The range of values of export share is between 0 percent and 28.5 percent in the sample, and hence domestic share varies between 71.5 percent and 100 percent.

To examine more directly if Japanese exporters change export price by responding to U.S. price, an additional structural model is constructed and estimated. Following the theoretical discussion of Eqs. (4.11) and (4.12), the Japanese price–cost margin (*JPCM*) equation in a structural form may include the U.S. price–cost margin (*USPCM*) instead of the U.S. structural variables. A Hausman test was conducted to test the hypothesis that *USPCM* is statistically independent of the disturbance term. The null hypothesis of zero correlation between *USPCM* and the disturbance term is rejected, implying that *USPCM* and *JPCM* need to be treated as simultaneously determined variables. To correct for a possibility of simultaneous bias, an instrumental variable estimator is used for *USPCM*. The *USPCM* instrument was obtained by regressing *USPCM* on the U.S. structural variables (Yamawaki, 1986).

The equation that explains the Japanese price–cost margin by using the *USPCM* instrument (*USPCMFIT*) is presented as Model (3) in Table 4.1. The coefficient for *USPCMFIT* is statistically significant and has a positive coefficient as expected. This result reinforces the previous finding on the positive effect of U.S. structural variables on the Japanese price–cost margin. Japanese exporters set export prices positively in reaction to local price in the U.S. market.

Estimates of Price–Cost Margins

Price–cost margins for domestic and export sales are estimated from Eq. (4.17) and the estimation result of Model (1) in Table 4.1. The ten industries for which the estimates of price–cost margins on exports for 1970 are the highest are listed in Table 4.2.[8] As expected, industries with high export shares in 1970, such as pottery products, tires, TV receivers, synthetic fibers, electric lamps, and watches, show high price–cost margins on export sales. The estimated price–cost margins on exports exceed

---

[8] Price-margins for export market were calculated from Eq. (4.17) by subtracting the estimates of price-margins for domestic market from actual price-cost margin for the industry. Price cost-margins for domestic market are estimated from Eq. (4.15). The estimates of price-cost margins for export market may be biased because price-cost margins for domestic market are not observable. Industries with high price-cost margins on export sales but with significantly low export share (<3 percent) are deleted from the list.

Table 4.2. *Estimates of price–cost margins for domestic and export sales, 1970,*
selected industries

Industry	SIC, Japan 1968	Price–cost margin domestic market 1970 (%)	Price–cost margin export market 1970 (%)
Vitreous Plumbing Fixtures	3041	32.5	44.7
Tires and Tubes	2811	22.8	37.6
Television Receivers	3543	26.9	37.3
Pens and Mechanical Pencils	3941	32.2	31.8
Organic Fibers	2643	27.1	31.3
Cellulose Manmade Fibers	2641	25.3	30.2
Paper Industry Machinery	3463	30.0	29.0
Electric Lamps	3531	22.8	27.7
Watches and Clocks	3771	23.3	26.7
Flat Glass	3011	51.8	26.4
Motor Vehicles	3611	21.0	11.8

Notes: The estimation method is described in the text. This table lists the ten industries where
the estimate of price–costs margins is the highest in the sample of sixty-nine industries, plus
the motor vehicle industries. Table 4.2 does not include industries where the export share is
lower than 5%.

the estimated price–cost margins on domestic sales for the first four
industries listed in Table 4.2.

Although the list in Table 4.2 shows a pattern in which industries
with large exports tend to enjoy high price–cost margins in the U.S.
market, there are exceptions to this pattern. The most notable is the motor
vehicle industry in the sample, where the estimated price–cost margins
for exports and domestic sales are 0.108 and 0.210, respectively. This
result for the motor vehicle industry in 1970 suggests that its profitability
in the export market was lower than the average for the manufacturing
industry (0.238) for that year. Although it is not feasible to evaluate if this
low-level of the price–cost margin was transitory given the nature of the
data used, it is at least not inconsistent with the result of export pricing
behavior in the 1970–1984 period that was presented in Chapter 2. The
export price behavior in passenger car market was classified neither as an
oligopoly nor as a price-taker. It is quite plausible that in the late 1960s and
early 1970s, the Japanese automobile industry was still at an infant stage
in the international market and was unable to command high price–cost

margins. On the other hand, the domestic market was protected from import competition by a number of measures, such as the currency value of Japanese yen that was set at a relatively low level against the U.S. dollar, the model approval system regulated by the government, and barriers to entry in distribution channels.[9]

4.4. A Case of Japanese Entry into the U.S. Luxury Car Market[10]

The analysis in the previous section showed that Japanese firms set export price in response to foreign rivals' price in the export market, which is in turn determined by the elements of market structure in that market. Cross-sectional analysis found that barriers to entry and concentration in the foreign market elevated foreign price above marginal costs and thus increased price–cost margins of Japanese firms that exported to the foreign market. Although this finding is useful, it is still very general and does not provide us with specific information about the way in which Japanese firms set export price in the U.S. market. To elaborate on this point, this section presents a case of Japanese entry into a specific U.S. market, namely Japanese entry into the U.S. luxury car market in the 1980s.

The U.S. Luxury Car Market

Japanese automakers grew markedly in the mid-1970s through the early-1980s, established themselves as the major automobile manufacturers in the world, and became known for their efficient production system and reliable products by the mid-1980s.[11] Three Japanese manufacturers, Honda, Nissan, and Toyota, entered subsequently into the luxury segment of the U.S. passenger car market in the late 1980s. The key features of their entry strategy were the establishments of new brand names, Acura (1986), Infiniti (1989), and Lexus (1989) and of new dealer networks for the marketing of these new brands. New brands were created for the

---

[9] See Chapter 9 of this book and Williamson and Yamawaki (1991).
[10] See Yamawaki (2002) for a statistical analysis of Lexus's entry and its effect on rivals' prices.
[11] See Clark and Fujimoto (1991) and Fujimoto (1999).

U.S. market to differentiate them from the traditional image commonly associated with their entry-level and middle-segment models. Among these three Japanese entrants, Toyota's Lexus was considered the most significant entry because it offered a model (LS 400) that was built from scratch based on a new platform. This model was designed with the intention to compete with European brands in this particular segment. Another important feature of Lexus was that it established a network of small numbers of well-focused exclusive dealers in order to assure a high level of sales per dealer and provide better customer service.

Before the entry of Japanese firms, the luxury sedan/coupe segment of the U.S. passenger car market was competed mainly between U.S. and European brands, such as Cadillac, Lincoln, Audi, BMW, Mercedes-Benz, and Jaguar. Although the U.S. parents of these brands, GM and Ford, are full-line producers and offer much wider range of models, the European producers, particularly BMW, Mercedes-Benz, and Jaguar (before the acquisition by Ford in 1989), are highly focused in the luxury/performance automobile segment. However, Audi offers a range of upscale models that share the same platforms with its parent's models (VW). The price range for BMW and Mercedes-Benz is set slightly higher than that of Audi in the U.S. market, reflecting the extent of product differentiation and the strength of brand. The three German firms manufactured cars for this particular segment almost exclusively in their main factories located in Germany and exported them to the U.S. market at the time of Japanese entry. Similarly, Jaguar produced all of its cars in the United Kingdom and exported to the U.S. market through the 1980s. The product range of the three German firms is highly overlapping, and they compete in virtually every subcategory (e.g., small-size, medium-size, and large-size sedans) within the luxury market.

Pricing and Market Share

Figure 4.1 shows the behavior of list price for the models in the large- and middle-size segments of this market between 1986 and 1997. Because Lexus is considered the most significant new competitor in this market,

US Dollars

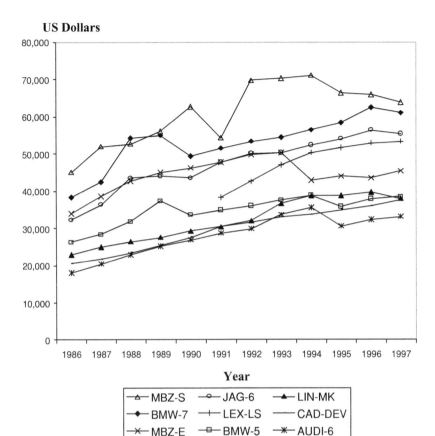

	MBZ-S	JAG-6	LIN-MK
	BMW-7	LEX-LS	CAD-DEV
	MBZ-E	BMW-5	AUDI-6

Figure 4.1. U.S. price of luxury cars, full-and medium-size segment, 1986–1997.
Source: Automotive News and *Ward's Automotive Yearbook.*
Notes: Price is average list price for base model excluding dealer options and is constructed based on the following models: BMW, 5-series (525/528) and 7-series (735/740); Mercedes-Benz, E-class (300/320), and S-class (420); Jaguar, XJ-6, Cadillac, DeVille; Lincoln, Continental; and Lexus, LS400. Abbreviations in the legend are: MBZ = Mercedes-Benz, JAG-6 = Jaguar XJ-6, CAD-DEV = Cadillac DeVille, LIN-MK = Lincoln MK VII/VIII, and LEX-LS = Lexus LS.

Lexus's prices are compared with the incumbents' prices. All of the prices are in terms of U.S. dollars and are the base prices before dealer options. Before the entry of Lexus, the prices of Mercedes-Benz S-class and BMW 7-series were the highest, followed by Mercedes-Benz E-class, Jaguar XJ-6, BMW 5-series, and the two U.S. brands, Cadillac and Lincoln. When Toyota introduced the Lexus LS-400, its U.S. price was substantially below the level set by its major competitor in its class (BMW 7, Mercedes-Benz S, and Jaguar XJ) and was even comparable to the level of a midsegment model such as BMW 5-series. However, LS400's price was much higher than the price levels set by Lincoln and Cadillac. Toyota increased LS-400's price gradually after entry, but its level was kept always below the price levels of its European rivals through 1997.

A similar pattern is observed for the price behavior of Lexus's mid-sized model (the ES). As shown in Table 4.2, the Lexus ES's entry price was set substantially below the levels set by its potential rivals such as the BMW 5-series and the Audi A6. It was even below the price level of BMW's smaller 3-series. This pattern suggests that the entry price of the Lexus ES was set at the level undercutting all the major competitors' prices in its size class and a smaller size class.

This observation is consistent with the prediction of the theoretical model presented in Section 4.2. The Japanese firm set its export price in response to the price set by its rivals in the export market. The level of foreign rivals' prices is, in turn, determined by the importance of product differentiation and brand recognition in this segment of the U.S. automobile market. It is important to note, again, that the ranking of price remained unchanged between BMW, Mercedes-Benz, Jaguar, and Lexus in the high-end market during this period, although Lexus's price increased over time. Another important observation from Figures 4.1 and 4.2 is that several years after Lexus's entry into the market, Mercedes-Benz, BMW, and Audi all reduced prices of their midsized models. The price of Mercedes-Benz's E-class was dropped markedly in 1994, deviating from the price level of Jaguar and becoming more comparable with the price level of the BMW 5-series.

Figure 4.3 shows the development of unit sales for the six incumbent firms and the new entrant in this market over the 1986–1997 period.

US Dollars

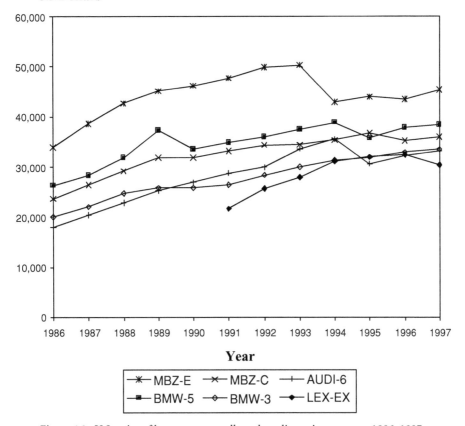

Figure 4.2. U.S. price of luxury cars, small- and medium-size segment, 1986–1997.
Source: *Automotive News* and *Ward's Automotive Yearbook*.
Notes: Price is average list price for base model excluding dealer options and is constructed based on the following models: BMW, 5-series (525/528) and 3-series (325/328); Mercedes-Benz, E-class (300/320), and C-class (C280/190); Audi, 5000/A6; and Lexus, ES300. Abbreviations in the legend are: MBZ = Mercedes-Benz and LEX-ES = Lexus ES.

Units

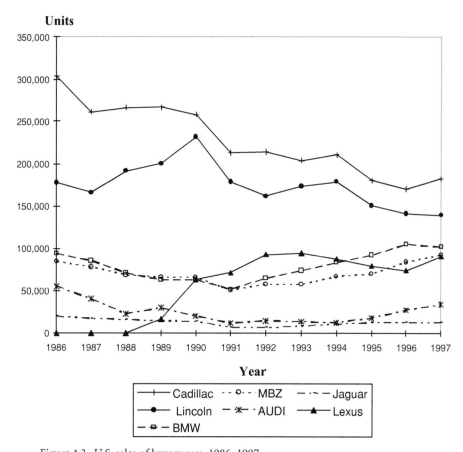

Figure 4.3. U.S. sales of luxury cars, 1986–1997.
Source: *Automotive News* and *Wards' Automotive Yearbook*.
Notes: Unit sales include all of the models sold in the U.S. market except convertibles, sports cars, and SUVs. MBZ in the legend indicates Mercedes-Benz.

It does not include unit sales of convertibles and SUV models because, at the time of Lexus's entry, these types of vehicles were not considered the brand's important substitutes. The most remarkable observation that emerges from Figure 4.3 is the rapid growth of Lexus's share in the market. Indeed, Lexus established its position in the market very quickly after entry. It entered the market in 1989, and its unit sales grew rapidly and reached its initial peak of 95,000 units by 1993. The behavior of unit sales for BMW over time is very similar to that of Mercedes-Benz. In fact, unit sales for BMW and Mercedes-Benz declined steadily during the 1986–1991 period, but regained growth in the subsequent period. Unit sales of both Cadillac and Lincoln show a declining trend over the 1986–1997 period, although Lincoln's unit sales were more volatile than Cadillac's sales after a sudden increase in 1990.

4.5. Conclusions

In this chapter, I developed a simple model of export price that takes into account elements of foreign market structure. It shows that export prices depend on foreign rivals' prices and elements of foreign market structure. The statistical analysis provided evidence that supports the following two hypotheses: (1) U.S. firms are likely to set the export price above marginal costs in the industries where the barriers to entry based on scale economies and product differentiation are high, given the level of concentration; and (2) Japanese exporters in the U.S. market, given such a relatively high U.S. price, match export price to the level of U.S. price. As a result of this interaction, the price–cost margin of Japanese exporters becomes high in this market. This finding suggests that it is important to take into account market structure of the foreign market when examining the price behavior of exporting firms. It is highly plausible that market performance of exporting firms is influenced by the elements of market structure in the destination market to which they export.

The descriptive analysis of Japanese entry into the U.S. luxury market reinforces this finding. A Japanese firm, attracted by potentially high profits in this market, entered into the market by offering a new concept. Although barriers to entry for de novo entrants may be very high in this market, the existing Japanese firm who was well-qualified to jump such barriers entered successfully into this segment of the market. Upon entering the market, the Japanese firm set prices to match incumbents' prices and kept these prices lower than their incumbents' prices. As a result, the Japanese firm gained market share rapidly and established its position as a strong competitor in the market.

5

Competitive Advantage and Export Performance

5.1. Introduction

The empirical analysis in the last three chapters dealt primarily with export pricing behavior. However, the case of Japanese entry into the U.S. luxury car market in the late 1980s suggests that export price strategy is just a part of the key success factors used to penetrate the international market. Indeed, the descriptive analysis of Chapter 4 suggests that the success of Japanese firms in the U.S. luxury car market depended on a number of factors in addition to its pricing strategy.

It is quite obvious, in the case of luxury automobiles, that the automaker has to offer an innovative product that is well designed and engineered in the export market where consumers are well-informed and sophisticated. A new product is developed by using many tasks including market intelligence, product design, engineering, and procurement, which are conducted both at the headquarters at home and at the R&D and design centers in the foreign market that the firm intends to enter. Foreign R&D and design centers often play crucial roles in the early stages of product development as they have a better understanding of the target consumer's preference and the local market trends. Production of luxury models is often done at a factory located in Japan where the automaker can source a layer of competitive advantages: firm-specific resources and capability that are not easily transferable to foreign locations and country-specific advantages, such as factor endowment and the existence of related and supporting industries. By the time the new model hits the export market, the firm should be ready for local sales and be involved in marketing, distribution, and service in that market. Although it is often ignored in the economic analysis of international trade, establishing a local support system is often among the most crucial factors for exporters to be successful in the foreign market. The automaker needs to set up an efficient and reliable distribution system to penetrate the new market. Just shipping products from the home country and leaving them at the foreign port does not guarantee any success in the foreign market. Local dealers need to be well-equipped with a pool of engaging sales and supporting work force. Local headquarters must support local dealers and provide them with a variety of services such as finance, warranty, technical support, and logistics. The involvement in local marketing, distribution, and service is crucial for success in the export market.

Although this description may oversimplify what automobile makers do to export their products, it at least suggests that a number of factors are at work to influence the likelihood of success in the export market. The aim of this chapter is to illustrate this point by deriving a simple model to examine the determinants of market share held by firms that supply imports to the foreign market, namely *import share*. This chapter then presents some evidence that supports the hypotheses on the determinants of import share predicted by this model.

There exists a large empirical literature that seeks to explain trade structure by the variables drawn from the factor-proportions (Heckscher–Ohlin) theory of trade.[1] Although this theory provides an important base for analysis of country-specific factors, the focus of this chapter is more on industry- and firm-specific determinants of trade performance. Therefore, the international rivalry model in this chapter uses the same approach used to derive the models discussed in Chapters 2 and 4 to emphasize these two sets of factors. The international rivalry model departs from the traditional premise of perfect competition by treating firms as oligopolists and assumes that home and foreign firms may engage in an oligopolistic interaction in the international market. This means

---

[1]   For example, see Deardorff (1984) for a survey. See Leamer (1984), Urata (1983), Balassa and Noland (1989) for empirical analysis of the influence of factor endowments on trade for Japanese industries.

that the model takes into consideration the elements of market structure as determinants of trade performance.

Treating market shares of domestic and foreign exporters in the world market as a Cournot-equilibrium outcome of international oligopoly is not particularly new in the theoretical literature of international trade as already described in Chapter 2 (Brander, 1981; Lyons, 1981; Brander and Krugman, 1983; Helpman and Krugman, 1985). This chapter presents a model for empirical analysis inspired by this line of theoretical models.

5.2. A Model[2]

The assumption used in this model is very similar to the theoretical models of Chapters 2 and 4. We assume that there are two countries, one domestic and one foreign, and that a monopolist controls each market before trade takes place. We assume further that products produced by firms in these two countries are differentiated due to embedded national characteristics, making products imperfect substitutes between the two national markets. With the products differentiated, each monopolist behaves as if its home market is segregated and distinct from the foreign market. Once a trade takes place between the two countries, the monopolist forms oligopolistic conjectures with the foreign rival about quantities. Thus, the major difference between the models in this chapter and previous chapters is the different treatment in the choice of a decision variable.

The international rivalry model allows for the possibility that both domestic and foreign firms undertake investments in advertising, R&D, and tangible capital in a manner analogous to the Spencer and Brander (1983) and the Krugman (1984) formulations. Thus, in the first stage, firms choose the levels of advertising, R&D, and capital stock, and in the second stage firms choose output levels. The second-stage equilibrium is determined, therefore, by taking the levels of advertising, R&D, and capital stock as given in the first stage. The payoff to each firm then is expressed as a function of all of the levels of strategic variables set by both firms.

---

[2] This section draws from Yamawaki and Audretsch (1988).

The prices of the domestic firm's product in the domestic market and in the foreign market are denoted by P_d and P_f, respectively, and the prices of the foreign firm's products in the domestic market and the foreign market are denoted by $P_d{}^*$ and $P_f{}^*$, respectively. A_d and A_f are the domestic firm's advertising budget invested in the domestic and foreign markets, and $A_d{}^*$ and $A_f{}^*$ are the foreign firm's advertising budget invested in the domestic and foreign markets, respectively. Advertising messages are assumed to be county-specific messages, and exporters need to make additional investments abroad. The domestic firm produces output D for domestic consumption and output X for exports. Similarly, the foreign firm produces output D^* for exports to the domestic market and output X^* to remain in its own market. The inverse demand functions for the domestic firm in its home and foreign markets are given by

$$P_d = P_d\,(D,\ D^*,\ A_d,\ A_d{}^*), \tag{5.1}$$
$$P_f = P_f\,(X,\ X^*,\ A_f,\ A_f{}^*). \tag{5.2}$$

Similarly, the inverse demand functions for the foreign firm in the domestic and foreign markets are given by

$$P_d{}^* = P_d{}^*\,(D,\ D^*,\ A_d,\ A_d{}^*), \tag{5.3}$$
$$P_f{}^* = P_f{}^*\,(X,\ X^*,\ A_f,\ A_f{}^*), \tag{5.4}$$

where the asterisks denote the variables associated with the foreign firm. Prices are assumed to fall as the domestic firm's output and the rival firm's output increase. In addition, prices are assumed to increase as the domestic firm's advertising increases, but to fall as the rival firm's advertising increases. It is assumed that the marginal costs of the domestic and foreign firms are given by

$$c = c\,(W,\ K,\ Z), \tag{5.5}$$
$$c^* = c^*(W^*,\ K^*,\ Z^*), \tag{5.6}$$

where c is the constant marginal cost, W is wages, K is capital stock, and Z is the level of cost-reducing R&D. Marginal costs are assumed to decrease as capital stock and R&D increase but to increase as wages increase.

The total profit of the domestic firm is

$$\Pi = P_d D + [P_f/(1+t^*)] \, X - c \, (D+X) - gX - rK - A - Z,$$
(5.7)

where t^* is the ad valorem import tariff rate levied in the foreign market, g is a constant per unit transportation cost, r is the cost of capital, and $A = A_d + A_f$. The total profit of the foreign firm is

$$\Pi^* = P_f^* X^* + [P_d^*/(1+t)]D^* - c^*(D^* + X^*)$$
$$- g D^* - r K^* - A^* - Z^*,$$
(5.8)

where t is the import tariff rate levied in the domestic market, and $A = A_d^* + A_f^*$. Because of the assumption of constant marginal costs, the profit-maximizing choice of D is independent of X and, similarly, D^* is independent of X^*.[3] The first-order conditions for profit maximization define the domestic and foreign firms' reaction functions as

$$D = f \, (D^*; W, K, Z, A_d, A_d^*),$$
(5.9)
$$D^* = f^* \, (D; W^*, K^*, Z^*, A_d, A_d^*, t, g),$$
(5.10)

where both functions are defined taking the levels of advertising, R&D, capital stock, wages, import tariffs, and transport costs as a given. To obtain equilibrium solutions, a set of conditions is imposed as described in the Appendix to this chapter. It is assumed that the reaction functions are sloping downward. The solutions for Eqs. (5.9) and (5.10) are given by

$$D = f \, (W, W^*, K, K^*, Z, Z^*, A_d, A_d^*, t, g),$$
(5.11)
$$D^* = f^* \, (W, W^*, K, K^*, Z, Z^*, A_d, A_d^*, t, g).$$
(5.12)

Because I assume that domestic and foreign products are differentiated, an equilibrium level of market share held by the foreign firm in the domestic market can be expressed in terms of inverse demand functions (5.1) and (5.3) and Eqs. (5.11) and (5.12),

$$m(y) = P_d^*(y)D^*(y)/[P_d(y)D(y) + P_d^*(y)D^*(y)],$$
(5.13)

[3] K and K^* are defined as capital stock for production rather than production capacity, imposing no constraints on production of D and X or D^* and X^*. This assumption is made to simplify the model.

where y is the vector of the predetermined variables. The partial effect on the equilibrium level of import share, $m(y)$, of a predetermined variable, is given by

$$\partial m/\partial y_i > 0 \text{ as } \partial D^*/\partial y_i > 0 \text{ and } \partial D/\partial y_i < 0, \qquad (5.14)$$

$$\partial m/\partial y_i < 0 \text{ as } \partial D^*/\partial y_i < 0 \text{ and } \partial D/\partial y_i > 0. \qquad (5.15)$$

Using the conditions described in the Appendix to this chapter, it follows that the foreign firm's equilibrium market share will increase and when it increases its own advertising, R&D, capital stock, and when the domestic firm increases its own wages. The foreign firm's market share will decrease when it increases its own wages, when the domestic firm increases its own advertising, R&D, and capital stock, when import tariffs increases in the domestic market, and when transport costs increase. That is, $\partial m/\partial A_d^* > 0$, $\partial m/\partial Z^* > 0$, $\partial m/\partial K^* > 0$, $\partial m/\partial W > 0$, $\partial m/\partial A_d < 0$, $\partial m/\partial Z < 0$, $\partial m/\partial K < 0$, $\partial m/\partial W^* < 0$, $\partial m/\partial t < 0$, and $\partial m/\partial g < 0$.

5.3. Determinants of Japanese Import Share in the U.S. Market

Specifications and Variables

We estimate Eq. (5.13), which identifies the equilibrium level of import share as a function of the vector of the strategic variables, by using data on Japanese imports in the U.S. market. Thus, the domestic market is assumed to be the United States, and the foreign market is assumed to be Japan in the empirical analysis below. A linear specification of the model is given by

$$USMJ = a + \sum b_{Ji}Y_{Ji} + \sum b_{USi}Y_{USi} + \sum c_k Y_k + \mu, \qquad (5.16)$$

where $USMJ$ is the share of Japanese imports in the U.S. market; Y_{Ji} and Y_{USi}, the explanatory variables for Japan and the United States, are constructed symmetrically between the two countries; Y_k represents the additional explanatory variables; μ is the disturbance term and $i = 1, \ldots, m$.

This specification differs markedly from the cross-commodity model used in the previous literature (see Deardorff, 1984) to explain import shares. The traditional approach, which is derived from the generalized factor-proportions model, employs only variables constructed for one country (Y_{USi}).[4] These variables are assumed to represent common industry characteristics across all countries, thus $b_{Ji} = 0$. The present model instead regards Y_{Ji} and Y_{USi} as variables that differ across two countries reflecting their past commitments and allows that $b_{Ji} \neq 0$.

The variable definitions are summarized in the appendix to this chapter. A_d and Z in Eqs. (5.11) and (5.12) are measured by the advertising/sales ratio, *AD*, and the R&D sales ratio, *RD*, in the statistical model. Two variables are used to measure the extent of strategic investment on tangible capital (K): the rate of growth of gross fixed assets at a constant price, *KGROW*, to measure precommitment of capital; and the rate of growth of shipments, *SGROW*, to measure committed supply capability at the margin. Labor costs (W) are measured by a proxy for unit labor costs, *ULC*, which is defined as nominal wages per production worker multiplied by the inverse of labor productivity.

In the theoretical model, it is assumed that a monopolist controls each market. Empirically, however, the extent of market structure varies from one industry to another. Therefore, we include a variable that measures the extent of market competition, the four-firm producer concentration ratio, *CR4*. As the statistical results in Chapter 4 show, the incumbent in a highly concentrated industry with high barriers to entry is likely to enjoy a high price in pretrade period. If domestic price exceeds marginal costs, the foreign firm will be interested in entering this market. Therefore, the import share is expected to have a positive relationship with the U.S. concentration ratio and a negative relationship with the Japanese concentration ratio. In addition, if non-Japanese imports are close substitutes for U.S. goods and Japanese imports, non-Japanese imports may inject additional Cournot players, who are not captured by the U.S. concentration ratio, into the market. Thus, we include the market share of non-Japanese imports, *USMNONJ*, to control for this additional effect.

As a proxy for transportation cost, we use the mile radius within which 80 percent of total industry shipments are made in the United States,

---

[4]   See Deardorff (1984), pp. 485–486.

DISTANCE, which was estimated by Weiss (1972). This variable measures the transportability of goods, reflected by overland shipment costs.[5] The extent of trade protection in the U.S. market is measured by the nominal rate of tariff protection, *USNOT,* and by an index of nontariff barriers, *USNTB.* Finally, the difference in product characteristics across industries is controlled by a dummy variable that has a value of one if the industry's major products are consumer's goods and a value of zero if producers' goods.

Because the model requires a symmetrical construction of variables between the United States and Japan, U.S. manufacturing industries were first matched to their counterparts in Japan. This matching procedure left me a sample of forty-two industries defined at a level comparable to the U.S. three-digit SIC level. Because it is more appropriate to assume that Japanese firms form Cournot conjecture with U.S. firms only when they penetrate in the U.S. market, I further selected twenty-four of the forty-two industries from this sample for which Japanese import share in the U.S. market exceeded 0.5 percent. Because the explanatory variables are assumed to be predetermined, a lag between the dependent variable and the explanatory variable is considered whenever possible. The choice of the length of the lag is mainly governed by the availability of data. Data sources are presented in the Appendix to this chapter.

Statistical Results

Table 5.1 presents the estimation result of the regression equations where the magnitude of the coefficients for *AD, RD, KL, KGROW, SGROW,* and *ULC* is restricted to being equal for Japan and the United States. The prefixes *J* and *US* attached to individual variables stand for Japan and the United States, respectively. All of the equations in Table 5.1 are estimated by the ordinary least squares (OLS) method.[6] The overall

---

[5] Data on ocean-shipping costs are available. See Clark (1981). However, the concordance between his industries and my industries is less than adequate for use in statistical analysis. Pugel (1978) finds the 80 percent radius a significant determinant of import share in the U.S. market.

[6] See Yamawaki and Audretsch (1988) for detailed accounts for the restrictions on the coefficients and the result of a Hausman test for simultaneity.

Table 5.1. *Regression equations explaining the share of Japanese imports in the U.S. market, 1977 (USMJ)*

Variable	1	2
JAD–USAD	1.679 (5.095)***	1.777 (5.884)***
JRD–USRD	0.972 (3.211)***	1.381 (4.130)***
JKGROW–USKGROW	0.016 (1.468)*	
JSGROW–USSGROW		0.007 (2.248)**
JULC–USULC	−0.140 (2.507)**	−0.130 (2.520)**
JCR4	−0.066 (2.494)**	−0.065 (2.687)***
USCR4	−0.001 (0.033)	−0.018 (0.554)
USMNONJ	0.163 (1.678)*	0.152 (1.731)*
DISTANCE	0.069 (4.620)***	0.065 (4.832)***
USNOT	0.001 (1.135)	0.001 (1.326)
USNTB	−0.021 (3.257)***	−0.0235 (3.864)***
CONSD	0.050 (3.748)***	0.051 (4.190)***
Constant	−0.006 (0.296)	0.004 (0.196)
Adj-R^2	0.788	0.824
F (11, 12)	8.757	10.775

Notes: *t*-test statistics are in parentheses. The levels of significance for one-tailed test are: *** = 1 percent, ** = 5 percent, and * = 10 percent.

significance and explanatory power of the statistical model are satisfactory, as shown in Table 5.1 where more than 75 percent of the interindustry variation in the dependent variable is explained.[7]

The coefficients for *AD* and *RD*, expressed as the difference between the two countries, are statistically significant and have the expected positive signs. Thus, an increase in *AD* and *RD* in the Japanese industries relative to its U.S. counterpart increases the Japanese market share in the U.S. market. However, an increase in *AD* and *RD* in the U.S. industry relative to its Japanese counterpart reduces the Japanese import share. This result provides evidence that supports the predictions of the theoretical model summarized by Eqs. (5.14) and (5.15).

The difference in the rate of growth of shipments, *JKGROW–USKGROW*, have a significant positive relation with Japanese import share, implying that a faster increase of investment in tangible

---

[7] See Yamawaki and Audretsch (1988) for the result of a test to examine if the results are dominated by a single influential observation in a small sample.

capital by Japanese firms relative to that by U.S. firms results in a larger Japanese share. The difference in the rate of growth of shipments, *JSGROW–USSGROW*, also has a significant coefficient with the expected positive sign. This result reinforces the result on *KGROW* and provides evidence that supports the predictions of the theoretical model.

The difference in labor costs is a significant determinant of the Japanese import share in the U.S. market. Its negative coefficient suggests that an increase in unit labor costs in the Japanese industry relative to the U.S. counterpart decreases the Japanese import share. Concentration is the only variable for which the coefficient was found to be different in magnitude between Japan and the United States. *JCR4* has a significant negative coefficient, and *USCR4* is insignificant in this specification.[8] To the contrary, the market share of non-Japanese imports, *USMNONJ*, has a significant coefficient with the expected positive sign, suggesting that non-Japanese imports inject additional Cournot-type players into the U.S. market who are not captured by *USCR4*.

The analysis in Chapter 4 shows that the profits of Japanese firms increase with the elements of Japanese market structure that correspond to noncompetitive price levels. Japanese firms' profits increase with the elements of U.S. market structure that correspond to the high price levels, which exceed the marginal costs and create positive profits for Japanese exporters to the U.S. market. The analysis of this chapter confirmed this finding by showing that the Japanese import share in the U.S. market increases with the competitive advantage of the Japanese industry and decreases with the competitive advantage of the U.S. industry. Competitive advantage was measured here by the relative levels of strategic variables, such as advertising, R&D, physical capital, and wages between the two countries. Although the previous literature has determined that the overall structure of Japanese–U.S. trade in the 1970s can be attributed at least to the traditional factor endowments (Audretsch and Yamawaki, 1988), the specific trade equilibrium in either a foreign market or a

---

[8] Sakakibara and Porter (2001) show that high concentration is positively associated with market-share instability, which in turn has a positive relationship with world export share of Japanese industries. Their result is not consistent with the result presented here.

domestic market is apparently well-explained by the international rivalry model presented in this chapter.

5.4. Exports and Japanese Involvement in U.S. Marketing, Distribution, and Service

One of the significant determinants of Japanese import share in the U.S. market was the advertising-to-sales ratio in the statistical analysis of the previous section. Although the Japanese advertising variable was constructed from advertising expenditures in the Japanese market, a more appropriate variable should be advertising expenditure in the U.S. market as the theoretical model suggests (demand functions (5.1) and (5.2)). The statistical analysis uses the variable constructed from advertising expenditures in Japan only because of the unavailability of data on advertising expenditures by Japanese exporters in the U.S. market. It is therefore assumed that Japanese firms allocate advertising expenditures between the Japanese and U.S. markets as a constant proportion of sales in each market. Because this treatment of Japanese involvement in advertising and marketing in the United States is not ideal, we will examine this issue more carefully by providing supplementary evidence in this section. The aim is to find a relationship between Japanese industries' trade performance and involvement in marketing, distribution, and service in the United States.

Descriptive Statistics

As the model presented in Chapter 4 suggests, an exporter faces barriers to entry into the foreign market. One of the significant barriers in the U.S. market was product differentiation by marketing and advertising. Although it was not explicitly analyzed in Chapter 4, another important source of entry barriers is setting up a scale-intensive distribution system.[9] An exporter may consider an option to work with import distributors in the local market or a large trading company at home to jump such distributional barriers. For Japanese exporters who intended to enter

---

[9] See Bain (1956) and Porter (1976, 1980). See also Williamson and Yamawaki (1991).

the U.S. market, using U.S. import distributors was less likely an option because U.S. importers were both markedly smaller and less efficient in stock turnaround and sales per employees compared to the distribution arms of U.S. manufacturers in a number of industries.[10] In some cases, the large Japanese trading companies (*Shosha*) provided an answer. In basic raw materials and related end products in food, fuel, fiber, metals, and chemicals, they offered extensive established networks and a depth of experience. However, they had been found to be less than satisfactory in supporting products that required extensive marketing and an after-sales service to consumers (Yoshino and Lifson, 1986). If Japanese exporters decided to invest in local distribution, they would have to be of a significant size to match the incumbent's size in distribution and efficiency.

Japanese manufacturing firms in some specific industries chose to commit their resources in the local market and established distribution subsidiaries, thereby engaging in marketing, organizing distribution channels, and providing customer services in the local market. Japanese firms invested a larger sum of resources in the wholesale trade sector of the United States than did other foreign firms by the end of 1986. Total assets held by U.S. affiliates in wholesale trade of Japanese nonbank companies were $38.8 billion and accounted for 45 percent of total foreign assets in the U.S. wholesale trade sector at the end of 1986. In wholesale trade, Japan was first, distantly followed by (West) Germany ($10 billion) and the United Kingdom ($12 billion), in the size of total assets of nonbank U.S. affiliates.[11] Table 5.2 shows that the share of U.S. distribution employees in total employment for Japanese firms in the United States was 46 percent in 1986 and the highest among the major foreign investors. Therefore, Japanese firms, unlike other foreign investors, concentrated their local operations on distribution activities during this period.

---

[10] For example, sales per establishment for *U.S.* import distributors as a percentage of manufacturer subsidiaries are 43 percent in electrical machinery and 37 percent in transportation equipment. U.S. Department of Commerce, Bureau of Census, *Census of Wholesale Trade*, vol. 1, 1987.

[11] This is according to the U.S. Department of Commerce, *Survey of Current Business, 68*, May 1988, table 12, p. 72.

Table 5.2. *Employment of nonbank U.S. subsidiaries by country of ultimate beneficial owner, 1986 (thousands of employees)*

Country of ultimate beneficial owner	All industries (1)	Manufacturing (2)	Wholesale trade (3)	(2) as % of (1)	(3) as % of (1)
All Countries	2964	1400	305	47.2	10.3
United Kingdom	637	332	44	52.1	6.9
Canada	601	272	20	45.3	3.3
Germany	305	155	48	50.8	15.7
The Netherlands	259	107	8	41.3	3.1
Japan	216	68	100	31.5	46.3
France	193	106	28	54.9	14.5
Switzerland	182	110	11	60.4	6.0

Source: U.S. Department of Commerce, *Survey of Current Business*, May 1988, table 10, p. 70.

The automobile companies, Toyota, Nissan, Honda, Mazda, and Fuji appear to be the largest distribution operations according to the employment data collected for U.S. distribution subsidiaries that were more than 50-percent owned by Japanese manufacturing companies across forty-four industries in 1986. The number of employees in U.S. distribution subsidiaries was more than 2,500 for Toyota and Nissan and exceeded 1,000 for Honda and Mazda. These companies are followed by the companies who are leading names in cameras, watches, office machines, and household appliances. In fact, per dollar of export sales, cameras, watches, clocks, toys, and musical instruments have the most employees in U.S. distribution relative to their size. In addition to a physical distribution function, these distribution subsidiaries provide after-sales service, user information and support, and sales force and customer education, and arrange marketing campaigns and point of sale promotions.

Statistical Analysis[12]

Employment data on U.S. distribution subsidiaries that were 50-percent or more owned by Japanese manufacturing companies were collected

[12] See Yamawaki (1991a) for full account on the statistical analysis.

for 1986. The employment figures at the subsidiary level were aggregated into the three-digit industry level. The full sample consists of
forty-four Japanese manufacturing industries matched with their U.S.
counterparts. This sample was used to test the hypothesis that Japanese
firms penetrate the U.S. markets more successfully in those industries
where they invest more in local distribution activities. Because distributional activities are subject to substantial expenses that must be sunk in
the local market, and the use of independent distributors is an inefficient route to distribute products, the foreign firm that enters the market
through export is put at a disadvantage against local incumbents. To
overcome the disadvantages that raise entry barriers, the foreign firm
must commit resources to the local distribution activity. Such commitment also signals to local customers that the firm's presence in the
local market is not transitory, and this commitment creates a goodwill
asset.[13] The failure to commit resources, therefore, becomes a deterrent to
exports.

Hence, we estimate the following equation to test this hypothesis:

$$\ln EXP = a_0 + a_1 \ln DIST + \sum_{j=1} a_{j+1} X_j + u, \qquad (5.17)$$

where *EXP* is total Japanese exports to the U.S. markets, *DIST* is total
employment in U.S. distribution subsidiaries of Japanese manufacturing
companies, *X* is the vector of exogenous variables, *u* is the disturbance
term, $j = 1, \ldots, m$, and a_1 is expected to have a positive sign. If the size of
U.S. distribution subsidiaries is determined by the size of exports to the
U.S. markets, the following relation should be considered in addition to
(5.17),

$$\ln DIST = b_0 + b_1 \ln EXP + \sum_{i=1} b_{i+1} Z_j + e, \qquad (5.18)$$

where *Z* is the vector of exogenous variables, *e* is the disturbance term,
$i = 1, \ldots, m$, and b_1 is expected to have a positive sign. All of the variables used in the statistical analysis are defined in Table A.5.2 in the
Appendix.

---

[13] See Bergsten, Horst, and Moran (1978). See also Pennie (1956) and McCulloch (1988)
for discussions on direct investments in distribution that promote exports.

Table 5.3. *Regression equations explaining total Japanese exports to the U.S. market (EXP) and total employment of personnel in U.S. distribution subsidiaries of Japanese manufacturing companies (DIST)*

	Dependent variable	
Variable	ln *EXP*	ln *DIST*
ln *DIST*	0.964 (3.48)***	
ln *EXP*		0.569 (1.32)*
ln *USEMP*	0.481 (2.87)***	−0.076 (0.23)
ln *JKL*	0.213 (0.73)	
ln *TRN*	−0.860 (1.40)*	
USRDS	−16.691 (1.35)*	30.678 (2.04)**
USGR		−0.117 (0.23)
CONSD		0.830 (1.36)*
Constant	4.626 (1.28)	1.027 (0.57)

Notes: Both equations are estimated by the two-stage least square (2SLS) method. The exogenous variables used for estimation are *USEMP, USRDS, USGR, CONSD, JKL,* and *TRN. t*-test statistics are in parentheses. The levels of significance are: *** = 1 percent, ** = 5 percent, and * = 10 percent.

In both equations, the total employment in the U.S. industry (*USEMP*) is included to control for the size of industry. The export equation includes capital intensity (*JKL*) in the Japanese industry, a proxy for transportation costs (*TRN*), and R&D intensity (*USRD*) as standard determinants of trade flows. The distribution equation includes R&D intensity (*USRDS*), a dummy variable that identifies consumer nonconvenience goods (*CONSD*),[14] and growth of the U.S. industry (*USGR*). These variables represent product and industry characteristics that determine the extent of U.S. distribution activities of Japanese firms.

Table 5.3 presents the estimation results of both equations. Equations (5.17) and (5.18) were estimated by the two-stage least squares (2SLS) method to correct the possible simultaneous bias.[15] In the *EXP* equation,

---

[14] See Porter (1976) for the definition of nonconvenience goods. This type of goods requires extensive customer service and auxiliary activities because their attributes are complex, durable, and often innovative. Thus, we expect that the manufacturer of this type of goods commits more to distributional activities.

[15] See Yamawaki (1991a) for the OLS estimates and issues on simultaneity.

the coefficient on *DIST* is statistically significant and has a positive coefficient as expected. The positive effect of *DIST* on *EXP* is robust even when the traditional trade variables (*JKL, TRN,* and *USRD*) and the size of industry (*USEMP*) are controlled in the regression equation. In the *DIST* equation, the coefficient of *EXP* is significant and has a positive sign as expected.[16] This result provides empirical evidence that supports the hypothesis that the Japanese involvement in U.S. distribution activities strongly promoted their exports to the U.S. market. Therefore, this finding strongly reinforces the previous section's findings on the effect of the competitive advantage of Japanese industries on their trade performance.

5.5. Conclusions

This chapter has presented a simple model of trade performance that relates import share with the competitiveness of domestic and foreign industries. The statistical analysis found that the Japanese import share in the U.S. market increases with the competitive advantage of Japanese industries and decreases with the competitive advantage of U.S. industries. It also sought to identify the causal influence of Japanese investments in distribution channels on Japanese exports. The results strongly support the influence of the Japanese investment in U.S. distribution activities on Japanese exports to the U.S. markets.

These findings are complement to the findings of Chapter 4 on the influence of Japanese and U.S. market structures on profits for Japanese exports to the United States. Price levels in the U.S. markets are determined by U.S. market structures. Japanese exporters set export price to match the U.S. price and earn positive profits in the markets where noncompetitive prices prevail. Because the U.S. markets that have noncompetitive price levels are likely to have high barriers to entry, Japanese firms that intend to export to such markets should have competitive advantages

---

[16] A Hausman test rejected the null hypothesis that *EXP* is independent of the disturbance term of *DIST* equation at the 10-percent level, suggesting that *EXP* needs to be treated as endogenous in the *DIST* equation. The OLS coefficient for *EXP* in a *DIST* equation is much larger and highly significant than the 2SLS estimate presented in Table 5.3. See Yamawaki (1991a).

to jump the barriers. Japanese exporters who have committed to intangible and tangible resources, such as R&D, distribution, marketing, service, production capacity, and increased operation efficiency relative to U.S. rivals, are likely the candidates who can jump U.S. entry barriers and reach the potential positive profits.

6

Entry into the European and U.S.
Manufacturing Industries

6.1. Introduction

Beginning the mid-1980s, Japanese firms vastly expanded their presence in the U.S. manufacturing sector through foreign direct investment (FDI). The flow of Japanese manufacturing FDI in North America surged from US$1.2 billion in 1985 to US$4.8 billion in 1987 and peaked in 1989 at of US$9.6 billion. Indeed, the investment flow during the period of 1985–1990 alone accounted for approximately 85 percent of the cumulative flow of Japanese manufacturing FDI into North America from 1967 to 1990. Japanese firms entered into a broad range of U.S manufacturing industries by establishing "green-field" plants and acquiring existing local firms. The presence of Japanese firms extended from food processing, chemicals, and steel products to general machinery, electronics, and automobiles.

The growing presence of Japanese firms was not a phenomenon peculiar to the U.S. markets. Japanese firms started investing extensively in European manufacturing industries as well during the 1980s. The flow of direct investment in manufacturing from Japan to Europe grew rapidly after 1987 and continued to grow beyond 1990. Japanese firms were present in various member states of the European Union (E.U.) extending from the United Kingdom and Germany to Spain and Portugal.[1]

---

[1] The extent and pattern of Japanese FDI during the late 1980s have been well-documented by previous research. See Dunning (1986), Graham and Krugman (1989), Froot (1991), Micossi and Viesti (1991), Jacquemin and Buigues (1991), and Yamawaki (1994). The determinants of Japanese FDI have been examined by Heitger and Stehn (1990), Mann (1990), and Drake and Caves (1992). See also Caves (1993).

Although Japanese manufacturing firms intensified their FDI during the late 1980s, their entry to the U.S. and European markets through FDI started much earlier – during the 1970s (Tsurumi, 1976). The pattern of early investments, however, differs significantly from the investments during the late 1980s in at least two important aspects. First, the finding of Drake and Caves (1992) shows that the interindustry variation of Japanese FDI in the United States during the 1970s is explained by economic factors that are different from those that explain the variation of FDI during the late 1980s. The importance of sales promotion and R&D to an industry increased and became significant determinants of Japanese FDI during the late 1980s. Kogut and Chang (1991), Hennart and Park (1994), and Pugel, Kragas, and Kimura (1996) find similar results for Japanese FDI and provide empirical evidence that supports the hypothesis that the accumulation of intangible assets in Japanese firms and their base industries motivated Japanese FDI during the 1980s.

Another significant characteristic of Japanese FDI during the 1980s that is distinguished from the pattern before 1980 is the frequent use of acquisitions by Japanese investors as a mode of entry (Froot, 1991; Yamawaki, 1994; Blonigen, 1997). Japanese firms entered U.S. and European manufacturing industries not only by establishing new plants but also by acquiring local concerns. One explanation for this increasing popularity of acquisitions among Japanese firms during the late 1980s is given by the appreciation of Japanese yen against the U.S. dollar after 1985 (Froot and Stein, 1991; Blonigen, 1997).[2] These two strands of findings clearly suggest that the pattern of Japanese FDI during the late 1980s differs from the earlier pattern due to the shifts in the competitive advantages of Japanese firms and the external economic conditions.[3]

Although previous research on the Japanese FDI in the late 1980s has contributed greatly to deepen our understanding of the motivation of Japanese firms to invest abroad, the majority of the findings are based on the experience in the U.S. market. As noted earlier, it was not just the U.S. market but also the European market in which Japanese firms invested in the late 1980s. An important question to ask is whether Japanese FDI

[2] See also Kogut and Chang (1996).
[3] See Caves (1993) for a survey of this literature on Japanese FDI up to 1993.

in Europe was motivated by the same factors as Japanese FDI in the United States. The existing empirical literature on Japanese FDI in Europe suggests, at least, that direct investments in the European Community (E.C.) by Japanese electronics firms in the late 1980s were motivated by the imposition of E.C. antidumping and other trade restrictions (Belderbos and Sleuwaegen, 1998).

The first aim of this chapter is to examine if the underlying motivation of Japanese firms to invest in European markets was the same as its motivation to invest the U.S. markets. I address this question by examining if the choice of acquisition as a mode to enter a new market is different between the two regions. The second aim of this chapter is to examine the effect of firm rivalry on FDI. In this chapter, I examine whether strategic interactions among sellers motivated them to invest heavily in the United States in the late 1980s.

6.2. The Data

For this purpose, a data set was constructed from the subsidiary level data compiled by Toyokeizai, *kaigai shinshutsu kigyo soran*, [*Directory of Japanese firms investing abroad*]. The data published in this corporate directory is based on questionnaire survey conducted by the publishing company and lists an extensive number of Japanese firms that own subsidiaries in foreign countries. For example, the 1991 survey covers 5,300 firms and their 12,500 subsidiaries distributed among 130 countries. The subsidiaries listed in this survey are those more than 10-percent owned by Japanese parents. Although the Ministry of International Trade and Industry (MITI) in Japan conducts a benchmark survey on the behavior of Japanese firms operating abroad and publishes a summary of this survey every 3 years, its original data at the individual subsidiary level are not easily accessible.[4] For this reason, the Toyokeizai data are used in this study.[5]

---

[4] MITI, *kaigai jigyo katsudo kihonchosa: kaigai toshi tokei soran*.
[5] One weakness of this data is that quantitative variables, such as sales, employment, and total assets, are occasionally missing for some companies. Although it is desirable to use these variables, this requirement reduces the sample size significantly. Therefore, the analysis presented in this chapter resorts primarily to qualitative information.

The sample of Japanese subsidiaries used in this study is generated by the following criteria: (1) the subsidiary is in manufacturing; (2) the Japanese parent firm is also in manufacturing;[6] (3) the subsidiary was established before 1991 and was in operation as of 1991; and (4) the Japanese parent owns more than 10 percent of the subsidiary. Out of the 12,522 subsidiaries listed in the 1991 Toyo Keizai survey data, 3,282 subsidiaries are located in the United States, and 2,549 subsidiaries are located in Europe. A further breakdown by sectors reveals that 1,054 U.S. subsidiaries and 524 European subsidiaries are in the manufacturing sector. From this sample, in manufacturing, 631 U.S. subsidiaries and 336 European subsidiaries are selected as a final sample for which all the selection criteria listed above are met.[7]

Table 6.1 presents a summary of the number of Japanese parent firms and their subsidiaries in the United States and Europe. In this sample, 391 Japanese firms own 631 subsidiaries in the United States, and 193 Japanese parents own 336 subsidiaries in Europe. These subsidiaries are classified according to three categories in terms of the geographic pattern, and their numbers are listed in rows 2–4 in Table 6.1. Japanese parents companies that own subsidiaries only in the United States account for 57.6 percent of the sample, but Japanese parent companies that own subsidiaries only in Europe account for 14.1 percent of the sample. The remaining 28.4 percent of the sample invested in both the U.S. and European markets by the end of 1990. An interesting observation on the third group of firms is that they own, on average, at least two subsidiaries each per region in contrast with one subsidiary per region for the first two groups of Japanese firms. Reflecting the underlying skewed distribution of Japanese parents toward the U.S. market in the sample, the distribution of subsidiaries between the two regions shows a similar pattern. In only 22 percent of the sample, European subsidiaries were owned by Japanese parents that had invested only in Europe by the end of 1990.

---

[6] This procedure eliminates subsidiaries owned by trading companies from the sample and makes interfirm comparisons among parents more sensible.

[7] See Yamawaki (1994) for a more detailed description of this data. The Japanese subsidiaries in the European sample are distributed among Austria, Belgium, Denmark, France, Germany, Ireland, Italy, the Netherlands, Spain, and the United Kingdom.

Table 6.1. *Ownership patterns for Japanese firms and their subsidiaries in the United States and Europe, 1990*

Type of parent firm	No. of parent firms	No. of subsidiaries			No. of subsidiaries per firm
		US	Europe	Total	
Firms that own subsidiaries in the US but not in Europe.	262 (57.6%)	345 (54.7%)		345 (35.7%)	1.32
Firms that own subsidiaries in Europe but not in the US.	64 (14.1%)		74 (22.0%)	74 (7.3%)	1.11
Firms that own subsidiaries both in the US and Europe.	129 (28.4%)	286 (45.3%)	262 (78.0%)	548 (56.7%)	2.22 (US) 2.03 (Europe)
Total	455 (100.0%)	631 (100.0%)	336 (100.0%)	967 (100.0%)	2.13

Notes: Shares of total numbers of firms are in parentheses. Percentages may not add up to 100 due to rounding errors. The Japanese subsidiaries in the European sample are distributed among Austria, Belgium, Denmark, France, Germany, Ireland, Italy, the Netherlands, Spain, and the United Kingdom.

Table 6.2 reports the distribution of parent firms by the year of entry and type of sequential entry process. The first three types of entry sequence correspond to the type of parents that invested in both the United States and Europe. Seventy-one firms out of these 262 firms first entered in the U.S. market and subsequently entered in the European market. However, fifty-two firms first chose the European market and later entered the U.S. market. Several interesting observations emerge from Table 6.2. First, Japanese firms that own subsidiaries either in the United States or in Europe entered in the markets more recent periods. More than 70 percent of them established their first subsidiaries in the two regions during the 1980s. Second, to the contrary, approximately 50 percent of the firms that entered both in the United States and Europe had established their subsidiaries by the late 1970s. Third, more than

Table 6.2. *Parent firms by year and sequence of entry in the United States and Europe*

	Total no. of firms	Year of first entry		
		Before 1970	1970–1979	1980–1990
Entered into the US first, then Europe.	71			
First entry into the US.		18	24	29
Subsequent entry into Europe.				
Before 1970		4	–	–
1970–1979		4	8	–
1980–1990		10	16	29
Entered in Europe first, then the US.	52			
First entry into Europe.		3	22	27
Subsequent entry in the US.				
Before 1970		3	–	–
1970–1979		0	5	–
1980–1990		0	17	27
Entered in the US and Europe in the same year.	6	0	2	4
Entered only the US.	262	11	43	208
Entered only Europe.	64	2	14	48

50 percent of the firms that entered the U.S. market before 1970 waited until the 1980s to establish their first European subsidiaries.[8]

6.3. Statistical Analysis of Entry Mode

Patterns

Table 6.3 reports the distribution of U.S. and European subsidiaries by method of entry. The most important pattern that emerges from this table

---

[8] For location decisions of Japanese firms in European manufacturing industries, see Yamawaki (1993), and Head and Mayer (2004). Yamawaki, Barbarito, and Thiran (1998) and Yamawaki (2006) compare the location decisions of Japanese firms and U.S. firms in European manufacturing. For evidence on sequential entry by Japanese firms, see, Kogut and Chang (1996) and Chang (1995).

Table 6.3. *Japanese subsidiaries by mode and year of entry in the United States and Europe, 1990*

	United States		Europe	
Total number of subsidiaries	631 (100.0%)		336 (100.0%)	
Subsidiaries established before 1980				
Total	114 (18.1%)	(100.0%)	81 (24.1%)	(100.0%)
Green-field	106	(93.0%)	74	(91.4%)
Acquisition	8	(7.0%)	7	(8.6%)
Subsidiaries established after 1980				
Total	517 (81.9%)	(100.0%)	255 (75.9%)	(100.0%)
Green-field	383	(74.1%)	184	(72.2%)
Acquisition	134	(25.9%)	71	(27.8%)

Notes: See the text for the description of data and sample selection.

is that Japanese firms, in general, prefer entry via green-field investment to acquisition. Indeed, 74 percent of total number of U.S. subsidiaries (383 out of 517 U.S. subsidiaries) and 72 percent of European subsidiaries (258 out of 336 European subsidiaries) established after 1980 are green-field investments. However, the remaining 26 percent of subsidiaries in the United States and 28 percent in Europe are established through acquisitions.

Second, the likelihood of Japanese firms to use acquisitions to enter U.S. and European markets was much lower during the 1970s. Of the 142 subsidiaries that entered the U.S. market via acquisition through 1990, 134 of these acquisitions took place after 1980. In Europe, of the seventy-eight entries that took place via acquisition, seventy-one of them took place after 1980. In other words, fewer than 10 percent of the entries were by acquisitions in both markets before 1980. This indicates clearly that acquisition had become much popular among the Japanese firms during the 1980s.

However, the frequency of Japanese firms to use acquisition is somewhat different between and Europe and the United States when their strategy is taken into consideration. Table 6.4 classifies Japanese entrants according to their diversification strategy. When a diversified entry is

Table 6.4. *Japanese subsidiaries by mode of entry and degree of diversification in the United States and Europe, 1990*

	United States		Europe	
Total number of subsidiaries	631 (100.0%)		336 (100.0%)	
Green-field entry				
Total	489 (77.4%)	(100.0%)	258 (76.8%)	(100.0%)
Horizontal	430	(87.9%)	234	(90.7%)
Diversified	59	(12.1%)	24	(9.3%)
Acquisition				
Total	142 (22.5%)	(100.0%)	78 (23.2%)	(100.0%)
Horizontal	105	(73.9%)	74	(94.9%)
Diversified	37	(26.1%)	4	(5.1%)

Notes: (1) Diversified entry is identified if the subsidiary's principal product is classified into the two-digit industry that does not contain the parent firm's principal product.
(2) Percentages may not sum up to 100.0 because of rounding errors.

defined as an entry into a two-digit industry that is different from the parent firm's principal industry, Table 6.4 shows that entry by acquisition is more frequently associated with diversified entry into the United States than into Europe. In fact, 26 percent of the total number of entries into the U.S. market through acquisition was by diversified entry, however, it was only 5 percent in the European market.

Table 6.5 reports Japanese entry counts by mode of entry for a cross section of the two-digit manufacturing industries to which the subsidiary's principal product is classified. A pattern that emerges from this table is that the frequency of Japanese firms to use acquisitions differs across industries. Japanese firms are likely to acquire European firms that produce nonelectrical machinery and transportation equipment, but they are likely to acquire U.S. firms that produce food, chemicals, and electrical machinery.

Hypotheses

The descriptive analysis in Section 6.3 suggests that the overall frequency to use acquisition by Japanese firms is comparable between the U.S. and European markets, but the motivation to use acquisition may differ in the two markets. The aim of this subsection is to find out how it is

Table 6.5. *Japanese acquisitions and green-field investments in the United States and Europe, by industry, 1990*

Industry	United States			Europe		
	Total	Green-field	acquisition	Total	Green-field	acquisition
Food processing	40	22	18	6	3	3
Textiles	7	6	1	9	8	1
Apparel	3	2	1	9	4	5
Lumber	1	1	0	0	0	0
Furniture	5	3	2	2	1	1
Paper	3	3	0	0	0	0
Printing	2	2	0	0	0	0
Chemicals	58	39	19	33	24	9
Rubber products	7	4	3	6	2	4
Plastic products	29	25	4	16	14	2
Stone, clay, and glass	19	11	8	8	3	5
Iron and steel	20	16	4	3	2	1
Nonferrous metals	27	22	5	6	6	0
Fabricated metals	8	7	1	1	1	0
Nonelectrical machinery	88	66	22	61	42	19
Electrical machinery	147	117	30	99	90	9
Transportation equipment	127	113	14	35	21	14
Instruments	13	9	4	13	12	1
Miscellaneous	27	21	6	29	25	4
Total	*631*	*489*	*142*	*336*	*258*	*78*

Notes: The Japanese subsidiaries in the European sample are distributed among Austria, Belgium, Denmark, France, Germany, Ireland, Italy, the Netherlands, Spain, and the United Kingdom.

different between the two regions by estimating a statistical model. As summarized earlier in this chapter, the existing literature on Japanese FDI has found there are at least three motives for Japanese firms to invest in the United States. First, Japanese firms that possess strong intangible assets transfer them internationally at a low opportunity cost for use in the host-country market (Drake and Caves, 1992). Second, strong intangible assets possessed by U.S. firms attract Japanese firms who intend to acquire such assets in the host country (Kogut and Chang, 1991). Third, the appreciation of the Japanese yen against the U.S. dollar after 1985 increased the market opportunity in the U.S. market as U.S. assets became more valuable (Blonigen, 1997) and as the purchasing power of Japanese firms over yen-denominated U.S. corporate assets increased (Froot and Stein, 1991).

Kogut and Chang (1991) addressed the question of whether Japanese firms entered a foreign market to acquire specific assets possessed by local firms and examined the influence of Japanese and U.S. R&D expenditures on Japanese entry counts in U.S. manufacturing industries between 1967 and 1987. Although their statistical results showed a strong positive effect of U.S. R&D expenditures on Japan–U.S. joint ventures, its effect on Japanese acquisitions of U.S. firms was found statistically much weaker. Kogut and Chang then concluded that U.S. technology is likely to attract Japanese investors to form Japan–U.S. joint ventures but not necessarily to motivate them to acquire U.S. firms.

By using Japanese FDI-intensity measured by subsidiary employment as a dependent variable, Pugel, Kragas, and Kimura (1996) reexamined the Kogut–Chang study. Their regression analysis did not find any statistical significance on both U.S. and Japanese R&D expenditures as determinants of Japanese FDI by acquisition. Hennart and Park (1993) show indirect evidence for the asset-seeking motive of Japanese FDI that the R&D intensity of Japanese parent is negatively related to the probability that the Japanese firm enters by acquiring U.S. firms. It is quite plausible that their data were too short to capture the major cause of the acquisition wave of Japanese firms in the U.S. market that started around 1986 and peaked in 1989. On the other hand, Blonigen (1997) shows much stronger evidence that is consistent with the asset-seeking behavior by the Japanese firm. His study indeed confirms that Japanese acquisitions in the U.S. markets during the period of 1975–1992 are positively correlated with periods of a weaker U.S. dollar only in industries where R&D expenditures are high.

I will examine the determinants of entry mode of Japanese firms for both the U.S. and European markets and test the null hypothesis that the determinants of entry mode are the same between the two markets.

Specifications and Variables

The hypothesis that the Japanese firm is motivated to enter the U.S. and European markets by acquiring going local firms when the firm's base industry is less endowed with productive assets than its foreign counterparts is tested by estimating a model of choice of entry mode used in previous research (Caves and Mehra, 1986; Kogut and Singh, 1988; Zejan, 1990; Hennart and Park, 1993). The probability of entry through acquisition instead of entry by establishing a green-field plant is estimated by a logit model and explained by a set of independent variables: (1) a variable that measures the extent of technological advantage in the home-base industry relative to its foreign counterparts; (2) variables that control for characteristics of the parent and subsidiary; (3) variables that control for changes in foreign exchange; and (4) variables that control for industry-specific factors.

Technological Advantage in the Home Base Industry

To test the main hypothesis, a variable that measures interindustry variance in the extent of technological advantages possessed by the source country *relative to* those possessed by its foreign counterparts is needed in statistical specification. A variable that measures industry R&D intensity constructed only from data for the source country is not suitable because it measures only interindustry variance in technological opportunity for that country. To tackle this measurement problem, Yamawaki and Audretsch (1988), and Kogut and Chang (1991) have proposed to use R&D intensity variables constructed from data for *both* the source and host countries to measure the extent of technological advantage of the source country *relative to* that for the host country. Previous research on international competitiveness (e.g., Cantwell, 1989) has suggested a cross-industry index of revealed technological advantage as an alternative measure of competitiveness in technology. The extent of technological advantage, RTA, is defined by $RTA_{ijt} = (P_{ijt}/\sum_j P_{ijt})/(\sum_i P_{ijt}/\sum_i \sum_j P_{ijt})$ where P_{ijt} is the number of patents granted in the United States in industry i to residents of country j in year t. This variable is constructed for the Japanese industry at the three-digit level to which the parent firm's primary product is classified. Because the acquisition wave of Japanese firms started around 1986, this variable is constructed with lag as an average over the 7 years preceding 1986. This variable thus measures the technological advantage of Japanese home-base industry *relative to* its counterparts abroad and is expected to show a negative relationship with entry by acquisition.[9]

Market Structure of the Entered Industry

Previous theoretical research (Gilbert and Newbery, 1992) on the build-or-buy decision has suggested that, in mature industries, entry by building new plant is relatively unattractive because it may create excess capacity and thus lower market price. By the same token, acquisition is preferred in concentrated industries because entry via new plant requires a large amount of sunk costs of entry and has a large negative impact on industry profits. Two variables are introduced to control for these factors in the statistical specification. *SCALE* controls for the effect that a large-scale entry inflicts on the market price and measures the subsidiary's employment share in the entered industry. *SCALE* is expected to have a positive relationship with the probability of entry through acquisition.[10]

The growth rate of shipments in the entered industry, *GROW*, provides a control for the demand condition in the entered industry. With *SCALE* controlled, *GROW* is predicted to be negatively related to entry through acquisition because slow growth amplifies the extent to which a large-scale entry creates excess capacity and disturbs the market price condition.[11]

The causality running from large-scale entry to choice of entry mode assumed here may require careful treatment in the statistical analysis. Although the choice of acquisition over new plant building is influenced by scale of entry, it is plausible that the firm's decision on the mode of

---

[9] The recipients of U.S. patents include all the non-U.S. residents as well as U.S. firms.

[10] Another variable suggested is the degree of concentration of the entered industry. This variable, however, is not included in the statistical analysis because concentration ratios for a cross section of industries are unavailable for most of the European countries as well as for the E.U. market as a whole.

[11] On the contrary, a strategic consideration may derive different predictions on these variables. The MNE that intends to grow quickly in the international market would simply prefer acquisition to building new plant because entry via acquisition is much quicker. In this case, rapid growth in the entered market may encourage quick entry through acquisition (Caves and Mehra, 1986).

entry simultaneously affects the scale of entry. The option to build a new plant may force the firm to start from scratch with at relatively small size, but acquisition may make it feasible to operate at a large-scale from the beginning. In the statistical analysis, the coefficient for *SCALE* will be estimated by using an instrument to mitigate the bias associated with the possibility of simultaneity.

Characteristics of the Parent and Subsidiary

Firm-specific characteristics are controlled by the variable that measures the extent of the parent firm's prior experience abroad, *EXPRNC*, and by the variable that identifies the parent firm's experience with the subsidiary's new product market, *DIV*. The mature parent firm with profound previous foreign experience may have accumulated the know-how and the ability to establish and manage foreign subsidiaries from scratch and thus have the incentive to enter through green-field new plant (Caves and Mehra, 1986; Kogut and Singh, 1988). The coefficient for *EXPRNC* is expected to have a negative sign.

The binary variable *DIV* identifies entry into the industry that is different from the parent firm's primary industry. If the firm does not possess a full range of intangible assets and skills to exploit in the new business abroad, it may consider the option of acquiring a local firm that possesses a stock of strong intangible assets and skills missing from the firm's existing bundle. *DIV* is therefore expected to have a positive relation to the probability of entry by acquisition.[12]

Time-Dependent Factors

Although the variables described in this chapter are expected to control for industry-specific and firm-specific characteristics, it is necessary to control for common market opportunities faced by Japanese firms at the time of entry. The study by Blonigen (1997) clearly suggests the importance of controlling for time-dependent factors present in acquisition data. In particular, Japanese FDI were heavily concentrated after 1985 in response to changes in exchange rates. Given the nature of the data set used, changes in exchange rates are controlled by *YENUSD*, which

---

[12] See Caves (1996), pp. 69–72, for an extensive survey on this issue.

measures the exchange rate expressed as the Japanese yen per unit of the U.S. dollar, *YENDM* that measures the Yen per unit of the German Mark, and *YENGBP* that measures the yen per unit of the British Pound. The exchange rate at the time of entry is used to construct these three variables.

Statistical Results

From the full samples of 631 subsidiaries in the United States and 336 subsidiaries in Europe, 371 U.S. subsidiaries and 198 European subsidiaries were further selected to construct the final sample for the statistical analysis based on the availability of information on parent firm and industry. The variable definitions and data source are listed in the Appendix of this chapter. Table 6.6 reports the logit results to explain the probability of Japanese entry by acquisition in the United States and Europe (*EMODE*). Models (1) and (3) include *YENUSD*, while Models (2) and (4) in Table 6.6 include time dummies instead. The coefficients for *RTA* are statistically significant and have predicted negative signs in all the equations in Table 6.6, suggesting that Japanese entrants into the U.S. and European markets are more likely to acquire existing firms if they are based in Japanese industries that hold small shares of international patents. This finding is consistent with the asset-seeking hypothesis that the Japanese firm whose base industry is at technological disadvantage is more motivated to acquire existing U.S. and European firms and seek their technological advantages. The estimated coefficients for *RTA* in Models (1) and (3) show that the change in the probability that Japanese subsidiary is established by acquisition at the sample mean is -0.15 for the U.S. sample and -0.12 for the European sample.

Another variable that shows similar effects between the U.S. and European samples is the variable that measures the parent firm's prior experience in the international markets. The coefficients for *EXPRNC* are significant in all of the equations in Table 6.6 and have negative signs, suggesting that Japanese firms are more likely to acquire existing local firms if their previous experience in the international markets is smaller. In other words, more experienced firms are likely to build new plants in the U.S. and European markets.

Table 6.6. *Logit estimates of entry mode, U.S. and Europe
(dependent variable: EMODE)*

Variable	United States		Europe	
	(1)	(2)	(3)	(4)
Constant	0.543	−0.517	−0.160	1.109
	(0.875)	(1.059)	(0.198)	(1.950)*
RTA	−0.852	−0.875	−0.666	−0.767
	(2.395)**	(2.355)**	(1.946)**	(2.112)**
SCALE[a]	0.001	0.001	1.222	1.328
	(2.310)**	(2.118)**	(1.130)	(1.183)
EXPRNC	−0.059	−0.059	−0.056	−0.050
	(2.985)***	(2.967)***	(2.136)**	(1.780)*
DIV	0.948	0.966	−1.927	−2.049
	(3.183)***	(3.156)***	(1.789)*	(1.884)*
GROW	−0.123	−0.185	−0.498	−0.425
	(0.204)	(0.297)	(1.066)	(0.916)
YENUSD	−0.004		0.006	
	(1.053)		(1.488)	
D86		0.606		−1.754
		(1.290)		(2.098)**
D87		0.183		−1.039
		(0.384)		(1.647)
D88		0.428		−0.990
		(1.048)		(1.510)
D89		1.240		−0.072
		(2.884)***		(0.158)
D90		1.130		0.296
		(2.537)**		(0.570)
Log likelihood	−200.43	−194.24	−108.10	−103.58
Likelihood ratio	0.093	0.121	0.113	0.150
Number of observations[b]	371	371	197	197

Notes: [a] *SCALE* is an instrumental variable estimator. [b] The number of positive observations is 105 in the U.S. sample and 61 in the European sample. Numbers reported in parentheses are *t*-test statistics. The levels of significance for a two-tailed test are: *** = 1%; ** = 5%; and * = 10%.

Turning to the variables that show different effects on the probability of Japanese firms to use acquisition in the two markets, the coefficient for *SCALE* is significant and has an expected positive sign for the U.S. sample, although it is not statistically significant for the European sample. Another marked difference is found between the two samples in the effect of diversified entry on mode of entry. Although the coefficient for *DIV* is statistically significant and signed positively as expected for the U.S. sample, it has an unexpected negative sign for the European sample. This result is consistent with the observation of the propensity to use acquisition in diversification from Table 6.4. Japanese firms used acquisitions more frequently to diversify into new industries in the United States than in Europe in the late 1980s. The significant positive coefficient suggests that the whole distribution of the probability that *EMODE* equals one over *RTA* is significantly higher in the case of diversified entry in the United States.

Finally, the result on the effect of the time-dependent variables appears to be different between the two samples. The coefficient for *YENUSD* has an expected negative sign for the U.S. sample, but it is insignificant. For the European sample, the coefficients for *YENDM* and *YENGBP* were both insignificant in unreported equations. When *YENUSD* is instead included to the specification for the European sample, its coefficient has a positive sign in but is insignificant. A marked difference emerges between the U.S. and European samples when *YENUSD* is replaced by a set of time dummies in Models (2) and (4) Acquisitions by Japanese firms are concentrated significantly in 1989 and 1990 in the U.S. sample, however such concentration was not observed for the same years in the European sample. The significant positive coefficients for *D89* and *D90* in the U.S. sample suggest that the whole distribution of the probability that entry occurs by acquisition is significantly higher over the independent variables for 1989 and 1990 in the U.S. sample. However, for the European sample, the constant is significant and has a positive sign, implying that Japanese acquisitions were more concentrated in the pre-1986 period.[13]

To test the null hypothesis that the estimated coefficients are the same between the U.S. and European samples, Table 6.7 presents the logit result including a set of interaction variables in the pooled U.S. and European sample. The null was tested for the coefficients for *RTA*, *SCALE*, *EXPRNC*,

---

[13] Dummies for 1984 and 1985 were also included in the specification in unreported equations. For the European sample, the coefficient for *D84* is significant and has a positive coefficient, which confirms the positive constant term.

Table 6.7. *Logit estimates of entry mode, pooled U.S. and European sample (dependent variable: EMODE)*

Variable	
Constant	0.061 (0.079)
RTA	−0.689 (2.113)**
SCALE[a]	−0.001 (1.049)
EXPRNC	−0.038 (1.657)*
DIV	−2.017 (1.885)*
GROW	−0.568 (1.274)
YENUSD	0.007 (1.633)
US*RTA	0.021 (0.051)
US*SCALE[a]	0.002 (2.501)**
US*EXPRNC	0.019 (0.636)
US*DIV	2.975 (2.686)***
US*YENUSD	0.010 (1.997)**
US	0.481 (0.496)
Log likelihood	308.63
Likelihood ratio	0.101
Number of observations[b]	568

[a]SCALE is an instrumental variable estimator. [b]The number of positive observations is 166 in the full sample. *t*-test statistics are in parenthesis. The levels of significance at a two-tailed test are: *** = 1%; ** = 5%; and * = 10%.

DIV, and *YENUSD* by including the interaction variables between these and a dummy (*US*) that identifies U.S. subsidiaries, *US*RTA*, *US*SCALE*, *US*EXPRNC*, *US*DIV*, and *US*YENUSD*. The coefficient for *US* is not statistically different from zero, suggesting that there is no difference in the overall frequency of Japanese firms to use acquisition in the United States and in Europe. This finding confirms our earlier conjecture from Table 6.3.

Among the interaction variables included in the estimated equation in Table 6.7, the coefficients for *US*SCALE*, *US*DIV*, and *US*YENUSD* are statistically significant, rejecting the null hypothesis that the estimated coefficients are the same between the two samples. The coefficient for *US*SCALE* has a positive sign, suggesting that the effect of *SCALE* is significantly larger in the United States than in Europe. Japanese firms are likely to use acquisition to enter at a large scale into the United States but not into Europe. The coefficient for *US∗DIV* has a positive sign, suggesting that the likelihood of Japanese to use acquisition is significantly high in the case of diversified entry into the United States. The effect of changes in the exchange rate is different in the two samples as expected. The coefficient for *US∗YENUSD* has a negative coefficient, suggesting that the appreciation of the Japanese yen against the U.S. dollar motivated Japanese acquisitions in the United States, but not in Europe. However, the null hypothesis of the equality of coefficients was not rejected for *RTA* and *EXPRNC*. The result on *RTA* suggests that the asset-seeking behavior of the Japanese firm is statistically not different between the U.S. and European markets.

6.4. Bunching in FDI

One of the most striking characteristics of Japanese FDI was the concentration of entry into the United States in particular years in the late 1980s. The statistical analysis showed that the likelihood of Japanese acquisitions was significantly higher in 1989 and 1990. Previous research has identified such bunching behavior in FDI by Japanese firms and attempted to provide explanations for it. Anecdotal evidence presented by Encarnation (1987) and Kester (1991) suggests that clusters of Japanese entries in particular industries and acquisitions in the United States during the late 1980s are associated with the imitating behavior of Japanese multinational enterprises (MNEs). A statistical study by Blonigen (1997) finds that exchange rate movements triggered common responses by Japanese firms to acquire local U.S. firms whose specific assets generate returns through the depreciation of the dollar. Yet, other studies find that Japanese firms tend to form clusters in particular regions when they enter into the United States and follow other members from the same vertical assembler-supplier group, *keiretsu*, (Head, Ries, and Swenson, 1994; Belderbos and Sleuwaegen, 1996). Generally speaking, these studies identify bunching of Japanese firms investing in the U.S. market. A question that has not been addressed yet, however, is whether certain traits of market structure influenced the decision of Japanese firms to imitate rivals' actions in investing in the United States. Did Japanese investors cluster in the United States because of their strategic interactions or because of their common responses to emerging opportunities?

Strategic Interactions and Bunching in FDI

Knickerbocker (1973) first provided an explanation for strategic behavior of oligopolistic firms in FDI and showed statistical evidence that supports the hypothesis that rivalry among U.S. MNEs motivates them to cluster in particular host countries and time periods. Bunching in FDI could occur as a common response to some shift in exogenous factors that raised the payoff to FDI for all competitors. Knickerbocker, however, found that certain firm- and industry-specific characteristics influenced the incidence of clusters in FDI. Most notably, he established a relationship between bunching in FDI and concentration in the domestic market, suggesting that oligopolistic interactions in highly concentrated U.S. industries motivated competitors to mimic rivals' actions.[14]

Consider these relations in the case of Japanese FDI in the United States. I begin by assuming that Japanese firms have similar resource endowments. I further assume that they face the same international market opportunity and experience some environmental shock common to all firms, such as changes in foreign exchange. When the Japanese yen appreciates against the U.S. dollar, Japanese firms see the market opportunity increase in the U.S. market as the proprietary assets of a potential U.S. target firm in R&D-intensive industries become more valuable (Blonigen, 1997) and as their purchasing power over yen-denominated U.S. corporations increases (Froot and Stein, 1991). Facing the increased opportunities in the U.S. market with a firm strategy constrained by the current level of resources, firms' reactions to such environmental shock are likely very similar each other (Collis, 1991; Teece et al., 1997). Suppose that one Japanese firm decides to invest in the U.S. market. Its domestic rivals recognize that the first-mover's action puts them at competitive disadvantage in the foreign and domestic markets. With new manufacturing and distribution subsidiaries established in the foreign market, the

---

[14] The Knickerbocker hypothesis has been tested in the previous literature. The implied positive relationship between entry concentration (or the extent of FDI) and seller concentration in the home market was confirmed by Flowers (1976), Caves et al. (1980), and Kogut and Chang (1991). See also Pugel et al. (1996). A follow-the-leader hypothesis, however, was not confirmed by Hennart and Park (1994) who used a dummy variable to identify loose-knit oligopolistic industries. Yu and Ito (1988) confirmed this hypothesis for the U.S. tire industry. See also Altomonte and Pennings (2003).

first-mover may be able to out-compete its rivals and gain market share at the expense of its rivals. Under these circumstances, firms decide to minimize risks by quickly matching rivals' actions (Knickerbocker, 1973; Peteraf, 1993).[15]

Previous empirical work (e.g., Orr, 1974; see Geroski, 1995 for a survey) on entry has used a model in which entry is hypothesized to occur when expected profits are high and barriers to entry (BTE) are low. Although the negative relationships between entry and entry barriers may be observed for domestic entrants, it is less likely that the same entry barriers deter the multinational entrant equally. If the multinational firm is likely the firm best equipped to jump barriers to entry into a market (Caves, 1971), the conventional negative effect of entry barriers on entry will be mitigated.[16] However, the industry with high entry barriers may attract the multinational entrant because of high profit potentials (see Chapter 4 of this book; Yamawaki, 1986). Our entry equation is then given by

$$E N_{it} = f\,[\Pi^e,\, E N_{k,t-1}], \qquad (6.1)$$

where EN_i denotes the decision by firm i to enter the market, EN_k is a vector of past entries by rivals to the same market, and Π^e is the expected industry profit which is defined by $\Pi^e = g(BTE, I)$, where I is a vector of industry-specific factors commonly observed the by all the entrants.

As noted earlier in this section, Knickerbocker (1973) finds that MNEs cluster in particular host countries and time periods, and such clusters occur in highly concentrated industries. This finding suggests that the reaction of firm i to rivals' entries into the foreign market in Eq. (6.1) depends on the degree of oligopolistic interactions. In other words, the competitive pressure to invest abroad felt by the firm is different between industries because of the difference in the underlying traits.

---

[15] Motta (1994), using a game-theoretic approach, has shown that the "follow-the-leader" hypothesis is indeed consistent with the prediction from a formal theoretical model. In a two-country setting, where one country's firms play a Cournot game in choosing between foreign direct investment, exports, and pure domestic operation, Motta shows that there are certain outcomes where bunching in foreign investment does occur. See also Head, Mayer, and Ries (2002).

[16] Gorecki (1976) and Shapiro (1983) provide evidence that supports this hypothesis.

Strategic Interactions and Entry Mode

Although the discussion so far was made with no distinction between entry by green-field investment and acquisition, it is important to take into consideration the effect of rivalry on entry mode. Caves (1991) presented a simple model to explain the incidence of clusters in international mergers. Assuming the importance of organizational specific assets in a concentrated industry, he shows that when a first-moving firm acquires a bundle of specific assets that relate to the opportunity set by way of a merger, the rivals imitate the first-mover's action by mergers in order to minimize their losses. These specialized assets include skills and technologies and are attached to the firm. These assets are not only the source of current cash flows but also carry option values from the preemption of future opportunities. When a rival seizes a newly emergent opportunity, the firm responds by imitating the rival's action.

If such specialized assets are obtained more easily by a way of merger and acquisition, we expect strategic foreign direct investment to occur more frequently in mergers and acquisitions than in new-plant investments. New-plant investments, instead, are likely to occur when a firm extends its activities abroad while exploiting transaction cost economies associated with the ownership of intangible assets. Therefore, strategic imitations are more likely to occur in acquisitions than in green-field investments.

Statistical Evidence

The strategic investment hypothesis suggests that the firm's reaction to rivals' actions depends on the degree of oligopolistic rivalry. This implies that the partial effect of EN_{it} with respect to $EN_{k,t-1}$ in Eq. (6.1) in the last section depends on the degree of competition. Because the partial effect is not observable from the data at hand, an entry concentration index (*ECI*) was constructed by modifying the method used by Knickerbocker (1973) to measure this effect. Concentrated entry is defined at the subsidiary level and measured by counting the number of U.S. subsidiaries established by domestic rivals within a specific time period preceding the Japanese firm's decision to establish a subsidiary in the U.S. market. This index differs from Knickerbocker's index in that it measures the extent of bunching observed by the firm within a specific time period *prior* to its entry, but Knickerbocker's index measures the extent of bunching within a specific time period observed *aggregately* for an industry. In other words, this index measures directly the extent of competitive pressure felt by a particular firm prior to its entry decision. An entry concentration index is computed by dividing the number of entries that took place during the 5 consecutive years *prior* to the firm's entry, by the total of all subsidiaries that were established during the 1980–1990 period.[17] Two different indexes are constructed depending on the type of entry mode: the entry concentration index for acquisition (*AQECI*) and the entry concentration index for green-field entry (*GFECI*). Detailed accounts on the construction of these indexes are given in the Appendix to this chapter.

Because a necessary condition for strategic investment is a market structure that induces the competitors to recognize rivals' reactions, namely a small number of firms in the industry, seller concentration, *CR8*, is used to test the strategic investment hypothesis. The extent to which the rivals in an industry respond to each other is thus expected to increase with concentration. However, this relationship should be much stronger in acquisitions rather than in green-field investments.

To test this hypothesis, several additional variables are included in the specification to control for industry-specific factors and the common responses by Japanese firms suggested by the exiting literature. As observed by previous research (Blonigen, 1997), Japanese foreign direct investments were heavily concentrated in the late 1980s responding to changes in time-dependent variables such as exchange rates and Japan's aggregate economic growth. The time-dependent effects of exchange rates are measured by *YENUSD* and by the time dummies as in the previous analysis of this chapter.

GROW measures industry shipment growth in the destination industry in the United States to control for industry-specific common responses by Japanese firms to the same favorable market opportunity observed in

---

[17] Knickerbocker (1973) computes an entry concentration index for a given industry as a total of the all the markets entered. In this study, only the U.S. market is considered in the analysis.

Table 6.8. *OLS estimates of determinants of pressure to respond to rivals' entries into the United States*

	Acquisitions AQECI (1)	Green-field investments GFECI (2)
Constant	0.444 (3.666)***	0.748 (11.068)***
CR8	0.213 (1.568)*	0.025 (0.330)
GROW	−0.083 (0.876)	−0.005 (0.125)
GROUP	0.154 (1.284)	0.022 (0.528)
YENUSD	−0.002 (3.108)***	−0.003 (9.754)***
D90	0.250 (4.281)***	0.253 (6.408)***
Adjusted R^2	0.243	0.383
F	7.675	33.874
N	105	266

Notes: Numbers reported in parentheses are *t*-test statistics. The levels of significance for a one-tailed test are: *** = 1%, ** = 5%, * = 1%.

the United States. The dummy that indicates the supplier in the vertical corporate group (*keiretsu*), GROUP, is included to identify the clustering behavior among the members of the same vertical supplier-assembler group suggested by Head, Ries, and Swenson (1994) and Belderbos and Sleuwaegen (1996). The coefficient for this variable is expected to have a positive sign.

Table 6.8 shows the estimation results of the determinants of the extent of competitive-pressure felt by Japanese firms prior to their entries into the United States. Model (1) in Table 6.8 is the estimate for the sample of Japanese acquisitions, and Model (2) is the estimate for the sample of Japanese new-plant investment. The dependent variables, AQECI and GFECI, measure the extent of competitive pressure felt by the firm prior to its entry into the United States. The coefficient for CR8 is statistically significant and has an expected positive sign for the sample of Japanese acquisitions, but it is insignificant for the new-plant FDI sample. The positive effect of CR8 remains significant even after time-dependent factors are included the AQECI equation. These findings, therefore, suggest the importance of strategic interaction in Japanese acquisitions in the United States.

On the contrary, Japanese green-field investments were bunched in particular years as a common response to some external shift such as an appreciation of the Japanese yen against the U.S. dollar. In the *GFECI* equation, the most significant coefficient is for *YENUSD*. Japanese firms that were well-qualified to establish new capacity felt strong pressure to move into the United States when the economic environment shifted. However, Japanese firms in highly concentrated industries faced stronger competitive pressure to acquire local firms as a result of strategic interaction.

6.5. Conclusions

The statistical results of studies in this chapter found that Japanese firms entered the United States and Europe by acquiring existing local firms if their base industries in Japan held small shares in international patents. This finding thus supports the hypothesis that Japanese firms, whose base industries are at disadvantage, are more motivated to enter the U.S. and European markets through acquisition to seek local technological assets. It also found that whole distribution of the probability of acquisition by Japanese firms over technological advantages is statistically not different between the U.S. and European markets. This finding of seeking U.S. and European technology through acquisition is more decisive than the evidence found in the previous research.

Despite this similarity between the two markets, the acquisition behavior of Japanese firms is different in the degree of diversification and the response to changes in the Japanese yen against the U.S. dollar and European currencies. Japanese firms diversified more extensively in the United States than in Europe, and their preferred mode for this end was acquisition. And, they responded to the appreciation of the Japanese yen against the U.S. dollar differently in the United States and Europe. Their response was to acquire local firms in the United States, but not in Europe. Finally, the timing of acquisitions was markedly different in the two regions. Japanese firms used acquisition more commonly in the 1980s than in the 1970s in both the United States and Europe. However, Japanese acquisitions in the United States were highly concentrated in 1989 and 1990, but they were not highly concentrated in Europe.

7

Strategic Interactions in Cross-Market Entry

7.1. Introduction

A natural sequence to the analysis of bunching in FDI among Japanese firms in Chapter 6 is the analysis of oligopolistic rivalry among Japanese firms and their foreign rivals in cross-market FDI. Although the Knickerbocker hypothesis suggests oligopolistic interactions among the firms domiciled in the same country, international oligopolists may interact with each other across international boundaries. Several pioneering studies on the incidence and behavior of the MNE pointed out that the local firm is often motivated to invest in the home market of the foreign firm to defend the local firm's home market from competition injected by the foreign firm (Hymer, 1960; Kindleberger, 1969; Caves, 1971; Wilkins, 1974; Vernon, 1977). This notion of defensive FDI was strongly associated with the rapid expansion of foreign direct investment by European firms in the United States during the late 1960s and the 1970s (Franko, 1976). Graham (1978) first tested the hypothesis of retaliatory defensive FDI by using time-series data on European investment for a cross-section of U.S. manufacturing industries and provided some evidence that supports this hypothesis. He argued that when the foreign firm enters into the home market of the local firm, a disruption in the stable environment occurs in a local oligopoly. This will subsequently stimulate rivalry among the local firms and the foreign entrant, and the local firms would consider an option of entering the home market of the foreign firm for retaliation and defense.

Do Japanese firms enter into the U.S. market in response to the entry of U.S. firms into the Japanese market? Do U.S. firms enter into the Japanese market by matching the moves of Japanese firms entering into the U.S. market? Do Japanese firms interact with European firms in FDI? These questions are appealing as little is known about how local firms and their foreign rivals interact with each other in FDI across national boundaries. There are, however, some issues to be addressed before I test the defensive hypothesis of cross-market FDI. First, more recent theoretical research shows that the pattern of two-way FDI or intrain-dustry FDI can occur without invoking the retaliatory defensive behavior of international oligopolists.[1] Brainard (1993), Markusen and Venables (1996), and Markusen (2002) present models of location choice by MNEs where single-product firms choose to consolidate production at home and exploit scale economies, or to produce in proximity to serve local customers. Under the assumptions of imperfect competition, fixed costs associated with local production, and trade costs, their models show that when proximity is more important than scale economies, intraindustry FDI occurs between symmetric nations. Baldwin and Ottaviano (2001) present a specific model of intraindustry FDI where multiproduct, final-goods firms use trade costs to reduce intervariety competition by placing production of some varieties abroad. If the multiproduct firms produce two or more products in the same country, their products would com-pete with each other and induce intervariety cannibalization under the assumption of imperfect competition. Their study shows that such a pat-tern of intraindustry FDI is commonly observed in industries such as transport equipment, chemicals, pharmaceuticals, and processed foods within Europe. However, they suggest that because there is very little intraindustry FDI between the United States and Japan, their model of multiproduct, horizontal goods firms is less relevant for the FDI pattern by Japanese firms.

Second, the low level of intraindustry FDI in Japan reflects the low level of inward FDI in Japan. It is a well-established fact that the stock of inward foreign direct investment (FDI) in Japan accumulated through the 1990s is significantly lower than that in other industrialized countries in

[1] The prevalence of intraindustry FDI among industrialized countries is documented by Norman and Dunning (1984) and Erdilek (1985).

North America and Europe. Why is FDI in Japan low? Which Japanese business practices become barriers to entry for foreign firms? Existing studies addressed these questions in response to the preeminence and provided at least the following two general conclusions: (1) the level of FDI in Japan is significantly lower than would be justified by Japan's factor endowments relative to European and Asian countries (Eaton and Tamura, 1994); and (2) because the economic model is unable to predict the low level of FDI in Japan, distinctive features of Japanese industrial organization should provide an explanation to the puzzle (Encarnation and Mason, 1990; Encarnation, 1992; Mason, 1992; Lawrence, 1991, 1993; Ito and Maruyama, 1992; Weinstein, 1996). Although these studies offer a number of important hypotheses on structural impediments peculiar to Japan, empirical test has thus far been limited to inferences from small data samples defined at the levels of sectors or industries (e.g., Lawrence, 1993; Wakasugi, 1996).[2]

One implication of the low level of inward FDI in Japan is that even when foreign firms recognize mutual dependence with their Japanese rivals, they would not choose to invest in the Japanese market because of the existence of entry barriers. If there were no institutional barriers to FDI in Japan, with Japan's relatively large market size and traditional trade costs, oligopolistic foreign firms would consider investing in Japan as an option and use trade costs to cover the fixed costs associated with local production. The existence of potential barriers to FDI, however, is likely to elevate the fixed costs of local production, which reduce the benefits of FDI associated with avoiding trade costs. This suggests, therefore, that the defensive motive of FDI may not be observed for the foreign firms investing in Japan.

7.2. Statistical Analysis of Retaliatory Entry into Foreign Markets

I test two complementary hypotheses: (1) the Japanese firms enter the home market of the foreign firms in response to the entry of the foreign firms in Japan; and (2) the foreign firms enter the Japanese market in response to the entry of the Japanese firms in the home market of

---

[2] Kogut (1996) presents some descriptive evidence on the importance of firm-specific factors in explaining the performance of foreign firms in Japan.

the foreign firms. These two hypotheses are tested by using a panel of European, U.S., and Japanese entries into European, U.S., and Japanese markets between 1980 and 1990 for thirty manufacturing industries. The data on Japanese entry into the U.S. and European markets are obtained from the same data source as used in Section 6.4. The data for U.S. and European entries in Japan are described in Section 7.3.

We estimate the following fixed effect model inspired by Graham's (1978) original model:

$$FDI^{kl}{}_{it} = \alpha_i + \phi_t + \sum_{s=1}^{3} \beta_s FDI^{lk}_{it-s} + u_{it},$$

where subscript k denotes country k, subscript l denotes country l, and subscript i denotes industry i. FDI^{kl} is the number count of FDI entries in country l by firms originating from country k, and FDI^{lk} is the number count of FDI entries in country k by firms originating from country l. Subscript t denotes time, and time lags of 3 years are taken into account for FDI, thus $FDI^{lk}{}_{it-1}$, $FDI^{lk}{}_{it-2}$, and $FDI^{lk}{}_{it-3}$, and α_i is the intercept that varies across cross section units, and ϕ_t is time trend.

Table 7.1 presents the fixed-effects estimation results of the statistical model above. Models (1) and (2) estimate the response functions of the Japanese firm to the U.S. entry and the European entry in Japan, respectively. The coefficients for *USFDIinJ* lagged 1 year and 2 years are statistically significant and have positive signs, and the coefficient for *EUFDIinJ* lagged 2 years has a positive sign and statistically significant. The estimated reaction coefficients are larger for *USFDIinJ* than *EUFDIinJ*, suggesting that Japanese firms respond more strongly and immediately to the entry of U.S. firms in Japan. However, the coefficients for *JFDIinUS* and *JFDIinEU* are all insignificant in the equations that explain the U.S. entry and European entry in Japan. The results of Models (3) and (4) thus suggest that the U.S. and European firms do not establish subsidiaries in the Japanese market to retaliate to the Japanese entry in their home markets in the previous years.[3] Finally, the coefficients for time trend

---

[3]   The numbers of observation differ between Japanese FDI, U.S. FDI, and European FDI due to missing data. Models (1) and (2) are estimated for 1980–1990, and Models (3) and (4) are estimated for 1982–1990. To check if the difference in the estimation results was caused by the difference in estimation periods, all the equations were reestimated for the comparable time period, 1983–1990. For this smaller sample, the basic results remained unchanged. Japanese firms responded to U.S. entries, but U.S. firms and European firms did not respond to Japanese entries.

Table 7.1. *Fixed-effects estimates of FDI entry of Japanese firms in U.S. and European markets, and European and U.S. firms in the Japanese market, 1980–1991*

Independent Variable	JFDIinUS (1)	JFDIinEU (2)	EUFDIinJ (3)	USFDIinJ (4)
$USFDIinJ_{t-1}$	0.398 (2.774)***			
$USFDIinJ_{t-2}$	0.441 (3.081)***			
$USFDIinJ_{t-3}$	0.036 (0.249)			
$EUFDIinJ_{t-1}$		−0.004 (0.047)		
$EUFDIinJ_{t-2}$		0.199 (2.150)**		
$EUFDIinJ_{t-3}$		−0.081 (0.390)		
$JFDIinEU_{t-1}$			0.023 (0.607)	
$JFDIinEU_{t-2}$			0.007 (0.169)	
$JFDIinEU_{t-3}$			0.038 (0.829)	
$JFDIinUS_{t-1}$				0.032 (1.260)
$JFDIinUS_{t-2}$				−0.046 (1.579)
$JFDIinUS_{t-3}$				0.013 (0.437)
Time	0.203 (8.437)***	0.069 (4.967)***	−0.027 (2.062)**	−0.042 (2.540)**
Adj-R^2	0.481	0.324	0.101	0.325
N	331	331	271	271

Notes: Numbers reported in parentheses are *t*-test statistics. The levels of significance for a two-tailed test are: * = 10%, ** = 5%, and *** = 1%. Numbers of observation differ because of missing observations. Modes (1) and (7.2) are estimated for 1980–1990, and Models (3) and (4) are for 1982–1990. The number of industry is thirty for both periods.

are statistically significant and have positive signs for Japanese FDI, but they are negatively signed for U.S. and E.U. FDI. This finding reinforces the finding on the asymmetric pattern of FDI between outward FDI and inward FDI in Japan.

7.3. Entry and Exit of Foreign Firms in Japan

The Japanese firm responds to the entries of the U.S. and European firms into the Japanese market, but the U.S. and European firms do not enter into the Japanese market in response to the Japanese entry to their home markets. This finding is consistent with our earlier conjecture that the foreign firms were discouraged to enter the into Japanese market because of structural entry barriers in the Japanese market. A question that follows is who actually entered into the Japanese market and survived there. Another conjecture from Section 7.2 was that the foreign firms with some sort of advantage over local firms were able to jump barriers and enter into the Japanese market.

This section, therefore, addresses the question of who enters and survives in the Japanese manufacturing industries by using a sample of 366 European and U.S. subsidiaries that were established during the 1973–1994 period.[4] The empirical analysis is designed to examine two sets of hypotheses. The first set of hypotheses is derived from the discussion on the business practices and institutional factors distinctive in Japan: (1) the prevalence of corporate groups or *keiretsu*; (2) the complex and fragmented distribution system; and (3) the difficulty in hiring local personnel and the existence of wage differentials between foreign and Japanese firms. These three factors have been proposed by the previous studies as constituting important structural impediments to foreign firms in operating in Japan through the 1990s (Lawrence, 1991 and 1993; Weinstein, 1996).[5] We test the hypothesis that the likelihood of survival for foreign subsidiaries in Japan is low when these three institutional factors are important features in the industry. A second set of hypotheses is drawn from foreign entrants' advantages over local firms and strategic behaviors to organize various activities in Japan. The likelihood of survival in Japan should then be determined by various subsidiary-specific factors.

Structural Barriers in Japan

Corporate Group and Keiretsu

One of the most distinctive business practices in Japan was the role played by corporate groups or *keiretsu* particularly in the 1960s through the

---

[4]   For previous empirical studies on the postentry behavior and performance of multinational enterprises, see Barkema, Bell, and Pennings (1996), Mitchell, Shaver, and Yeung (1994), Baldwin (1995), Lee and Caves (1998), Yamawaki (1997), Mata and Portugal (1997), and Kimura and Fujii (2003).

[5]   There is a large literature that addresses the effect of institutional barriers, such as *keiretsu*, on international trade in Japan. See Fung (1991), Lawrence (1991), Saxonhouse (1993), Ueda and Sasaki (1998), Quiu and Spencer (2001), Harrigan and Vanjani (2003), and Head, Ries, and Spencer (2004).

early 1990s. Although the definition of corporate groups in Japan is often murky, at least two distinctive types of corporate groups are defined: (1) horizontal, financial groups (*kinyuu-keiretsu*); and (2) vertical, industrial groups (*sangyo keiretsu*). Financial groups are organized around major banks and tied through cross-shareholdings. It is also common for some of the group firm's board members to be executives of the main bank. On the other hand, industrial groups are organized around large industrial firms. The parent firm controls, and influences to some extent, business activities of the entire group that is consisted suppliers or subcontractors. It is common for the participating firm in the group to be linked with the parent and other firms hierarchically. Corporate groups offer the member firms competitive advantages by facilitating the collaborative development of new capabilities, the formation of joint ventures among the participating firms from different industries, the sharing of risks and information, and preferential in-group loans.[6]

Lawrence (1991, 1993) has put forward the hypothesis that the prevalence of corporate groups or *keiretsu* is likely to constitute impediments to FDI in Japan. He argued that the member of a corporate group favors doing business with other members within the same group, and therefore the presence of corporate groups is likely to discriminate against foreign firms relative to Japanese group firms. Using a data sample with very few observations, Lawrence (1993) showes that the sales of majority-owned affiliates of U.S. firms are significantly lower in Japanese industries where the share of financial groups is high. Although Lawrence's result is consistent with the hypothesis that the prevalence of corporate groups in Japan deters entry of foreign firms, Saxonhouse (1993) and Weinstein (1996) suggest an alternative interpretation that *keiretsu* firms are simply more competitive and drive the sales of foreign firms down without discriminating against them.[7]

---

[6] See Odagiri (1992) for more detailed accounts on corporate groups in Japan.
[7] See Horaguchi (1995), and Nakamura, Fukao, and Shibuya (1995) for further evidence on the effects of the prevalence of corporate groups on sales share of foreign affiliates in Japanese industries. Contrary to Lawrence (1993), their studies were unable to confirm the negative relationship between the sales of foreign affiliates and the sales of corporate groups. Weinstein and Yafeh (1995) test the hypothesis that *keiretsu* collude in product markets.

A key issue to the hypothesis proposed by Lawrence (1993) is whether corporate groups discriminate against foreign firms in favor of Japanese rivals. If such discrimination occurs against firms that are outsiders to corporate groups, foreign firms may be able to circumvent such a disadvantage by forming joint ventures with *keiretsu* member firms. Therefore, we propose a hypothesis that the foreign entrant that is affiliated with the Japanese corporate group has a higher probability of survival in Japan.

However, the existing study on divestiture and exit of joint ventures observes that joint ventures, on average, have a shorter lifespan than otherwise comparable business units under single control (Kogut, 1989). This observation suggests that joint ventures with Japanese partners may be terminated in the early years and, thus, result in a lower probability of survival in Japan.

Distribution

A second distinctive market structure in Japan that may constitute a structural impediment to entry into its market is the complex and fragmented distribution system (Williamson and Yamawaki, 1991; Ito and Maruyama, 1991). The Japanese domestic wholesale sector was highly fragmented with some 400,000 wholesalers during the period studied in this book. Across a wide spectrum of industries, manufacturers are forced to deal with distributors who are both smaller and have slower throughput than is common in the United States. Williamson and Yamawaki (1991) estimate that the average annual sales across a sample of wholesale establishments were only US$8.9 million at the end of 1980s.

The complexity of Japan's distribution channel has motivated some Japanese manufacturers to integrate downstream into distribution. Faced with the challenge of introducing new products through a complex distribution system, Japanese automobile, electrical machinery, and household appliance manufacturers progressively assumed control of wholesaling operations in the 1960s. As a result of these developments, the structure of Japan's distribution typically became dichotomized: the manufacturer controlled sector and the multistage independent distributor network. Trading relationships within this structure are complex and are characterized by the variable rebate system. A variety of rebates include a rebate based on absolute sales volume, incentives for meeting specific

sales targets, and a loyalty rebate. These differ according to the destination of sales, transportation requirements, transaction lot sizes, the levels
of inventory held by the wholesalers, and the extent of participation in
promotional campaigns (Williamson and Yamawaki, 1991).

The complexity of the Japanese distribution system has therefore
encouraged Japanese firms either to integrate forward into distribution
or to establish tight relationships with the distribution chain. These relationships enable the Japanese firms to exert control and use the channels
as a source of market intelligence. In addition, the integration into distribution may have increased the barrier to entry by increasing the amount
of sunken costs. Because the Japanese incumbent has committed to the
market and sunk substantial investment costs prior to the entry of foreign
firms, the revenue flow that warrants continuing its operation is smaller
than what would otherwise be required.

This feature of Japan's distribution forces the foreign entrant to make
a difficult decision: invest substantially and integrate distribution or
establish long-term relationships with independent wholesalers. Vertical integration requires a substantial amount of up-front investment
and commitment, which is risky and may result in high barriers to exit.
Establishing long-term relationships and building trust with independent
Japanese wholesalers are particularly difficult for the foreign entrant who
often lacks the knowledge of the business practice and culture in Japan
(Baron, 1997).[8] It does not require a large up-front investment, but it
may result in loss of control and higher operational costs.

The choice of entry mode depends not only on the investment and
operational costs incurred but also on the type of assets involved. The
transaction-cost model developed by Coase (1937) and Williamson
(1971) predicts that the firm's choice among modes of transactions of
intermediate goods depends on the attributes of assets involved. If transaction of intermediate goods require substantial investments in specialized assets by the buyer and seller, the high costs incurred by switching
from one partner to another gives them an incentive to form long-term
contracts. If the costs of negotiating and monitoring long-term contracts

---

[8] The case of Kodak in Japan provides an example of this problem.

are substantial, the firm internalizes transaction of the intermediate good through vertical integration (Caves, 1996).[9]

The discussion here suggests that Japan's distinctive distribution system may have served to deter entry of foreign firms into the Japanese market. It is, therefore, crucial for foreign entrants to find strategies to mitigate the effects of such barriers. Although it is not clear a priori whether integration into distribution generally increases the likelihood of survival, the transaction-cost model suggests that integration into distribution is particularly important in the industry that involves transactions of specialized assets. Yamawaki (2004a) finds evidence that foreign affiliates in Japan tend to integrate into distribution in the industry where proprietary intangible assets, such as marketing expertise, play an important strategic role.

Labor Market

The third source of competitive disadvantage that foreign firms may face in Japan is the difficulty in attracting competent personnel and the existence of labor-cost differential with Japanese firms. Weinstein (1996) has pointed out that high-quality Japanese workers are more likely to be reluctant to work for foreign companies than Japanese ones because of differences in training mechanisms and the inability of foreign firms to commit to long-term employment. Japanese companies typically provide on-the-job training for their workers, and workers remain at the same firm long after the training is completed. To prevent quitting, Japanese companies pay their workers low initial wages in return for training and long-term employment. Weinstein (1996) shows that foreign firms in Japan typically pay starting salaries for college graduates that are on average 6 percent higher than in Japanese firms but face a greater probability of a much shorter tenure.

The wage differential between foreign firms and domestic firms in Japan is thus likely to put foreign firms at disadvantage relative to Japanese rivals and force them to earn lower profits. Therefore, we propose a hypothesis that the foreign entrant to Japanese industry, where the

---

[9] It provides a survey on vertical integration by the multinational enterprise.

imperfection of labor market is such that it puts them at disadvantage relative to Japanese firms, has a low probability of survival.

Competitive Advantages of Foreign Firms in Japan

As shown in the Section 7.2, the U.S. and European firms do not enter the Japanese market in the form of a defense of their home markets. Likewise, the proximity-concentration model and the multiproduct horizontal FDI model do not explain the patterns of intraindustry FDI between Japan and the United States and between Japan and Europe. Japan's structural barriers are likely to be the reason for the low level of inward FDI and thus the low level of intraindustry cross-market FDI. There is, however, a puzzle for this line of discussion. Major U.S. and European MNEs have invested and survived in certain Japanese industries despite the barriers to entry in Japan.[10] What explains the presence of such foreign MNEs in Japan? The classic theory of horizontal MNEs is helpful and provides us some answers to this puzzle. The classic theory of the incidence of MNEs is that the firm that possesses proprietary intangible assets, such as technological expertise, marketing expertise, or managerial skills, would exploit these assets and invest in foreign markets. Without advantages accrued from these intangible assets, the firm would be at a disadvantage in the foreign market relative to local firms (Hymer, 1960; Kindleberger, 1969; Caves, 1971; Horst, 1972).[11]

The hypothesis that MNEs must have some sort of advantage over local firms is particularly relevant in Japan because foreign MNEs operate at disadvantages relative to local Japanese firms that are protected by institutional barriers. Inspired by recent research of Bernard, Eaton, Jensen, and Kortum (2003), and Helpman, Melitz, and Yeaple (2004) on the relationship between firm heterogeneity and export-FDI activity, several researchers examined the relationship between productivity levels and different types of firm ownership in Japan by using a firm-level longitudinal panel data for the late 1990s. This emerging empirical

---

[10] Kiyota and Urata (2005) show that only 1.2 percent of the total number of firms in Japan in 2000 are accounted for by foreign-owned firms.

[11] For the new theory of MNEs that incorporate this approach into a framework of formal model, see Helpman (1984), Horstman and Markusen (1987), and Markusen (2002).

literature has produced several important findings: foreign-owned firms show higher total factor productivity (TFP) than domestically owned firms in Japan (Fukao, Ito, and Kwon, 2005; Kimura and Kiyota, 2006a); and M&As by foreign firms tend to improve target firms' TFP levels larger and quicker than M&As by Japanese firms (Fukao et al. 2005). These findings for the late 1990s indeed suggest that the foreign MNEs have some advantages over local firms to operate in Japan. Fukao et al. (2005) suggest that the factor underlying this relationship is the technology transfer from the foreign parent to Japanese subsidiary.

Data and Descriptive Statistics

Data

The data sample for this chapter is constructed from the survey data at the individual subsidiary level compiled jointly by Toyo Keizai and Dun and Bradstreet and published in *Gaishikei kigyo soran [Foreign Affiliated Companies in Japan: A Comprehensive Directory]*. This corporate directory has been published by Toyo Keizai since 1986.[12] It lists an extensive number of foreign firms that own subsidiaries and affiliates in Japan. For example, the 1995 survey covers 3,200 subsidiaries that are more than 20-percent owned by foreign parents and have equity larger than Y50 million. Although the Ministry of Economy, Trade and Industry (METI) in Japan conducts a benchmark survey on Japanese subsidiaries owned by foreign firms, the original information on individual subsidiaries was not accessible at the time of preparing this study.[13] For this reason, the Toyo Keizai–Dun and Bradstreet survey data are used in this study. Given the history of liberalization reforms in Japan, the year when major liberalization reforms were completed, 1973, was chosen as the first observation

---

[12] Although this directory is published annually, information provided is not necessarily updated annually. For a large number of sample firms, it is, therefore, not feasible to construct a panel data set.

[13] The empirical analysis presented in this section was originally conducted in 1998. See Yamawaki (2004b). METI first conducted the survey in for the 1991 fiscal year, again for the 1994 fiscal year, and annually thereafter. This microdata set is now accessible and used most recently by several researchers (e.g., Kimura and Kiyota, 2006a, 2006b; Fukao, Ito, and Kwon, 2005).

year for the statistical analysis.[14] Because the latest survey data available at the time of preparing this study is for 1996, this study sets 1996 as the last year of the observation period.

In the analysis that follows, an exit is observed at the subsidiary level and identified if a subsidiary that had been established during the period 1973–1994 disappeared from the list of subsidiaries in the subsequent years. Although this procedure identifies the subsidiary that exited, it is not able to find out whether the subsidiary was divested because of business failure or it was dissolved because the foreign firm achieved the goal it set when it entered the market. To circumvent this problem, additional information is obtained from various newspapers and is used to identify the subsidiary that failed and was then liquidated.

The sample of foreign subsidiaries is generated by the following criteria: (1) the subsidiary is in manufacturing; (2) the foreign parent firm is in manufacturing; (3) the subsidiary was established during the 1973–1994 period; (4) the subsidiary is owned by more than 20 percent by the foreign parent.[15] These criteria and an additional criterion on the availability of quantitative and qualitative information on individual subsidiaries and parents produce a sample of 366 subsidiaries in Japan. The Toyo Keizai survey counts a total of 555 entries in manufacturing after 1975. The sample prepared for this study thus accounts for approximately 65 percent of total entries during the observation period.

Among the 366 subsidiaries, 199 subsidiaries (54.4 percent) have U.S. parents, forty-nine subsidiaries (13.4 percent) have German parents, twenty-seven subsidiaries (7.4 percent) have UK parents, twenty-four subsidiaries (6.6 percent) have French parents, and twenty-two subsidiaries (6 percent) have Swiss parents. No subsidiary of Asia-based firms is found to be included in the sample. When these subsidiaries are grouped into the three-digit level of industrial classification, the

---

[14] Several liberalization reforms that started in 1967 and ended in 1973 permitted FDI with prior government approval in all but seventeen industries. Further liberalization reforms during 1974–1976 eliminated the restriction on the seventeen industries. With the reform of 1992, the requirement of prior notification was further changed to the requirement of ex post report. Trough the period of this study, only two manufacturing industries, petroleum and leather, were subject to governmental regulations.

[15] Subsidiaries that are divested subsequently after foreign parents are merged or acquired are eliminated from the sample.

electronic equipment and parts industry records the largest number of entries with thirty-seven subsidiaries (10.1 percent), followed by the organic chemicals industry with thirty-one entries (8.5 percent), the pharmaceutical industry with twenty-six subsidiaries (7.1 percent), the computer industry with twenty-two subsidiaries (6 percent), and the special industrial machinery industry with nineteen entries (5.2 percent).

Sample Selection Bias

Even though the data in this study were carefully screened, it was not feasible to rectify an important limitation on the data. Although the first Toyo Keizai survey data available is for 1985, it reports information on subsidiaries established before 1985. We are thus able to track the record of the subsidiaries established after 1973 through 1996. It is very difficult, however, to identify the subsidiaries that entered into the Japanese market after 1973 but exited before 1985 as they are not recorded by the Toyo Keizai data. This sample selection procedure resulted in the exclusion of affiliates that entered after 1973 and exited before 1985. This may become a potential source of selection bias in the statistical analysis for two reasons. First, the group of affiliates, which survived very long (entered between 1973 and 1985 and survived through 1985), is overrepresented in the sample. Second, this data base, therefore, loses the observations on infant mortality for affiliates that entered during the 1973–1985 period but includes infant mortalities of those that entered subsequently. In the statistical analysis in the next section, we will examine the homogeneity of determinants of survival between the pre- and post-1986 entrants.

Patterns of Exit

Table 7.2 reports the numbers of entering and exiting subsidiaries of foreign firms in the Japanese manufacturing industries by entry cohorts. The 1973–1979 cohort recorded the largest number of entries with 122 entry counts, which is followed by the 1980–1984 cohort with 105 entry counts. The table clearly indicates a trend of declining number of entry in more recent years. Of the 366 subsidiaries that entered into Japan in the 1973–1994 period, fifty-five subsidiaries in total were liquidated or divested due to business failure by 1996, accounting for 15 percent of the sample. The largest number of exits is observed for the subsidiaries of the

Table 7.2. *Exit of subsidiaries of foreign MNEs from Japanese manufacturing industries, 1973–1996*

	Entry	Exit (business failure)	Exit (unclassified causes)	Exit (total)
Entry cohort				
1990–1994	43 (100%)	5 (11.6%)	0 (0.0%)	5 (11.6%)
1985–1989	96 (100%)	10 (10.4%)	11 (11.5%)	21 (21.9%)
1980–1984	105 (100%)	30 (28.6%)	11 (10.5%)	41 (39.1%)
1973–1979	122 (100%)	10 (8.2%)	16 (13.1%)	26 (21.3%)
Total	366 (100%)	55 (15.0%)	38 (10.4%)	93 (25.4%)

1980–1984 cohorts, and their average exit rate through 1996 is 28.6 percent, which is distinctively higher than the exit rates for the other cohorts. This means that approximately one out of four subsidiaries established during the 1980–1984 period died in the subsequent years through 1996. The exit rate for the 1973–1979 cohort is the lowest with 8.2 percent. The exit rates for the 1985–1989 and 1990–1994 cohorts are comparable with 10.4 percent and 11.6 percent, respectively. Despite the fact that the 1980–1984 cohort omits the subsidiaries that exited before 1985, it shows higher exit rates than the 1985–1989 and 1990–1994 cohorts that include infant mortalities.

The fourth column of Table 7.2 shows the number of exits recorded by identifying the subsidiaries that entered the Japanese markets but were not listed in the Toyo Keizai survey data in subsequent years. The causes of these exits are not reported in the survey or in other sources. A total of thirty-eight subsidiaries are classified into this category, which account for 10.4 percent of the sample. The fifth column of the same table adds the numbers in the third and the fourth columns and counts a total of ninety-three exits, which accounts for 25.4 percent of the entire sample.

Statistical Analysis of Exit

Statistical Model and Variables
The empirical analysis in this section is motivated by the following theoretical framework to analyze entry and exit. The subsidiary's profits

are defined by Π_i (S_i, I_j), where S_i is a vector of state variables specific to the ith subsidiary and I_j is a vector of exogenous variables specific to industry j in which the ith subsidiary operates. The subsidiary that entered earns Π_i after entry. It decides to exit if losses exceed exit costs X_i. That is, a subsidiary exits from the market if $\Pi_i < -X_i$. Because the subsidiary's profits and exit costs are unobservable, I assume that Π_i^* + X_i^* is a linear function of vectors, S_i and I_j, $\Pi_i^* + X_i^* = \alpha + \beta S_i + \delta I_j + \varepsilon_i$. I then model that the probability that a subsidiary exits is a function of subsidiary specific characteristics, S_i, and industry specific characteristics, I_j.

The dependent variable, *EXIT*, is a binomial variable equal to one if the subsidiary of the foreign firm entered in the Japanese market between 1973 and 1994 and exited before 1996, and zero if it survives through 1996. We use a probit model to identify the determinants of *EXIT*.[16] As discussed earlier in this section, the data used suffer from important limitations because the period of survival varies depending on the year of entry. In addition, the data base loses the observation of infant mortality for affiliates that entered during the 1973–1985 period. We attempt to mitigate this problem by dividing the sample into two subsamples, the 1973–1985 entrants and the 1986–1994 entrants.

EXIT is explained by a set of independent variables, S_i and I_j: (1) variables that test the impediment hypotheses; (2) variables that test the competitive advantage hypotheses; (3) variables that control for subsidiary-specific characteristics; (4) variables that control for industry-specific characteristics; and (5) variables that control for parent-specific and source country effects. All the explanatory variables are constructed for 1994, if the subsidiary survived, and for the last year before exit if they exited before 1994. The subsidiary's primary product is classified to the three-digit industry classification in Japan.

---

[16] It is more appropriate to use a hazard-function model rather than a probit model to analyze the probability of exit. However, duration data sets required to test our hypotheses on entry barriers are not easily available for foreign subsidiaries in Japan. The years of entry and exit for foreign subsidiaries are observable, but subsidiary-specific and industry-specific data are available only sporadically for some years between the time of entry and the time of exit.

Structural Impediments

The hypothesis on the entry-deterring effect of corporate groups is tested by the two variables that identify foreign firms that form joint ventures with Japanese *keiretsu* firms. The first variable, *KEIRETSU*, identifies Japanese partners that belong to the presidents' club of the leading six financial corporate groups, Mitsui, Mitsubishi, Sumitomo, Fuyo, Sanwa, and DKB, that existed during the time period of this study. The second variable, *JV*, identifies joint ventures with Japanese partners who do not belong to the six corporate groups but include members of vertical industrial *keiretsu*, such as Hitachi, Matsushita, Toshiba, Fujitsu, Mitsubishi Electric, Toyota, and Nissan. If forming joint ventures with *keiretsu* firms and Japanese partners mitigates the disadvantage of being outsiders, the coefficients for these two variables should have negative signs. On the other hand, if joint ventures are terminated in the early years, the coefficients of these two variables will have positive signs.

The second hypothesis of structural impediments is tested by the two variables, *VIDIST* and *DISTSIZE*. The first variable, *VIDIST*, is constructed at the subsidiary level and identifies subsidiaries that integrate forward into distribution and/or have exclusive distribution agreements with Japanese partners. The sign of its coefficient is indeterminate a priori. Vertical integration into distribution may mitigate the distribution barrier established by vertically integrated Japanese competitors. On the other hand, it may expose the affiliate to risk because it requires a substantial amount of fixed investment,[17] and it is expected to show a negative coefficient for the industry where intangible assets are important. The second variable, *DISTSIZE*, is constructed at the three-digit industry level and measures the size of independent wholesalers in Japan relative to those in the United States. A small value of *DISTSIZE* indicates that Japan's distribution is more fragmented, and its stock turnover is lower relative to the United States. If Japan's fragmented distribution

[17] The empirical finding by Asaba and Yamawaki (2005) on the profitability of Japanese subsidiaries of foreign MNEs shows this complexity. Subsidiary profits increase as the subsidiary's reliance on its own distribution channel increases in the low-growth industry. On the contrary, subsidiary profits increase as the subsidiary's sales to independent wholesalers increase in the high-growth industry.

puts foreign firms at disadvantage, this variable will have a negative coefficient.

The industry-specific variable, *WAGEDIF*, which measures the difference in average wage and salary per employee between foreign-owned firms and Japanese firms in the same three-digit industries, tests the hypothesis on the disadvantage in the labor market. The hypothesis suggests that *WAGEDIF* will have a positive coefficient. On the other hand, if the foreign firm is efficient and, therefore, can afford to pay higher wage and salary to its employees, the positive effect of *WAGEDIF* on the probability of exit will be offset, and *WAGEDIF* may have an opposite sign.

Competitive Advantage

The hypothesis that the Japanese subsidiary of the foreign firm that possesses competitive advantages to operate in Japan is likely to survive is tested by the subsidiary's export share, *EXPORT*. Although export share does not directly measure the effect of proprietary intangible assets on firm survival, recent empirical studies in the literature of firm heterogeneity and export-FDI activity show a positive correlation between productivity and the propensity to engage in foreign activities. In particular, exporters tend to exhibit higher productivity than nonexporters before the firms actually engage in exports (Bernard and Jensen, 1999, 2004; Helpman, Melitz, and Yeaple, 2004; Kimura and Kiyota, 2006a).[18] To the extent to which this empirical regularity is present in our data, a high export share may indicate that the subsidiary has some sort of advantage in Japanese manufacturing.

In addition to export share, the subsidiary's import procurement share, *IMPORT*, is included to test the hypothesis that the subsidiary that engages in the intrafirm trade and has access to the parent's global advantages at their home base and third-country market by importing and exporting has a competitive advantage in Japan and thus is likely to survive. Previous research has shown that large foreign MNEs possess certain advantages through their global configurations of business

---

[18] Kimura and Kiyota (2006a) also show that firms that exit from foreign markets tend to show relatively low TFP growth.

activities and their capabilities to draw on location-specific and organization-specific advantages (Dunning, 1996; Graham, 1996; Kogut, 1996). Foreign affiliates with large import procurement shares are most commonly observed in the Japanese industries such as pharmaceuticals, medical equipment, and computer and electric equipment.[19] The both coefficients for *EXPORT* and *IMPORT* should therefore be negatively related to *EXIT*.

In addition to these two variables that measure the extent to which the subsidiary engages in international activities, we introduce the dummy variable that identifies the subsidiary that does not hold substantial manufacturing capacity in Japan, *NOPLANT*. If the multinational firm locates manufacturing activities in different countries to exploit their location-specific advantages, it will be able to circumvent significant difficulties in Japan associated with organizing networks of local suppliers to procure materials and intermediate goods, and holding large production capacity and local work force. This implies that *NOPLANT* will have negative coefficients.

Control Variables

The subsidiary-specific factors are controlled by the following two variables: (1) the subsidiary's employment size, *SUBSIZE*; and (2) its parent's employment size, *PARSIZE*. The theoretical study by Jovanovic (1982) predicts that the probability of survival is positively correlated with the firm's age and size because of the underlying difference in efficiency across firms of different ages and sizes. Previous empirical studies on firm exits, including those by Evans (1987) and Dunne, Roberts, and Samuelson (1988), found evidence consistent with this prediction and found that small, new firms have high mortality rates, and thus the probability of survival increases with size and age.[20] Existing empirical studies

---

[19] The average share of imports in total procurement is 76.7 percent in pharmaceuticals, 75.2 percent in medical equipment, and 65.3 percent in computer and electronic equipment for foreign-owned subsidiaries in the sample. For evidence of the growing importance of intrafirm trade, see Casson et al. (1986) and Andersson and Fredriksson (2000).

[20] See Caves (1998) for a survey on the literature of entry and exit. For evidence of entry and exit for different countries, see, for example, Mata and Portugal (1994), Wagner (1994), Geroski (1995), and Baldwin (1995).

on multinational enterprises have also found evidence consistent with this finding that new and small subsidiaries are more likely to be divested (van den Bulcke et al. 1980; Yamawaki, 1997; Mata and Portugal, 1997; Kimura and Fujii, 2003). Therefore, this standard framework is used to control for the influence of size on the probability of exit.

The previous finding that entrant business units face high levels of infant mortality for industrialized countries suggests that barriers to survival of some form exist commonly across different countries. These barriers may not necessarily be country-specific but may be industry-specific (Audretsch, 1995; Baldwin, 1995). The industry-specific factors are controlled by the following three variables: (1) the advertising/sales ratio, *ADSL*; (2) the R&D/sales ratio, *RDSL*; and (3) the Herfindahl index of seller concentration, *HI*. Entry into the highly advertising intensive consumer-goods industry requires a substantial amount of investment sunk in advertising. In particular, foreign entrants may find large investments necessary because they need to establish new brands and reputation, adapt products and advertising campaigns specifically to the consumer's taste in the host country, and invest in distribution. If such a requirement entails significant disadvantages on foreign entrants, the probability of exit in such an industry will be positively related to *ADSL*.[21] In addition, our discussion on vertical integration into distribution suggests that we need to control for the type of product to assess its effect to mitigate the barriers associated with Japan's distribution system.

The extent to which the technological environment influences the ability of new firms to survive was shown in the previous research. The industry R&D/sales ratio was found to be associated with a higher rate of hazard in a large U.S. sample (Audretsch, 1995). To control for the industry-specific effect of R&D intensity, we add *RDSL* to the specification and expect its coefficient to have a positive sign.

Encarnation (1992), and Encarnation and Mason (1990) have argued that Japanese firms in oligopolistic industries collude against foreign firms and therefore succeed in holding dominating positions in their domestic markets. However, Lawrence (1993) found evidence

---

[21] On the other hand, once successfully entered and persevered, such sunk investment may become a barrier to exit.

contradicting this collusive hypothesis. The obvious mechanism is that an oligopoly elevates price substantially above marginal cost, making entry profitable, given the entry barriers. Chapter 4 of this book finds evidence that suggests the existence of such mechanism for the Japanese firms that export to the oligopolistic industries in the United States. The Japanese exporter in the U.S. market that is characterized by high barriers and high concentration shows a higher profitability than the exporter to the low barrier, low concentration industry. To test the collusive hypothesis and the entry-inducing price hypothesis, the Herfindahl index of seller concentration (*HI*) is included in the specification.

Finally, the effects of economic and other conditions in parents' source countries on the performance of their Japanese subsidiaries are controlled by a country-specific dummy variable. *USD* identifies U.S.-owned firms, which account for approximately 55 percent of the sample. The definitions and sources of all the variables are provided in the appendix of this chapter.

Statistical Results

Table 7.3 presents the estimation result of the probit analysis. Model (1) uses the full sample of 246 subsidiaries,[22] and Model (2) uses the sample of subsidiaries that were established between 1973 and 1985. Model (3) uses the sample of subsidiaries established after 1986. The three equations are estimated using the same specification that includes all the explanatory variables discussed in the previous section. Estimating the full model would allow us to test the entry-barrier hypothesis against the competitive-advantage hypothesis.

The homogeneity of determinants of survival between the pre- and post-1986 entrants was examined by dividing the full sample into the two subsamples: the 1973–1985 entrants and the 1986–1994 entrants. The results presented in Table 7.3 shows clearly that the group of firms that survived very long (established between 1973 and 1985 and survived through 1985) is overrepresented in the full sample. However, a significant difference emerges in the estimated coefficients when the 1973–1985 entrants are compared to the result of the 1986–1994 entrants that

---

[22] The number of observation is reduced to 246 from 366 because of missing variables.

Table 7.3. *Probit estimates of determinants of exit (dependent variable: EXIT)*

Variable	1 (1973–1994 entrants)	2 (1973–1985 entrants)	3 (1986–1994 entrants)
Intercept	−0.105 (0.128)	0.330 (0.323)	−0.264 (0.124)
SUBSIZE	−0.299 (3.107)***	−0.355 (2.850)***	−0.344 (1.521)
PARSIZE	−0.036 (0.659)	0.027 (0.387)	0.109 (0.839)
KEIRETSU	0.298 (0.844)	0.368 (0.824)	0.217 (0.290)
JV	0.370 (1.241)	0.241 (0.667)	0.334 (0.446)
VIDIST	−0.075 (0.270)	−0.160 (0.456)	−0.321 (0.459)
DISTSIZE	−0.003 (0.514)	−0.004 (0.554)	−0.003 (0.215)
WAGEDIF	0.020 (0.037)	−0.361 (0.516)	1.292 (1.090)
NOPLANT	−0.212 (0.870)	−0.289 (0.833)	−0.127 (0.217)
EXPORT	−0.017 (2.256)**	−0.040 (2.284)**	−0.014 (1.271)
IMPORT	−0.006 (1.606)	−0.003 (0.719)	−0.014 (1.808)*
ADSL	9.944 (0.874)	7.157 (0.452)	17.194 (0.796)
RDSL	6.425 (1.187)	−1.282 (0.170)	19.798 (1.836)*
HI	−2.013 (0.669)	1.520 (0.376)	−14.005 (1.847)*
USD	−0.006 (0.025)	0.371 (1.256)	−0.596 (1.184)
Log likelihood	−90.264	−57.716	−24.57
Likelihood ratio index	0.119	0.160	0.270

Notes: The number of observations is 246 in Model (1), 167 in Model (2), and 79 in Model (3). The number of positive observations is thirty-six, twenty-four, and twelve, respectively. Numbers reported in parentheses are *t*-test statistics. The levels of significance for a two-tailed test are: * = 10%,** = 5%, and *** = 1%.

includes infant mortalities. The hypothesis that the coefficient vectors are the same in the two subperiods between 1973–1985 and 1986–1994 is rejected.[23]

The estimated coefficients for the five entry-barrier variables, *KEIRETSU, JV, VIDIST, DISTSIZE,* and *WAGEDIF* are all statistically insignificant in both subsamples. A chi-squared test cannot reject the hypothesis that the sum of these five coefficients is zero for both sub-periods.[24] The finding of Model (2) suggests, first, that the presence of

---

[23] The hypothesis that the difference between the estimated coefficients is zero in the two periods is tested by constructing the Wald statistics. The test statistics have a value of 31.22 with 15 degrees of freedom. The 1 percent critical value from a chi-squared test is 30.58. On the basis of the Wald test, we would reject the hypothesis that the same coefficient vector applies in the two subperiods 1973–1985 and 1986–1994.

[24] The Wald statistics has a value of 0.0076 for Model (2) and 0.674 for Model (3).

structural barriers in Japan did not affect the likelihood of survival for the affiliates that entered between 1973 and 1985 and survived through 1985. However, it is not ascertained for this group of firms that infant mortalities were not caused by the existence of barriers to entry in Japan. To the contrary the finding of Model (3) suggests that the structural barriers did not affect the likelihood of survival for the affiliates that entered after 1986 and that they were not the cause of infant mortalities in this group of firms.

The coefficients for the two international variables, *EXPORT* and *IMPORT*, have the expected negative signs in both subperiods. The coefficient for *EXPORT* is statistically significant at the 5-percent level in Model (2) for the 1973–1985 entrants, but the coefficient for *IMPORT* is significant at the 10-percent level in Model (3) for the 1985–1994 entrants. A chi-squared test rejects the hypothesis that the coefficients for *EXPORT* and *IMPORT* are jointly zero for Model (2) at the 5-percent level of significance and for Model (3) at the 10-percent level of significance.[25] This result provides evidence that supports the hypothesis that the foreign affiliate that engages in export is more likely to survive in Japan. This finding is consistent with the recent findings on the positive relationship between productivity and foreign ownership in Japan (Fukao, Ito, and Kwon, 2005; Kimura and Kiyota, 2006b). It also provides evidence that support the hypothesis that the foreign subsidiary that has an access to the parent's global sourcing advantage and exporting opportunities is more likely to survive in Japan. The result of Model (3) further suggests the importance of import procurement when the affiliate is relatively young in the Japanese market. When the affiliate survives the infant stage, it becomes crucial to establish an export base in Japan for its long-term survival.

The most significant difference in the determinants of survival between the subsamples of the 1973–1985 entrants and the 1986–1994 entrants is found in the effects of R&D intensity and seller concentration. The coefficient for *RDSL* is statistically significant at the 10-percent level and has an expected positive sign for the 1986–1994 entrants, while it is insignificant for the 1973–1985 entrants. The coefficient for *HI* is significant at the

---

[25] The Wald statistics have a value of 4.956 for Model (2), and 3.292 for Model (3).

10-percent level and has a negative sign for the 1986–1994 entrants, but it is insignificant for the 1973–1985 entrants.[26] These findings suggest, for the 1986–1994 entrants, that foreign affiliates in highly R&D-intensive industries and in less-concentrated industries are less likely to survive in Japan. The finding of negative effect of the industry R&D–sales ratio on the likelihood of survival is consistent with the results found in the existing literature (e.g., Audretsch, 1995).

The positive effect of seller concentration on the likelihood of survival is consistent with the hypothesis that foreign MNEs possess proprietary assets and hence competitive advantages over the local firms enter the entrenched Japanese market. Japanese incumbents in highly entrenched oligopolistic industries elevate prices and make entry potentially profitable if foreign entrants can jump over the high entry barriers. On the other hand, entry into low concentration industries in Japan is less attractive because of potentially low profitability. This result reinforces my earlier evidence that supports the prediction of the model developed in Chapter 4 of this book. Although the result in Chapter 4 showed the U.S. influence of an oligopoly on Japanese entry, the result in this chapter shows the Japanese influence of an oligopoly on foreign entry into Japan.

Although the industry-specific factors such as *RDSL* and *HI* are insignificant determinants of survival for the 1973–1985 entrants, the coefficient for subsidiary size, *SUBSIZE*, is highly significant and has a negative size. When foreign affiliates survive long in Japan, they are likely to be large in employment size. However, subsidiary size is statistically insignificant as a determinant of survival for the 1986–1994 entrants for which the industry effects are more important.

I also tested the hypothesis that the effect of integration into distribution on firm survival is stronger in industries where intangible assets are important. An interaction variable between *VIDIST* and *ADSL* is added to the specification in estimation. However, the coefficient for this interaction variable is insignificant.

---

[26] The coefficients for *RDSL* are statistically different at the 5-percent significance between the two subsamples. The coefficients for *HI* are statistically different at the 1-percent significance between the two subsamples.

7.4. Entry and Exit Patterns of Domestic Firms

One question that remains unanswered in the statistical analysis of the previous section is of whether the observed pattern of exit is unique to the foreign firms in Japan. In other words, is the likelihood of exit high also relevant for Japanese firms in highly R&D-intensive and less concentrated industries? Unfortunately, we are unable to answer this question because data to perform the same test that was performed in the last section are not available easily. However, the previous research on firm exit and entry in Japan provides us with some indirect evidence that confirms such pattern for Japanese firms. Using gross entry data for twenty Japanese industries in the period of 1986–1991, Kawai and Urata (2002) during found that the determinants of average annual gross entry rates differ between different size classes. For small firms with one to nine employees, the entry rates are significantly lower in industries with high R&D intensity than in industries with low R&D intensity. To the extent that R&D intensity measures the height of entry barriers, this finding suggests that relatively small Japanese firms are at a disadvantage in highly R&D-intensive industries. The negative effect of R&D in gross entry rates disappears for firms larger than twenty employees.

Yamawaki (1989) found that Japanese firms in R&D-intensive industries face strong competitive pressure by estimating the speed at which short-run excess profits and losses are eroded over time.[27] The speed of profit erosion (λ) was first estimated for 376 Japanese firms for the 1964–1982 period and for 413 U.S. firms for the 1964–1982 period. The estimates were then aggregated into forty-two, three-digit industries matched between Japan and the United States. And, the determinants of the estimated λ coefficients were identified from the cross-section data. When the differences in the estimates of λ between Japan and the United States were regressed on market structure variables, R&D intensity and seller concentration were indeed found as significant determinants. R&D intensity showed a negative relationship to the difference in λ between Japan and the United States, suggesting that excess profits in Japanese industries

---

[27] $\Pi_t = \alpha + \lambda \Pi_{t-1} + \mu_t$, where Π_t is profit at time t, and λ measure strength of competitive forces of entry. See Yamawaki (1989), and Odagiri and Yamawaki (1986) for detailed discussion on this model.

decay at a higher speed and thus the incumbents in Japan find it more difficult to maintain their market positions in the long-run than do the firms in the United States. To the contrary, the effect of seller concentration on the difference in the speed of profit erosion between Japan and the United States was positive, suggesting that high concentration fosters the persistence of profits and weaker competitive forces in Japan.

Finally, Yamawaki (1991b) shows that entry and exit in Japanese manufacturing industries are cyclical and respond to fluctuation of business conditions. Using a panel of 135 three-digit industries for the 1979–1984 period, I found that net entry is sensitive to industry demand fluctuations as well as aggregate demand fluctuations and responds negatively to the costs of capital. The responses of net entry into business environments were also found to vary with market structure. High sensitivity of net entry to cyclical business conditions implies that competitive pressure is injected into an industry with a cyclical pattern.[28]

7.5. Conclusions

This chapter first examined the pattern of strategic interactions between Japanese firms and their U.S. and European rivals in intraindustry cross-market FDI. The statistical analysis found that Japanese firms responded to the entries of U.S. and European firms in the Japanese market by entering in the U.S. and European markets. However, no evidence was found for a pattern of retaliatory response by the U.S. and European firms seeking to establish subsidiaries in the Japanese market. The existence of structural barriers in Japan is considered to be a major factor that discouraged potential entry and thus retaliatory actions by foreign firms.

The statistical analysis of this chapter, however, does not find evidence that supports the hypothesis that the likelihood of exit is determined by the distinctive feature of Japan's business practices and industrial organization, such as the existence of corporate groups and complex distribution system, and the imperfection in labor market. To the contrary, foreign

---

[28] For the pattern of exit in the 1990s and the effect of government policy on exit in Japan, see Nishimura, Nakajima, and Kiyota (2005).

firms that possess proprietary assets jump over the barriers and enter the Japanese market. These firms tend to show lower mortality rates in Japan.

This chapter finds that the likelihood of survival in Japan is higher when foreign firms are able to export from Japan and take advantage of the parents' global sourcing networks and exporting opportunities. Foreign firms must have some advantage to offset disadvantages relative to locally based firms in Japan. A high export share may indicate the subsidiary's possession of technological expertise and managerial capability to enhance productivity. In addition, the subsidiary in Japan that engages in intrafirm trade between its parent and other affiliates within the same multinational entity is likely to exploit the MNE's organizational advantages created from locating various value-chain activities in different countries and thereby offseting the Japan-specific disadvantages. Thus, Japanese firms responded by establishing subsidiaries in the U.S. and European markets to respond to the early entries of the U.S. and European firms that possessed proprietary assets and hence had significant advantages to operate in Japan.

Finally, this chapter finds that the industry-specific factors such as high R&D intensity and low seller concentration are the determinants of exit for the group of firms that are relatively new in the industry. However, such industry-specific effects are found to be insignificant for the group of firms that have survived for a long time in Japan.

8

Responses of Foreign Firms to Japanese
Competition

8.1. Introduction

As Japanese firms in engineering-intensive industries expanded their international operations in the late 1980s, their product focus also shifted from low-end products to middle-range products, and further to high-end products. The most notable example of such upward shifts in product segments was observed in the automobile industry in the late 1980s. Although Japan's automobile manufacturers succeeded in penetrating the international markets based on their competitive advantages in production efficiency and product quality in small-size and middle-range passenger vehicles,[1] they were not yet a major competitive force in the high-end luxury car segment in the late 1970s and the early 1980s. Contrary to the low-end and midsegment, European manufacturers were historically strong competitors in the high-end luxury segments worldwide. In the U.S. passenger car market, German, British, and U.S. firms had been the major players in the luxury segment after World War II. A notable change in market structure, however, occurred in the late 1980s when Japanese firms entered the luxury segment of the U.S. passenger car market. Chapter 4 investigated their entry process in the U.S. market and described how Japanese firms took advantage of their competitiveness and implemented a policy to set export price at a level that undercut incumbents' price. When measured by market share, the newly established brands of Japanese automakers, such as Toyota's Lexus, were

---

[1] See Clark and Fujimoto (1991) and Womack, Jones, and Roos (1991).

no doubt very successful in penetrating the U.S. market that had been entrenched by the existing European and U.S. luxury brands.

What happened to the foreign rivals specializing in luxury automobiles in the U.S. market after Japanese firms entered their segment successfully in the early 1990s? Did the European and U.S. incumbents with established brands respond to the new competition initiated by Japanese firms? Did they lower prices to challenge the Japanese competition? Or, did they accommodate Japanese entry and raise prices? The focus of previous chapters was the behavior of Japanese firms and their response to foreign rivals' actions. The focus now shifts to foreign rivals' reactions to Japanese firms' actions and how they responded to new competition. This chapter thus examines how the European and U.S. incumbents in the U.S. luxury car market responded to new competition by changing their prices, if they ever did.

8.2. Competitive Interactions between Incumbents and New Entrants

The descriptive analysis in Chapter 4 showed how Lexus's price was set relative to rivals' price when the new brand was launched by Toyota into the U.S. market. Figure 4.1 in Chapter 4 showed that Lexus's average list price at the time of entry was set significantly below German competitors' price within the same category and more comparable to the price of models classified in the lower category. However, at least two noticeable changes occurred in the pricing behaviors of Japanese and German competitors around 1994. First, Lexus raised prices gradually after 1991 up until 1994. After 1994, the rate of price increase became somewhat smaller. Second, Mercedes-Benz lowered the price of its E-class passenger cars in 1995 and suppressed the rate of price increase in the S-class after 1994. At the time of Lexus's entry, the price of the E-class model exceeded the price of the Lexus's LS400 despite the idea that the E-class model is considered one size smaller than Lexus's LS400. Although these observations are descriptive, they seem to suggest that after its initial success, Lexus started raising its sales price in the U.S. market, and that the German competitor responded to new competition by reducing the price of its product that was competing potentially with the new entrant's primary product. There are at least three questions that need to be addressed based on this finding: (1) do all the incumbents firms respond to entry? (2) do their responses differ significantly one from another? (3) and do they reduce or maintain their prices in response to entry?

Previous Studies

Entry Deterrent Pricing

Previous theoretical studies of strategic behavior generally assume an asymmetry of firms in an industry and suggest that incumbents' response to entry is firm specific rather than industry specific. The classic dominant-firm pricing model and a dynamic limit-pricing model (Gaskins, 1971) assume typically an asymmetry of pricing and investment behavior between a dominant firm and fringe firms in an industry. In the dynamic limit-pricing model, a dominant firm with a large market share regulates the entry and expansion of small firms so as to maximize its long-run profits. Small firms in the industry behave collectively as a competitive fringe and behave as price-takers.

More recent work analyzes the strategic behavior of a firm assuming asymmetry between firms in their competitive advantages, which are in turn created by structural traits specific to each firm. A model of predatory pricing based on reputation effects suggests that differences in firms' beliefs about their rivals can result in entry deterrence (Kreps and Wilson, 1982; Milgrom and Roberts, 1982). The incumbent who has high costs may be able to build a reputation as a firm that responds to entry with low prices if it lowers its price in response to entry. The incumbent preys to signal information about itself as a low-cost firm. The entrant who infers information about by the incumbent's costs observing its pricing behavior may then decide not to enter. In this reputation model, the reputation that a firm acquires is clearly specific to the firm, and the firm is prey to signal information about its own production costs and product quality.

In the early limit-pricing models (Bain, 1956; Modigliani, 1958; Sylos-Labini, 1962), the key assumption was that the entrant believes that the incumbent will maintain its output after entry occurs. This threat to produce the same level of output after entry occurs is not credible because it is not profit maximizing for the incumbent when both the incumbent and entrant have identical costs. To make the threat credible, an incumbent needs to commit to a low price after entry. The key to making the incumbent's behavior credible is to invest in excess capacity (Spence, 1977; Dixit, 1980). An asymmetry between firms is important in this model in that the incumbent has committed itself to a large sunk investment so that its threat is credible. Again, it is assumed that one firm has an advantage over its rivals in the same industry, and its advantage is specific to the firm.

That a firm's response to rivals in an industry depends on the firm's ability to respond has been shown decisively in the previous theoretical literature. Kreps and Scheinkman (1983) has developed a two-stage game in which capacities are set in the first-stage by the oligopolists, and production takes place in the second-stage subject to capacity constraints generated by the first-stage decisions. Their model shows that competitive outcomes depend on the sequence in which decisions are taken and on the way in which earlier decisions shape firm-specific advantages and, in turn, determine the payoffs associated with later decisions (Martin, 2001).

In summary, all of these studies incorporate the notion that firms are different from rivals in an industry in that they possess advantages and disadvantages over others, and firms interact with each other in the industry. One firm's response to entry, therefore, may be different from another firm's response because of the underlying differences in their characteristics. To examine these issues of firms' responses to entry, it is necessary to use firm data in empirical analysis.

Strategic Groups

The theory of strategic groups argues that firms in an industry are likely to differ systematically in their structural characteristics, such as the degree of vertical integration and diversification; the extent to which they advertise and brand their products; whether or not they use captive distribution channels; whether they are full-line or narrow-line sellers; whether they operate in the national market or only regionally; and whether they are multinational firms. Although these characteristics are specific to firms and distinguish one firm from another, some firms closely resemble others in the industry and recognize their mutual dependence. The industry, therefore, contains subgroups of firms with different characteristics, which are then referred to strategic groups (Caves and Porter, 1977).

Because strategic groups within an industry are characterized by differing structural characteristics, their competitive positions in face of entry are different each other. One group may be well entrenched and protected from new competition, but another may find new competition more a threat. Barriers to entry then become specific to the group rather than specific to the industry, and barriers to mobility between groups may be erected.

This theory suggests, therefore, that one incumbent's response to entry may differ from another incumbent's response, and that the differences are determined by their strategic positioning in the industry. When they are in the same strategic group, their responses will be similar. However, when they belong to different strategic groups in the industry, their responses will be significantly different one from another. Their behavior is thus determined by factors specific to individual firms as well as mobility barriers.

Evidence from Previous Empirical Studies

Empirical evidence on the pattern of incumbents' response to entry has been derived from studies using surveys and statistical methods. Among the earlier studies using survey results, Biggadike (1976) found that 46 percent of the sample of diversifying entrants perceived no response by incumbents, and Yip (1982) found that none of his sample of entrants perceived responses by incumbents. Of the 293 U.S. managers who responded to the questionnaire survey by Smiley (1988), nearly half considered it important to respond to entry. Using a similar survey result in the UK, Singh, Utton, and Waterson (1997) indicated that almost 50 percent of the respondents would normally use none or only one of the wide set of actions once entry has occurred.

Among the previous literature using a statistical approach, Cubbin and Domberger (1988) found that the incumbents responded to entry with increasing advertising expenditures in 40 percent of the forty-two advertising-intensive UK industries they studied. Lieberman (1987b) studied the postentry investment behavior of incumbent firms in U.S.

chemical industries and observed an increase in capacity after entry. Thomas (1999) studied incumbents' response to entry in the U.S. ready-to-eat cereal industry and found that incumbents are more likely to respond to entrants with an aggressive price response. He also found that incumbents are more likely to respond when the scale of entry is greater.[2]

Some of these and other studies address the question of who responds to entry and suggest that both industry-specific factors and firm-specific factors are important in determining incumbents' response. Yamawaki (1985), using historical data on firms, shows that the pricing and investment behaviors of a dominant firm are significantly different from those of fringe firms within an industry. Asymmetric firm behavior was observed in the U.S. Steel industry, when U.S. Steel responded to a capacity expansion of Bethlehem Steel, although Bethlehem Steel did not respond to an expansion of U.S. Steel. The work of Cubbin and Domberger (1988) shows that incumbents are more likely to respond when they are dominant firms in static markets, which suggests that incumbents' responses to entry are likely to be firm-specific and also likely to depend on market structure.

Lieberman (1987b) shows that incumbents are likely to increase capacity in concentrated industries, suggesting that market structure is important in shaping incumbents' decision to respond to entry. Bunch and Smiley (1992) analyzed more directly the question of who deters entry, but their major concern was to identify industry characteristics, rather than firm-specific characteristics, as important factors in determining the propensity to deter entry. Their statistical analysis found that for new products strategic entry deterrents are used more often when markets are concentrated, are populated with large firms, and are R&D intensive. These studies provide evidence that incumbents are more likely to respond to entry when their markets are concentrated. Finally, Thomas (1999) found that the incumbents' response differs between entry by new firms and entry by existing firms. The incumbent firms in the U.S. cereal industry are likely to accommodate other incumbents on price

---

[2] Lieberman (1987a) and Masson and Shaanan (1986) tested the hypothesis that the incumbent builds excess capacity to deter entry.

and new product introductions but would use advertising to deter new entrants.

In the empirical literature of strategic groups, previous studies have primarily focused on the identification of strategic groups and the relationships between strategic groups and profits at industry, group, and firm levels, rather than strategic groups' reaction to new entry. Caves and Pugel (1980) found that the behavior of firms within an industry varies across different groups in the extent of advertising, foreign investment, exports, and capital expenditure. Although the link between an industry's strategic group structure and industry performance has been found, empirical evidence on the link between group membership and firm profitability has not been well-established (e.g., Porter, 1979; Fiegenbaum and Thomas, 1990). Various forms of rivalry within groups and between groups (Cool and Dierickx, 1993) are considered to be a missing element necessary to establish a link between group membership and firm profitability. The previous literature in this field has not examined response differences to new competition among incumbents of different strategic groups.

In summary, these studies suggest that incumbents, in general, respond to entry infrequently (Geroski, 1995) and that their decisions to respond depend on industry as well as firm characteristics. Few of these empirical studies, however, have addressed the issues of response differences to entry among incumbents in an industry and among incumbents of different strategic groups within an industry.[3]

Hypotheses

The theoretical models based on game theory offer a general hypothesis that an incumbent firm's response to entry is different from other incumbents' responses. Response differences among incumbent firms are predicted because firms differ in their resource endowments and thus differ in their structural characteristics. The theory of strategic group offers another general hypothesis that an incumbent firm's response to entry is

---

[3] Haskel and Scaramozzino (1997) found evidence that conjectural variations among firms, measured by physical and financial capacity, depend on the ability of other firms to react.

different from another incumbent firm's response, but their responses are more similar when both firms belong to the same strategic group than when they belong to different groups. Reaction differences among groups arise because differences in firm characteristics are more distinctive between groups than within a group. The firms within the same strategic group are more homogeneous in resources and characteristics, which induce similar behavior among them. Therefore, we have two general hypotheses on incumbent firms' response to entry:

Hypothesis (1): The extent to which an incumbent firm responds to entry is different across firms within the industry.

Hypothesis (2): The extent to which an incumbent firm responds to entry is the same within group but different between groups within the industry.

The evidence from the previous studies suggests that incumbent firms are less likely to respond immediately to entry. Geroski (1995) suggests that these facts may be consistent with the behavior of incumbents who do not change their preentry output levels after entry (the Sylos Postulate). The alternative hypothesis he suggests is that incumbents ignore entrants at least until they are well-established. This hypothesis implies that incumbents do not perceive immediate threats from entrants when they are still small and new in the industry. Incumbents are more likely to respond when entrants become large and grab a recognizable size of market share. This chapter tests the two hypotheses by using product and firm data and applying this data to a fixed-effect model in the statistical analysis.

8.3. Statistical Analysis of Price Reactions

Statistical Model

The model used in this chapter is derived from the model of export pricing under oligopoly with differentiated products introduced in Section 2.2.2. The exporting firm maximizes its total profits that originate from domestic and export markets in terms of home currency. The export price equation was derived from the first-order condition for this problem and given in Chapter 2 as

$$P_f = [\varepsilon/\varepsilon - 1 - \varepsilon\eta\sigma(P_{f*}/P_f)(s/1 - s)]C'/e, \qquad (8.1)$$

where $\varepsilon = - (\partial X/\partial P_f) (P_f/X)$, $\eta = - (\partial P_f / \partial X^*) (X^*/P_f)$, $\sigma = \partial X^*/ \partial X$, P_f is the price of the domestic firm's product in the export market in terms of the foreign currency, P_f^* is the price of the foreign rival firm's product in the export market, and s is the firm's market share in the export market, $s = P_f X/(P_f X + P_f^* X^*)$. The firm produces output D for domestic consumption and output X for export. Similarly, the foreign rival produces output D^* for export and output X^* for consumption in its own market. Prices are assumed to fall as the domestic firm's output and the rival firm's output increase.[4]

In Eq. (8.1), the mark-up in the export market is defined by the bracket term and is a function of the parameters of the demand functions (ε and η), the conjectural variation (σ), market share (s), and foreign rival's price P_f^*.[5] Equation (8.1) yields the price formula:

$$P_f = \lambda C'/e, \tag{8.2}$$

where λ is the mark-up term. Assume that the mark-up term is determined by

$$\ln \lambda = a_0 + a_1 \ln P_f^* + a_2 \ln s. \tag{8.3}$$

Taking the logarithm of Eq. (8.2), and substituting the Eq. (8.3) into it, the basic price equation for the exporter is given by

$$\ln P_{fit} = \alpha_i + \phi_t + \beta_{1i} \ln P_{f^*jt} + \beta_{2i} \ln s_{it} + \beta_{3i} \ln e_{it} + \beta_{4i} \ln c_{it} + u_{it}, \tag{8.4}$$

where α_i is a firm-specific fixed effect, ϕ_t is a time-specific effect, c_{it} is the marginal cost, and u_{it} is an iid error term.

The response of the exporter to a change in rivals' price is estimated by the coefficient for P_f^* in Eq. (8.4). Hypothesis (1) implies that β_1 differs across different firms, and the Hypothesis (2) implies that β_1

---

[4] Because all the exporters locate production facilities for the luxury passenger models investigated in this chapter in their home countries, the impact of local cost factors on the exporter's price as suggested by Gros and Swenson (1996) is assumed to be unimportant.

[5] The conjectural variation approach is generally rejected from a theoretical point of view (e.g., Shapiro, 1989). However, Dockner (1992), Sabourian (1992), Lapham and Ware (1994), and Cabral (1995) have provided a formal justification for using the conjectural variation approach on practical grounds. These studies have shown that, under certain conditions, the outcome of a static conjectural model is consistent with the outcome of a dynamic model.

differs among different groups of firms. A positive sign for this coefficient suggests that the exporter follows rivals' price changes, and a negative sign suggests that the exporter lower price strategically when rivals increase price. A negative sign for the coefficient for the exchange rate, β_3, suggests that changes in currency values are passed through on local price, and a positive sign implies that changes in currency values are adjusted by changes in the mark-up.

Because the price data in this chapter is defined at the level of individual model, Eq. (8.4) is specified, taking into account additional factors, as

$$\ln P_{fkt} = \alpha_k + \phi_t + \sum_{j}^{m} \beta_{1j} \ln P_{f^*jt} + \beta_{2k} \ln s_{it} + \beta_{3k} \ln e_{it} + \beta_{4k} \ln c_{it}$$
$$+ \beta_{5k} \, New \, Model + u_{kt}, \tag{8.5}$$

where subscript k denotes model k, and subscript i denotes firm i that produces model k. Because exporter i competes with several rivals in the U.S. market, P_f^* is constructed for individual rivals, $j = 1, \ldots, m$. A binary variable, *NewModel*, is added in Eq. (8.5) to control for the introduction of a new model in a specific product class. The time-specific effect is modeled in a general way by including a time trend in estimation. All the coefficients are specified to vary across different models and will be tested if they differ across models, firms, and groups.

Data and Variables

The data sample in this chapter is constructed at the level of individual luxury models offered in the U.S. market. Three German brands, BMW, Mercedes-Benz, and Audi, one British brand, Jaguar, and two U.S. brands, Cadillac and Lincoln, are included in the sample because these brands are considered to be major competitors of Toyota's Lexus. The number of models included in the sample varies across firms according to the availability of continuous price series within a particular model class over the 1991–2001 period and by the offering, in the U.S. market, of models by individual firms. For example, three models are included for BMW (3-series, 5-series, and 7-series) and Mercedes-Benz (C-class, E-class, and S-class); but only one model is used as a sample for Audi

(A6). Although these firms currently produce and sell other types of luxury cars, such as sports cars, convertibles, and SUV models for the U.S. market, these models are not included in the statistical analysis of this chapter. This is because Lexus at the time of entry in 1989 was primarily targeted at the sedan/coupe segment of the market.

All of the variables are constructed annually for the period of 1991–2001. The first observation year, 1991, was chosen because official price data for Lexus models are available after 1991. Import price is expressed in units of the destination market's currency (US$), although costs are expressed in units of the source country's currency. The foreign-cost variable is measured as the source country's aggregate hourly earnings (*Wage*). The exchange-rate variable is measured as the average annual nominal exchange rate (*Exchange Rate*) and is expressed in units of the exporter's currency per U.S. dollar.[6] The definitions of the variables used in the statistical analysis are described in detail in the appendix of this chapter.

Statistical Results

A fixed-effects model of Eq. (8.5) was estimated for individual makes. Table 8.1 presents the fixed-effects estimates of the coefficients for $P^*_{f\,t-1}$ for the major German and Japanese competitors in the U.S. market. In estimation, rivals' lagged prices are nested in the specification of Eq. (8.5). Because both own price and rival's price are expressed in logarithm, the estimated coefficient is interpreted as the elasticity of own price with respect to rival's price. Several interesting findings emerge from Table 8.1. First, the pattern of reaction to rivals' lagged prices differs between makes. For the two German firms, BMW and Mercedes-Benz, the hypothesis, $\alpha, \beta = \alpha_i, \beta_i$, is rejected at the 1-percent level of

---

[6] In the auto industry, labor costs may be considered effectively fixed. This is particularly the case for Japan, where the "lifetime" employment system was in effect in the years of the study and for the E.U., where labor-management relationships were institutionalized. This consideration, however, does not affect importantly the specification of estimating equations because the exchange rate, e, and costs, c, are included in an additive way in Eq. (8.1). The coefficient for e is expected to measure the response of the markup to fluctuations in foreign exchange.

Table 8.1. *Estimated elasticity of price with respect to rivals' price for BMW, Mercedes–Benz, and Lexus, 1991–2001*

Independent variable: Lagged Rival's Price	Dependent variable: *Price*		
	BMW	Mercedes-Benz	Lexus
BMW		0.488(1.396)	−0.519(2.913)****
Mercedes-Benz	0.258(2.688)**		−0.059(0.627)
Lexus	0.101(0.642)	−0.397(1.870)*	
Number of observations	33	33	31

Notes : *t*-test statistics are in parentheses. The level of significance at a two-tailed test is: *** = 1%; ** = 5%; and * = 10%. The elasticity is estimated by β_{1j} in Eq. (8.5). A fixed-effects model was used to estimate Eq. (8.5) for individual firms. The estimation period is for 1991–2001. The number of observations for Lexus is thirty-one because the price of its *GS* model was available after 1993.

significance, suggesting that the incumbents respond to rivals' prices differently. This result provides evidence that supports Hypothesis (1).

Second, Table 8.1 shows that BMW responds positively to Mercedes-Benz's price, but it does not respond to Lexus's price. The elasticity of own price to Mercedes-Benz's price is 0.258, implying that a 1-percent increase in Mercedes-Benz's price will lead to a 0.26 percent increase in own price. However, Mercedes-Benz does not follow the pricing of BMW. The German firm, however, is likely to change price strategically in response to a change in Lexus's price. The elasticity of Mercedes-Benz with respect to Lexus's price is −0.397, which implies that a 1 percent increase in Lexus's price will lead to an approximately 0.4-percent decline in Mercedes-Benz's price. This result of negative response by Mercedes-Benz to Lexus's price confirms our earlier finding from Figure 4.1. Third, Lexus responds to negatively to BMW's price, but it does not follow Mercedes-Benz's price. The estimated elasticity of own price with respect to BMW's price for Lexus is −0.519, implying that a 1-percent increase in BMW's price will lead to a 0.52 percent decrease in Lexus's price. What is the economic intuition that underlies such behaviors? The asymmetric behavior that BMW responded to Mercedes-Benz's price, but Mercedes-Benz did not respond to BMW's price appears to suggest that Mercedes-Benz was the price leader, at least, among the German firms in the luxury segment of the U.S. market in the period studied in this chapter. An

Table 8.2. *Estimated elasticity of price with respect to rival's price for Audi, Jaguar, Cadillac, and Lincoln, 1991–2001*

Independent variable: Lagged rival's price	Dependent variable: *price*			
	Audi	Jaguar	Cadillac	Lincoln
BMW	0.562(2.420)	0.143(0.324)		
Mercedes-Benz	1.147(3.055)*	−0.423(2.157)*		
Cadillac				0.919(3.172)***
Lincoln			−0.006(0.029)	
Lexus	0.490(3.152)*	1.027(3.371)**	0.179(0.599)	0.201(0.752)
Number of observations	11	22	22	22

Notes: *t*-test statistics are in parentheses. The level of significance at a two-tailed test is: *** $= 1\%$; ** 5%; and * $= 10\%$. The elasticity is estimated by β_{1j} in Eq. (8.5). A fixed-effects model was used to estimate Eq. (8.5) for individual firms. The estimation period is for 1991–2001. The number of observation differs between the firms due to the difference in the number of models included in the sample.

increase in price by Mercedes-Benz was followed by a price increase of BMW. When Lexus's share increased markedly in the few years after its entry, Mercedes-Benz had to respond to the new competition by cutting its price around 1994. Hence, the elasticity of Mercedes-Benz with respect to Lexus's price has a negative value. And, as suggested by the negative value of the elasticity, Lexus's strategy was to set price strategically to take advantage of the high price set by German rivals in the U.S. market.

To test the hypothesis that Mercedes-Benz behaved as a price leader among the German firms, Table 8.2 shows the estimated elasticity of its own price with respect to rivals' prices for Audi. As expected, its elasticity with respect to Mercedes-Benz's price is positive and statistically significant with a value 1.147. Because a *t*-test cannot reject the hypothesis that the estimated elasticity value is not different from 1, this result suggests that a 1 percent increase in Mercedes-Benz's price will lead to a 1-percent increase in Audi's price. Although Audi does not respond to BMW's price, it responds to Lexus's price positively. The elasticity with respect to Lexus's price is 0.49, suggesting that its response to Lexus's price is statistically smaller than response to Mercedes-Benz's price. This

Table 8.3. *Fixed-effects estimates of Lexus price in the U.S. market, 1991–2001*

Variable	Dependent variable: *Lexus price*
Mercedes-Benz Price$_{t-1}$	−0.059(0.627)
BMW Price$_{t-1}$	−0.519(2.913)***
Market Share	0.191(3.816)***
Exchange Rate	−0.277(5.053)***
Wage	4.379(9.015)***
New Model	−0.041(3.500)***
Time	−0.016(3.125)***
Adj-R^2	0.992
N	31

Notes: *t*-test statistics are in parentheses. The levels of significance for a two-tailed test are: *** = 1%; and ** = 5%.

finding is consistent with the pattern that Mercedes-Benz behaves as the price leader among the German firms.[7]

Table 8.2 also shows the elasticities for other luxury brands in the U.S. market. The most notable finding there is the pricing behavior of U.S. brands, Cadillac and Lincoln. It appears that the both brands do not respond to Lexus's price and thus one indifferent to new competition. However, Lincoln responds to its domestic rival's price significantly. The estimated elasticity with respect to Cadillac's price is 0.919 and is statistically not different from 1. This suggests an asymmetric behavior of Cadillac and Lincoln, and that Cadillac behaves as a price leader. A 1-percent increase in Cadillac's price will lead to a 1-percent increase in Lincoln's price. The both U.S. brands do not respond to German prices at all when they are included in the model specification. This result implies that the U.S. firms behave differently from their German and Japanese competitors, which provides evidence that supports Hypothesis (2).

Table 8.3 presents the fixed-effects estimates of Eq. (8.5) for Lexus in 1991–2001. All the coefficients except for Mercedes-Benz's price are

[7] Mercedes-Benz does not respond to Audi's price when Audi's price is also included in the model specification.

statistically significant. As already explained, BMW's lagged price has a negative relationship with Lexus's current price. The coefficient for market share has a positive sign, suggesting that Lexus increased price as its share increased in the U.S. market. The coefficient for the exchange rate has a negative sign with a value of 0.277, suggesting that a 1-percent appreciation of the Japanese yen against the U.S. dollar was passed through on local price with a 0.28 percent increase during the period of 1991–2001. The coefficient for *New Model* is negative, implying that Lexus does not increase price when they introduce new models in the U.S. market, given other factors.

8.4. Market Share and Exchange Pass-Through

The previous section investigated the price reaction of incumbents to Lexus price. Although we found some evidence that incumbents responded to new competition by changing price, incumbents' response may take a more subtle form than direct response in price. Instead of reducing price directly, the incumbent may choose to keep the price level constant but reduce the mark-up when the value of their home currency appreciates against the value of local currency. An appreciation of home currency increases costs at home and gives an incentive for incumbents to squeeze the mark-up.[8] Yamawaki (2002a) tests this hypothesis by using a variable interacted between the exchange rate and the entrant's market share and estimating the following equation:

$$\ln P_{kt} = \alpha_k + \phi_t + \beta_{1k} \, Entry_t + \beta_{2k} \ln e_{it} + \beta_{3k} \ln c_{it} \qquad (8.6)$$
$$+ \beta_{4k} Entry_t * \ln e_{it} + \beta_{5k} \, Tax_t + \beta_{6k} NewModel_t + u_{kt},$$

where Entry is the entrant's market share, and the coefficient for the interaction variable, *Entry**ln *e*, tests the maintained hypothesis on exchange pass-through. Tax controls for the structural break that may be imposed by the luxury car tax and gas guzzler tax in 1991.[9]

Using the data for 1986–1997, the author estimated a fixed-effects model of Eq. (8.6) (Table 8.4). The coefficient for the exchange rate is

[8] See Feenstra (1989), Knetter (1989, 1993), and Goldberg and Knetter (1997) for the existing literature on exchange pass-through.
[9] See Yamawaki (2002) for a detailed account on the statistical model.

Table 8.4. *Fixed-effects estimates of luxury car price of German models in the U.S. market, 1986–1997*

Variable	Dependent variable: German car price
Entry	−2.410(2.107)**
Exchange Rate	−0.741(4.101)***
Wage	0.159(1.657)
Entry Exchange Rate*	6.093(3.252)***
Tax	−0.040(0.870)
New Model	0.032(1.469)
Time	0.014(2.297)**
Adjusted R-squared	0.950
Number of Models	9
N	84

Notes: *t*-test statistics are in parentheses. The levels of significance for a two-tailed *t*-test are: * = 10%, ** = 5%, and *** = 1%.

statistically significant and has a negative sign, indicating that the German firms increase local prices when their home currency appreciates against U.S. dollar. Although such behavior of passing changes in currency values on local price is observed for the preentry period, it is significantly constrained during the postentry period. Indeed, the coefficient for the interaction variable, *Entry*Exchange Rate*, is highly significant and positively signed. Evaluated at the value of *Entry* during the preentry and postentry periods, the pass-through coefficient for the preentry period is –0.74, although it ranges between –0.20 and 0.23 in the postentry period. The German exporters were able to enjoy increasing their prices approximately by 7 percent when the German mark appreciated by 10 percent before Lexus entered in the U.S. market. However, new competition injected by Lexus changed their behavior in the U.S. market. The German firms' response was initially modest, and the firms reduced their pass-through responding to the entry of Lexus. As Lexus's market share increased gradually and reached to 15 percent of the U.S. market, they could no longer afford to ignore the potential threat and squeezed mark-ups approximately by 2 percent when German mark appreciated by 10 percent.

8.5. Conclusions

This chapter examined the questions of whether and how incumbents respond to entry. The statistical analysis finds that the incumbent's response to entry is specific to the firm. The responses of incumbents to the new entrant's price differ markedly between firms. Some firms reacted strategically by counteracting, and others responded in a way to accommodate the new firm. And yet, others did not respond to new competition at all. The incumbents' responses may take a more subtle form when they export from their home countries to the destination market. The European exporters, particularly the German car manufacturers, are likely to adjust their mark-ups in the destination market when their home currencies appreciate to compete with the Japanese rivals. The incumbent exporter thus squeezes the mark-up to neutralize the effect of an increase in cost at home on local currency price particularly when it faces new competition.

One interesting finding from this chapter is that the entry of Lexus into the U.S. market has changed the nature of competition in the industry. The three German firms presumably set prices following the leadership of Mercedes-Benz. As Lexus's market share increased after entry, Mercedes-Benz could not ignore the impact of competition from Lexus so Mercedes-Benz responded to it competitively. Thus, Japanese entry into an entrenched export market triggered oligopolistic interactions and intensified rivalry.

9

Exit in the U.S. Manufacturing Industries

In Chapter 6, I examined the pattern of Japanese entry in the European and U.S. manufacturing industries in the late 1980s when the explosive increase in the flow of FDI was observed. What happened to those Japanese firms that rushed into Europe and the United States? Did they already exit from these markets? In fact, a number of Japanese firms that entered in the U.S. and European industries in the 1980s have left these markets by now. The purpose of this chapter is two-fold: first, it examines the pattern of Japanese exit from the United States through 2000; second, it tests several hypotheses on the relationship between concentrated entry and exit patterns.

9.1. Patterns

The data used to describe the exit pattern of U.S. subsidiaries of Japanese firms is constructed from the subsidiary level information published in Toyo Keizai, *kaigai shinshutsu kigyo soran* and described fully in Chapter 6. The sample of Japanese subsidiaries used in this chapter is generated by the following criteria: (1) the subsidiary is in manufacturing; (2) the Japanese parent firm is in manufacturing; (3) the subsidiary was established during the 1985–1990 period; and (4) the Japanese parent owns more that 10 percent of the subsidiary. These criteria and the unavailability of some of quantitative data on subsidiary, parent, and industry characteristics produce a sample of 316 subsidiaries in the United States. The 1985–1990 period records the highest concentration of Japanese entries into the U.S. market in any 5 consecutive years in history. The yen

Table 9.1. *Numbers of Japanese entries and exits by year of entry,*
United States

Year of entry (1)	Number of entries (2)	Number of exits (3)	Number of nonlisting affiliates (4)	Exits/Entries (3)/(2) (5)	Total disappearance rate (3) + (4)/(2) (6)
1985	24	4	3	0.167	0.292
1986	45	8	14	0.178	0.489
1987	52	8	8	0.154	0.308
1988	87	8	18	0.092	0.299
1989	59	9	9	0.153	0.305
1990	49	9	15	0.184	0.490
Total 1985–1990	316	46	67	0.146	0.358

appreciated against the U.S. dollar by 39 percent in real terms between 1984 and 1985.[1]

A follow-up study of these Japanese entrants was conducted through the year 2000 to examine if they exit from the U.S. market in the subsequent period after entry. Column 3 of Table 9.1 shows the number of exits by year of entry for this sample of U.S. subsidiaries of Japanese firms. Out of the 316 subsidiaries established between 1985 and 1990, 46 subsidiaries exited in the U.S. market by 2000. This sample shows that Japanese firms on average exit from the U.S. market within 8 years after entry. The exit rate, defined by the ratio of number of exits divided by the number of entries, is the highest for the 1990 cohort with 18.4 percent and the lowest for the 1988 cohort with 9.2 percent. The overall exit rate for this sample is 14.6 percent.

Although the forty-six cases are clearly identified as exits, there exist a number of U.S. subsidiaries that are dropped from the Toyo Keizai list through 2000.[2] If we consider these missing subsidiaries as exits as well, the exit rate increases markedly for every entry cohort. Column 4 of

[1] The real exchange rate is constructed by using the nominal exchange rate and consumer price indexes.
[2] There are other cases where the names of affiliates are changed. Such cases are not included in this list.

Table 9.1 reports the number of these missing subsidiaries, and column 6 shows the exit rates using the sum of numbers listed in columns 3 and 4. The highest exit rate is recorded for the 1990 cohort with 49 percent and the lowest exit rate is recorded for the 1985 cohort with 29.2 percent. The average rate for the entire sample is 35.8 percent, suggesting that at least one out of three entrants has already exited or dropped from the list of U.S. affiliates of Japanese firms.[3] When the confirmed exits and those dropped from the directory are compared, a significant difference between the two groups exists in terms of ownership control. Those dropped out from the directory are likely to be the subsidiaries established as joint ventures. And, in this group, the likelihood of exit is significantly higher for the joint venture subsidiary than wholly-owned subsidiary.[4] It appears, therefore, that those dropped from the directory include a number of joint ventures that were dissolved.

9.2. Hypotheses on Concentrated Entry and Exit[5]

One of the most distinctive patterns of Japanese FDI in the United States during the late 1980s is the concentration of entries in a particular time period. In this section, we ask specifically whether concentrated entries by Japanese investors into the U.S. manufacturing industries turn out subsequently to have higher mortality rates. Japanese firms that export to the U.S. market with high barriers to entry and, therefore, high price, earned higher profits than those exporting to the low entry-barrier market (Chapter 4). Facing such opportunity for high profitability, Japanese firms scrambled to the U.S. market through direct investments by matching rivals' moves. Although some Japanese MNEs were well qualified to jump over barriers to enter certain U.S. markets, others may have faced high hazards as a consequence of such bunching behavior.

The question of why a decision maker imitates others' actions has received much attention in the theoretical literature in economics and strategic management in recent years. As introduced in Chapter 6,

---

[3] See Yamawaki (1997) for some evidence on early exits of Japanese firms in Europe and United States.
[4] Statistically significant at the 5-percent level.
[5] This section heavily draws on Yamawaki and Asaba (2005).

Knickerbocker (1973) first provided an explanation for bunching behavior of oligopolistic firms in foreign direct investment and showed statistical evidence that supports the hypothesis that rivalry among multinational enterprises motivates them to cluster in particular host countries and time periods. Recent theoretical research on herd and imitation behavior, however, addresses this issue with much wider scopes and applications than the older literature on the MNE. Economic theories on herd behavior, or information cascade, (Banerjee, 1992; Bikchandani, Hirshleifer, and Welch, 1992; Brandenburger and Polack, 1996) argue that a decision maker, under uncertainty and with imperfect information, mimics others' actions even if it results in suboptimal outcomes. If information is costly to obtain and rivals' actions are easy to observe, imitation is likely to occur. Another line of theoretical literature on herd behavior argues that the existence of agency costs may discourage managers to take independent actions that deviate from industry norms (Scharfstein and Stein, 1990; Zwiebel, 1995).

The strategic management literature argues that firms adopt similar behaviors because of competitive interaction. When firms are constrained by their resource endowments and have comparable resource endowments with each other, firms imitate others' actions when facing the same business opportunity and environment (Collis, 1991; Peteraf, 1993; Teece, Pisano, and Shuen, 1997). In a formal theoretical model, Head, Mayer, and Ries (2002) show that risk-averse firms in an oligopoly that operate with the same technology and face the same demand curves and cost uncertainty abroad would engage in a competitive process with matching the moves of their rivals.

Competitive Processes and Concentrated Entry

A simple model of entry presented in Chapter 6 showed the following entry equation:

$$\text{EN}_{it} = f\left[\Pi^e, \text{EN}_{k,t-1}\right], \tag{9.1}$$

where EN_i denotes the decision by firm i to enter the market; EN_k is a vector of past entries by rivals to the same market; and Π^e is the expected industry profit, which is defined by $\Pi^e = g(BTE, I)$, where I is a vector of industry-specific factors commonly observed the by all the entrants.

Actual industry profits (Π) are assumed to be negatively related to the number of firms in the industry.[6] This means that profits decline as more firms enter the market in a particular time period ($\Sigma_t \Sigma_j EN_{jt}$), and the number of firms (N) increases in the industry,

$$\Pi_t = \Psi[N_t(\Sigma_t \Sigma_j EN_{jt}), I], \text{ where } t = -1, -2, \ldots, -\text{m}.$$

The firm decides to exit if losses exceed exit costs (C). That is, the firm exists from the market if $\Pi < -C$. The exit decision for firm i can be then given by

$$EX_{it} = \Omega[N_t(\Sigma_t \Sigma_j EN_{jt}), I] \qquad (9.2)$$

This means that hazard increases for the Japanese entrants as they cluster in the U.S. market in a particular period of time and entry is highly concentrated. In addition, entrants clustering in industries where barriers are high may face high failure rates because of the high risk associated with the industry characteristics that underlie the high barriers to entry (Lieberman, 1989). This factor becomes particularly acute when firms with comparable resource endowments compete with each other. Competition should be very intense because rent can be easily eroded without resource heterogeneity (Peteraf, 1993).

Information Cascade and Post-Entry Performance

Theoretical research on information cascade argues that it is optimal for a manager, having observed the actions of those ahead of him, to follow the behavior of the preceding firm without regard to his own information. His choice then will not result in efficient use of information and lead the firm to make the inefficient choice (Banerjee, 1992; Bikhchandani et al. 1992). This model then suggests that the arrival of a first Japanese firm to invest in the U.S. market conveys positive information about the market and attracts the followers in Japan. The followers decide to enter the U.S. market because the firm preceding them entered the market, and this choice may be inefficient and, hence, suboptimal.[7] The positive

---

[6] For example, see Cowling and Waterson (1976) for a formal model that shows the negative relationship between the number of firms and profitability.

[7] Kennedy (2002) tests this hypothesis for the U.S. TV broadcasting industry.

information conveyed by the first investor thus outweighs the negative payoff externality.[8] We, therefore, expect that entry into a market motivated by herd behavior based on information cascade is likely to result in business failure.

Is information cascade more often associated with acquisitions or new-plant investments? Previous research on acquisitions suggests that firms that follow an initiator are more likely to use acquisitions than building a new plant when they enter a foreign market while matching the initiator's action (Dubin, 1976).[9] Acquisitions are obviously a quick way to enter a market because investments in new facilities require relatively long gestation and shakedown periods. In addition, up-front investment costs required for a green-field investment project may be much higher than the cost of acquiring a local firm. More to the point of information cascade: firms that intend to build new facilities abroad may be required to engage in intensive feasibility studies and evaluate the results of pilot projects before making decisions on large irrevocable investments. They may even form joint ventures with local partners with an aim to learn about the preference of local consumers and the behavior and performance of suppliers and workforce, and to get access to distribution and logistic networks prior to their full-scale entry into the local market.[10] Therefore, firms that invest in green-field plants are likely to obtain specific data and information and use them to evaluate their investment projects before their entry. This observation suggests that the herd-like behavior based on information cascade is more often associated with acquisitions than green-field investments.

The competitive effect of bunching (the market-crowding hypothesis) and the inefficiency of herd behavior based on information cascade (the

---

[8] Caves (1991) proposes a general model that assumes the presence of organizational specific assets in a concentrated industry to explain the bunching of international horizontal mergers during the 1978–1988 period. If the first-moving firm acquires a bundle of specific assets that relate to the opportunity set by way of a merger, the rivals imitate the first-mover's action by mergers.

[9] Caves and Mehra (1986) found some evidence, albeit weak, of the behavior of the foreign MNE that uses acquisition to enter the U.S. market in order to speed up its response to the first-movers from the same home country and industry. See Hennart and Park (1993) for evidence on Japanese firms.

[10] An example is Toyota's joint venture with GM at the NUMMI plant.

herd hypothesis), both predict a positive relationship between concentrated entry and the likelihood of exit. Equation (9.2) shows that concentrated entry will reduce profits and hence increase the hazard of exit. Entry by green-field (new-plant) investments will increase the number of establishments in the entered industry and thus reduces the prospective profits given the downward-sloping demand curve. On the other hand, entry by acquisition does not change the number of firm in the industry and may not necessarily create excess capacity and lower prices (Gilbert and Newbery, 1992). However, acquisitions of existing firms by foreign firms often revitalize the acquired plants and result in improvement in efficiency (Lichtenberg and Siegel, 1987; Fukao, Ito, and Kwon, 2005). Therefore, $\Sigma_t \Sigma_j EN_{jt}$ in Eq. (9.2) should be decomposed into green-field entry (*GFEN*) and acquisition entry (*AQEN*). The market-crowding hypothesis predicts that concentrated entry increases the likelihood of exit for green-field investors but not necessarily for acquisition entry.

The model of herd behavior predicts that firms are more likely to engage in acquisitions than green-field investments under information cascade, and hence that they are likely to show higher likelihood of exit. To test this hypothesis, we include a variable that identifies whether the entry is by acquisition or is by green-field investment, EMODE, in Eq. (9.2). We expect that entry by acquisition would show a high propensity to exit than entry by green-field investment. Incorporating these effects of bunching on exit, our Eq. (9.2) is rewritten as:

$$EX_{it} = \Omega[\,N_t(\Sigma_t \Sigma_j GFEN_{jt}, \Sigma_t \Sigma_j AQEN_{jt}), EMODE_{it-k}, I\,], \qquad (9.3)$$

where *EMODE* denotes the choice of entry mode by firm (i).

Hypotheses
We develop the following hypotheses that are motivated by the discussion above:

(1) The likelihood of exit for Japanese firms is high when they cluster in the U.S. market in particular time period. It is thus expected to have a positive relationship with concentrated entry.

(2) The likelihood of exit is higher for Japanese firms that acquire local U.S. firms and facilities rather than those Japanese firms that invest in new plants.

(3) Japanese firms that imitate rivals' actions and follow their entries are more likely to use acquisition than green-field investment to enter the U.S. market.

The relationships between concentrated entry and postentry performance are examined by testing Hypotheses (1) and (2). The effect of herd behavior on the choice of entry mode will be examined by testing Hypothesis (3).

9.3. Statistical Analysis

Concentrated Entry and Postentry Performance Specifications and Variables

I estimated exit behavior by using a probit model of the probability that a subsidiary of the Japanese firm exits from the U.S. market.[11] Our dependent variable, *EXIT*, is a binary variable equal to one if the subsidiary exited between 1990 and 2000; zero if it survived through 2000. We eliminated those firms dropped from the subsidiary from the sample. Because our sample consists of subsidiaries established between 1985 and 1990, we divided the sample into two subsample periods in estimation to examine if the exit behavior of the 1985–1987 cohort is different from that of the 1988–1990 cohort. I expected a stronger effect of concentrated entry on exit behavior for the 1988–1990 entrants because they are likely to be the entrants that imitated and followed the earlier entries of the 1985–1987 cohort after the Japanese yen appreciated against the U.S. dollar in 1985.

The probability of exit is explained by a set of independent variables as suggested by Eq. (9.3) in the previous section.

---

[11] It is more appropriate to use a hazard-function model to examine the probability of exit. However, duration data required to run a hazard-function model were not easily accessible for Japanese subsidiaries in the U.S. market at the time of this study. The years of entry and exit may be observable, but subsidiary-specific and industry-specific data required for this study are only sporadically available.

Concentrated Entry

Our model suggests that concentrated entry in a particular time period reduces industry profitability and thus forces the firms in clusters to quit the industry in the subsequent period. To measure the market-crowding effects of *EN*, *GFEN*, and *AQEN* in Eq. (9.3), we constructed entry concentration indices, *ECI*, *GFECI*, and *AQECI* by modifying the method used by Knickerbocker (1973). This measure of concentrated entry is defined at the subsidiary level and measured by counting the number of U.S. subsidiaries established by domestic rivals within a specific time period preceding the Japanese firm's decision to establish a subsidiary in the U.S. market. As described in Chapter 6, this index measures more closely the extent of competitive pressure felt by a particular firm prior to its entry decision. Five-year entry concentration indexes are computed by dividing the total number of entries that took place during the 5 consecutive years prior to the firm's entry, by the total of all subsidiaries that were established during the 1980–1990 period.[12] *GFECI* is computed from entries by green-field investments only and does not include entries by acquisition, but *AQECI* includes only acquisitions. *ECI* includes both types of Japanese entries. Detailed accounts of the construction of these indexes are given in the Appendix of this chapter.

Entry Mode

We test the hypothesis that entry by acquisitions will increase hazard of exit by *EMODE*, which is a binary variable equal to one if the firm enters the U.S. market by acquiring a local firm; zero if the firm enters by establishing a green-field plant. Although this variable identifies whether the firm used acquisition or not when it entered the U.S. market, it does not necessarily show the firm acquired a local firm as a response to a rival's preceding acquisitions in the U.S. market. We examine this issue by estimating a model of the probability that the firm adopts acquisition as an entry mode in response to its rivals' actions in the next section.

---

[12] Knickerbocker (1973) computes an entry concentration index for a given industry as a total of the all the markets entered. In this study, only the U.S. market is considered in the analysis.

Control Variables

The industry-specific factors are controlled by the following three variables: (1) the R&D/sales ratio, *RDSL*; (2) the capital/labor ratio, *KL*; and (3) the growth rate of industry shipment in the post-entry period, *GROWP*. The extent to which the technological environment influences the ability of new firms to survive was shown in previous research of business turnover. The industry R&D/sales ratio was found to be associated with a higher rate of hazard in a large U.S. sample (Audretsch, 1995). The capital/labor ratio is included to control for the effect of the capital committed to an activity on exit. The heavier the proportion of fixed investment to durable assets, the less likely is exit (Caves and Porter, 1976). Industry growth is computed using shipments of the entered industry for the postentry period of 1987–1996 and is expected to control for the current and future state of industry growth.

The subsidiary-specific variables are controlled by the following two variables: (1) subsidiary's employment size relative to the size of entered industry, *SCALE*; and (2) parent's prior experience in foreign direct investment, *EXPRNC*. The theoretical study by Jovanovic (1982) predicts that the probability of exit is positively correlated with firm's age and size because of the underlying difference in efficiency across firms of different ages and sizes.

Statistical Results

Table 9.2 presents the estimation results of a probit model of the probability of exit for the full sample of the Japanese firms that entered into the U.S. market between 1985 and 1990, and for the subsamples of the 1985–1987 entrants and the 1988–1990 entrants. We test the hypothesis that concentrated entry increases the likelihood of exit by examining the coefficient for *ECI*. The coefficient for *ECI* is statistically insignificant in any equations in Table 9.2.

This result remains unchanged when we replace *ECI* with *GFECI* and *AQECI* in Table 9.3. Concentrated entry by establishing new plants did not affect the likelihood of exit of Japanese entrants by changing the number of firms and hence profitability in the industry. The extent of bunching in acquisitions also did not affect the likelihood of Japanese

Table 9.2. *Probit estimates of determinants of exit with ECI*
(dependent variable: EXIT)

	1985–1990 Entrants (1)	1985–1987 Entrants (2)	1988–1990 Entrants (3)
Constant	−1.001 (2.294)**	−1.466 (2.255)**	−0.178 (0.211)
ECI	−0.184 (0.412)	0.268 (0.255)	0.222 (0.337)
EMODE	0.386 (1.930)*	0.360 (1.055)	0.502 (1.870)*
RDSL	0.177 (0.121)	−2.349 (0.838)	3.004 (1.435)
KL	−0.014 (0.723)	0.022 (0.848)	−0.122 (2.095)**
GROWP	0.448 (1.822)*	0.894 (2.028)**	0.238 (0.772)
SCALE	−0.029 (0.512)	0.108 (0.955)	−0.151 (0.659)
EXPRNC	−0.062 (0.584)	−0.194 (1.120)	−0.028 (0.190)
Log likelihood	−114.23	−45.19	−61.60
Likelihood ratio index	0.040	0.082	0.107
Number of observations	249	96	153

Notes: The number of positive observations is forty-six in Model (1), twenty in Model (2), and twenty-six in Model (3). Numbers reported in parentheses are *t*-statistics. The levels of significance for a two-tailed test are: * = 10%, ** = 5%, and *** = 1%.

exit in the United States. These findings thus reject the market-crowding hypothesis of the effect of bunching on exit hazard.

However, the coefficients for *EMODE* have expected positive signs for the full sample and the subsample of the 1988–1990 entrants. This finding suggests that acquisitions by the 1988–1990 entrants turn out to have higher mortality rates than acquisitions by the earlier 1985–1987 entrants. Although this result is consistent with the herd hypothesis and the possibility of inefficient choice made on acquisition by the imitators, it dose not provide direct evidence that supports the hypothesis that the likelihood of exit is higher for acquisitions under information-cascading herd behavior. Ravenscraft and Scherer (1987) and Kaplan and Weisbach (1992), suggest that acquisitions, in general, are likely to be divested within short periods of time after they are completed. It is therefore important to examine whether Japanese firms that exited had acquired local firms in response to rivals' preceding acquisitions.

Table 9.3. *Probit estimates of determinants of exit with GFECI and AQECI (dependent variable: EXIT)*

	1985–1990 Entrants (1)	1985–1987 Entrants (2)	1988–1990 Entrants (3)
Constant	−0.911 (2.122)**	−1.171 (1.795)*	−0.263 (0.314)
GFECI	−0.392 (0.999)	−1.379 (1.449)	0.449 (0.814)
AQECI	0.030 (0.078)	0.567 (0.564)	−0.236 (0.464)
EMODE	0.402 (1.996)**	0.325 (0.914)	0.493 (1.812)*
RDSL	0.128 (0.087)	−2.266 (0.735)	3.223 (1.525)
KL	−0.014 (0.755)	0.016 (0.575)	−0.120 (2.109)**
GROWP	0.441 (1.764)*	1.044 (2.262)**	0.312 (0.955)
SCALE	−0.032 (0.525)	0.097 (0.797)	−0.159 (0.706)
EXPRNC	−0.062 (0.586)	−0.200 (1.127)	−0.045 (0.296)
Log likelihood	−113.79	−43.83	−61.28
Likelihood ratio index	0.043	0.110	0.111
Number of observations	249	96	153

Notes: The number of positive observations is forty-six in Model (1), twenty in Model (2), and twenty-six in Model (3). Numbers reported in parentheses are t-test statistics. The levels of significance for a two-tailed test are: * = 10%, ** = 5%, and *** = 1%.

Herd Behavior and Entry Mode

In this section, we test the hypothesis that Japanese firms imitate rivals' decisions to acquire U.S. firms when large number of rivals have already entered the U.S. market in a particular period of time. The model of entry mode presented in Chapter 6 will be used to test this hypothesis.

Specifications and Variables

The dependent variable, *EMODE*, equals one if the entry occurred by acquisition, and equals zero if the entry occurred through green-field investment. The main variables to test the maintained hypothesis are the concentration indices introduced in the previous section (*GFECI* and *AQECI*). They are defined at the subsidiary level and measured by counting the number of rivals' entries in the United States within a specific time period preceding the Japanese firm's decision to establish a subsidiary in the U.S. market. Under the herd hypothesis, we expect these two variables have positive relationships with the probability of choosing acquisition as a mode of entry. All other subsidiary- and industry-specific variables included in the model specification are the same as those variables used in Chapter 6.

Although *AQECI* and *GFECI* measure firm-specific motives to use acquisition, it is necessary to control for common market opportunities faced by all of the Japanese firms at the time of entry. The result in Chapter 6 clearly suggests the importance of controlling for time-dependent factors present in entry data. To control for the common response to environmental change by Japanese firms, we introduce a variable that measures the exchange rate expressed in units of the Japanese yen per unit of the U.S. dollar, *YENUSD*, at the time of entry in the model specification. This variable is expected to distinguish the herd behavior based on the information cascade from the common response to changes in the exchange rate.

Statistical Results

The estimation result of a logit model explaining the probability that entry occurs through acquisition against green-field investment is presented by Model (1) in Table 9.4. The coefficient for *AQECI* is statistically insignificant, but the coefficient for *GFECI* is significant and has a positive sign. This result suggests that the Japanese firm is more likely to choose acquisition when a large number of rivals have already entered the U.S. market by establishing new subsidiaries in the years prior to its entry. This positive relationship is observed even after we control for time-related effects by *YENUSD*. To the extent that *YENUSD* controls for common response to some external shift, the positive coefficient for *GFECI* suggests the presence of herd-like behavior.

This result is important in that it shows that Japanese firms do not choose green-field investments in response to rivals' earlier entries. Their decisions to invest in new plants are made based on their technological capabilities, previous international experience, and business strategy to specialize in their primary products. However, Japanese firms are likely to use acquisition when: (1) they see rivals enter the U.S. market by establishing new plants; (2) their home industries are at technological disadvantage; (3) parents' prior foreign experience is limited; and (4) they

Table 9.4. *Logit estimates of determinants of entry mode and diversified entry*

	Dependent variable	
	EMODE (1)	DIV (2)
Constant	−0.248 (0.224)	−1.071 (1.268)
EXPRNC	−0.366 (2.371)**	0.557 (2.053)**
RTA	−0.747 (1.913)*	−0.336 (0.837)
GROW	−0.800 (1.207)	0.793 (1.577)
DIV	1.055 (3.263)***	
RDSL		−6.994 (1.086)
KL		−0.081 (2.641)**
SCALE[a]	0.241 (0.647)	
PSIZE		0.146 (0.801)
GFECI	1.238 (2.301)**	0.083 (0.137)
AQECI	0.028 (0.056)	1.383 (2.463)**
YENUSD	0.002 (0.318)	−0.013 (1.506)
Loglikelihood	175.625	148.093
Likelihood ratio index	0.091	0.114

Notes: (1) *SCALE* is an instrumental variable estimator. (2) The number of observations is 316, and the number of positive observations is ninety-five in Model (1) and seventy in Model (2). Numbers reported in parentheses are t-test statistics. The levels of significance for a two-tailed test are: * = 10%, ** = 5%, and *** = 1%

diversify beyond their primary industries in the U.S. markets. This finding provides some evidence that supports the hypothesis that Japanese firms that imitate rivals' actions are likely the ones who do not own competitive advantages and who are more likely to use acquisitions than green-field investments. These findings imply that Japanese firms that use acquisitions as a mode of entry into the U.S. market indeed face a higher degree of hazard in the postentry period. The results on exit behavior found in the previous section confirms this hypothesis.

Model (2) in Table 9.4 is the estimated result of a logit model of diversified entry to examine if Japanese diversification in the United States is associated with rivals' prior entries. The coefficient for *AQECI* is statistically significant and has a positive sign, suggesting that the decision to diversify is affected by rivals' prior acquisitions in the United States. However, the coefficient for *GFECI* is statistically insignificant. This result reinforces our earlier finding on the herd behavior in acquisition because

Table 9.5. *Probit estimates of determinants of exit with EMODE∗DIV*
(dependent variable: EXIT)

	1985–1990 Entrants (1)	1985–1987 Entrants (2)	1988–1990 Entrants (3)
Constant	−0.678 (1.522)	−0.990 (1.461)	0.274 (0.297)
GFECI	−0.438 (1.104)	−1.461 (1.538)	0.412 (0.724)
AQECI	−0.001 (0.002)	0.793 (0.776)	−0.398 (0.754)
EMODE	0.068 (0.280)	−0.065 (0.138)	0.104 (0.317)
EMODE∗DIV	1.009 (2.817)***	0.963 (1.423)	1.105 (2.328)***
RDSL	0.047 (0.032)	−2.186 (0.682)	3.046 (1.445)
KL	−0.014 (0.730)	0.013 (0.480)	−0.137 (2.187)**
GROWP	0.326 (1.244)	0.927 (1.919)*	0.187 (0.553)
SCALE	−0.039 (0.700)	0.085 (0.674)	−0.114 (0.729)
EXPRNC	−0.126 (1.145)	−0.243 (1.335)	−0.149 (0.916)
log likelihood	−109.76	−41.78	−58.52
Likelihood ratio index	0.076	0.132	0.148
Number of observations	249	96	153

Notes: The number of positive observations is forth-six in Model (1), twenty in Model (2), and twenty-six in Model (3). Numbers reported in parentheses are *t*-test statistics. The levels of significance for a two-tailed test are: * = 10%, ** = 5%, and *** = 1%.

it shows that Japanese acquisitions are indirectly motivated by rivals' acquisitions in the United States prior to their entries. Rivals' actions gave positive information on the U.S. corporate market and motivated Japanese imitators to diversify into the U.S. industries by acquiring local firms.

Finally, Table 9.5 presents the estimation results of the likelihood of exit that include an interaction variable *EMODE∗DIV* and *EMODE*. The coefficients for the interaction variable are statistically significant and have positive signs for the full-sample and for the subsample of the 1988–1990 entrants, suggesting that diversified acquisitions have a higher degree of hazard than nondiversified acquisitions, especially for the late entrants. Their coefficients are much larger than those estimated for *EMODE*, which become insignificant when *EMODE∗DIV* is added to the specification. This finding reinforces our earlier finding of high mortality rates associated with herd-like behavior.

9.4. Conclusions

This chapter examined herd-like behavior exhibited by multinational enterprises in foreign direct investments and its effect on postentry performance. Using data on Japanese firms that entered the U.S. manufacturing industries in the late 1980s, the empirical analysis found that Japanese firms choose acquisitions to enter the U.S. market by matching their domestic rivals' U.S. entries prior to their entries. Their postentry performance measured by exit is inferior to the performance of those firms that entered by establishing green-field plants. The likelihood of exit is statistically higher for the Japanese firm that used acquisition to enter the U.S. market particularly in the 1988–1990 period.

The analysis of the determinants of entry by acquisition further shows that diversifying firms are also motivated to use acquisitions in response to rivals' entries preceding their entries, after controlling for common response to some external shift. However, Japanese firms are less likely to invest in new plants in response to rivals' actions. This result, hence, suggests the herd-like behavior by Japanese firms in acquisitions, which is consistent with bunching under information cascade. Overall, the statistical results provide evidence that is more consistent with the herd hypothesis than the market-crowding hypothesis of postentry performance at least for the case of Japanese entrants in the United States in the late 1980s.

10

Interpreting the Empirical Findings

10.1. Major Findings

The first aim of this study is to explore how firms compete in international markets and to examine empirically the ways in which interfirm rivalry affects international trade and investment. The second aim is to explore the evolution of the export and foreign direct investment behavior of Japanese firms in the period between the late 1950s and the early 2000s. This study provides the first systematic account of the changing pattern of Japanese competitiveness in the international market. The central results of the statistical analysis pertain to the test of the hypothesis, which contends that Japanese firms' export and direct investment behaviors are influenced by market structure. The results, in many ways, are consistent with that hypothesis. Because the specific results are summarized in the concluding section of each chapter, only the major findings of this study are summarized here:

1. The export pricing behavior of Japanese industries differs by industry. Some of Japan's major export industries behaved as oligopolies in the international market during the 1970s and the 1980s. These industries are steel (plates and sheets), construction machinery, metal working machinery, radio and TV, photographic cameras, telecommunications equipment, tape and video recorders, audio equipment, and photographic films (Chapter 2).

2. Japanese industries were often accused of dumping. This study finds at least two types of industries alleged to engage in this practice: (a) the industries where export price is sensitive to

industry excess capacity and procyclical to domestic demand fluctuations (steel products and chemicals); and (b) the industries
where export price is insensitive to domestic demand conditions
(tape and video recorders, radio and TV receivers, semiconductors, and passenger cars). Iron and steel are most representative
of type (a), and their price behavior in the late 1950s through
the early 1970s is consistent with the prediction from the theoretical model of international price discrimination. On the other
hand, in some of the type (b) industries, which include Japan's
major export industries during the period studied (integrated circuits, semiconductors, tape and video recorders, and photographic
cameras), export price declined over time along the learning curve
(Chapter 3).

3. Japanese firms exporting to the U.S. markets where barriers to
entry were high and therefore seller concentration was high, earned
relatively high profits on exports in the late 1960s and in the early
1970s (Chapter 4).

4. Japanese exporters that invested in intangible and tangible assets,
such as R&D, distribution, marketing, and service, and production
capacity, and improved operation efficiency relative to their U.S.
rivals, were able to jump high entry barriers and attain positive
profits in the U.S. market (Chapter 5).

5. As competitive pressure from low-cost countries intensified,
Japanese firms shifted their product segments from the middle segment to the high-end segment. In the U.S. passenger car market,
the Japanese firms entered into the high-barrier luxury car segment in the late 1980s. The incumbent European and U.S. firms
did not respond to the new entry initially. The incumbent firms
started responding to the competitive pressure eventually, however,
by changing local prices and mark-ups (Chapter 8).

6. Japanese firms started investing in the United States and Europe
intensively after 1985. One of the most distinctive characteristics
of the later pattern of Japanese foreign investment compared to the
earlier pattern of Japanese foreign direct investment was the frequent use of acquisition. Japanese firms that invested in green-field
plants made their decisions based on technological capabilities,

previous international experience, and business strategy to specialize in their primary products However, Japanese firms used acquisition to enter the U.S. market when: (1) they saw their rivals enter into the market by establishing new plants; (2) their home industries were at technological disadvantage; (3) their parent company's prior foreign experience was limited; and (4) they diversified beyond their primary industries (Chapters 6 and 9).

7. Entry of Japanese firms into the U.S. and European markets was in part, motivated by early U.S. and European entries into the Japanese markets. However, the U.S. and European firms did not respond to Japanese entries in their home markets. The U.S. and European firms that jumped over entry barriers in Japan were those firms that possessed proprietary assets and benefited from their parent company's global operations. The presence of U.S. and European firms, however, remained very low, accounting for only a tiny fraction in the total number of firms in Japanese manufacturing (Chapter 7).

8. Japanese firms that acquired local firms in the U.S. market in response to their domestic rivals' actions in the late 1980s appeared to show a postentry performance that deviates statistically from the performance of firms that established new plants. The likelihood of exit is higher for Japanese acquirers than Japanese green-field investors (Chapter 9).

10.2. International Competition and Japan's Corporate and Economic Organization

This book does not intend to examine the source of Japanese firms' competitive advantages and disadvantages in international markets or to describe various aspects of Japanese firms and their management practices. The empirical results presented in Section 10.1, however, provide us with several strands to weave a pattern of Japanese competition in the world market over the period of the late 1950s through the 1990s. The underlying presumption is that the pattern of competition is linked to industrial market structure, the source of competitive advantage of firms, the source of comparative advantage of home and foreign countries, and to government policy. This section attempts to make an inference to establish such links.

Japanese Exports in the 1950s and the 1960s

Export Performance and Strategic Industry

After World War II, one of the most crucial economic questions Japan had to address was how to reconstruct her economy to achieve sustained growth given the domestic and international context. Japan is a typically resource-poor country and must trade to live. Given the overriding importance attached to economic growth, Japan needed to develop export industries. To this end, the Japanese government needed an industrial policy to select potential export industries, to allocate investment capital strategically to them, and to make strategic industries competitive (Komiya, Okuno, and Suzumura, 1988; Kosai, 1988; Tsuruta, 1988). Among those strategic industries were iron and steel, shipbuilding, machinery, heavy electrical equipment, chemicals, automobiles, petrochemicals, computers, and semiconductors.

The influence of Japan's industrial policy on economic growth has been debated in the existing literature.[1] One school argues that the government's industrial policy nurtured industrial development and made the difference in the rate of investment in certain economically strategic industries (Johnson, 1982; Zysman and Tyson, 1983). Another school gives the government's industrial policy much less weight as the driving force of rapid growth (Patrick and Rosovsky, 1976; Saxonhouse, 1979; Komiya, Okuno, and Suzumura, 1988). The latter school emphasizes instead the importance of private investment in human resources, technology, and physical investment in economic growth. It is probably true that the government provided a favorable environment and infrastructure, and some targeted industries such as steel and shipbuilding grew rapidly and succeeded in export markets. It is not clear, however, that the international success of Japan's major export industries in the 1960s through the 1980s was dependent on the government's specific industrial policy measures.

---

[1] For a survey, see Lincoln (1984) and Eads and Yamamura (1987).

Although some of the targeted industries were developed into success-ful exporting industries, many of Japan's industries that emerged in the 1960s, and achieved remarkable success in exporting, were not necessar-ily among the list of strategic industries. For example, sewing machines, cameras, bicycles, motorcycles, pianos, zippers, transistor radios, color TV, tape recorders, magnetic recording tape, audio equipment, fishing gear, watches and clocks, calculators, electric wire, machine tools, numer-ically controlled machine tools, textile machinery, agricultural machin-ery, insulators, communication equipment, ceramics, and robots flour-ished as Japan's exporting industries during the 1960s and through the 1980s. The majority of the firms in these industries started from scratch after World War II and developed their own competitive advantage with-out any particular benefits from industrial protection and promotion policies (Komiya, 1988).[2]

Price Discrimination and Cyclical Dumping

As described in Chapter 1, Japanese exports in iron and steel, machinery, electrical machinery, and shipbuilding grew remarkably beginning in the 1950s and continuing through the 1960s. Pricing behavior in the steel industry, a representative of its class of Japanese industries in the late-1950s through the early 1970s, was examined in Chapter 3. The most striking result was that when domestic seller concentration was high, Japan's steelmakers raised the domestic price of steel while they reduced the export price. This is not a direct evidence of price discrimination, but the presumption is that Japanese steelmakers were able to set prices differently between the home market and the export market. For a seller to practice price discrimination, three prerequisites must be satisfied. First, the seller must have some monopoly power to control price. Second, the seller must be able to segregate the home market from the export market

---

[2]   In a regression analysis explaining the cross-industry variance of U.S.-Japan trade balance in the late 1970s, Audretsch and Yamawaki (1988) showed that the Japanese industries, which had 10 percent or more of total depreciation covered by the special depreciation allowance in Japan between 1962 and 1973 also had a stronger trade balance. Such a statistical relationship does not necessarily mean that MITI's policies were actually responsible for the strong trade performance. It is conceivable that the MITI, in fact, had a policy of targeting industries that were strong and likely to succeed in the world market. See Saxonhouse (1983).

based on different price elasticities of demand – higher elasticity and less monopoly power in the export market than in the home market. Third, the opportunity for buyers in the home country to engage in arbitrage – buy the good abroad and import cheaply – is restricted.[3] These conditions are most likely to be satisfied when the domestic market is protected by transport costs, tariffs, and nontariff barriers.

During the 1950s and the 1960s, one of the pillars of Japan's trade policy was to protect and nurture those domestic industries that had good prospects for development. The government granted such strategic industries various subsidies, preferential tax treatment for depreciation, and preferential loans from government-affiliated banks, and protected them from foreign competition by import quotas and tariffs (Komiya and Itoh, 1988; Komiya, Okuno, and Suzumura, 1988). As a result of import restrictions, import penetration in Japanese industries was relatively low and its competition-enhancing effect was not important in most industries through the late 1960s (Uekusa, 1982). With imports restricted by the government, Japanese firms in highly concentrated industries were able to take advantage of the conditions that facilitated price discrimination in the 1950s and the 1960s.

Another finding from Chapter 3 was that when demand is unexpectedly weak and creates excess capacity, Japan's steelmakers lowered the export price while they kept domestic price unchanged. Although the export price generally falls when demand declines, the cyclical pattern and magnitude of price reductions may be exacerbated in part by excessive investment in capacity by Japanese firms and through various interventions by the government. In order to avoid excess capacity and price competition, the Ministry of International Trade and Industry (MITI), from the 1950s through the 1960s, intervened in the decision-making process of firms in price setting, quantity setting, and investment. The administrative guidance of the MITI, which aimed to coordinate investment in capacity through collusion among firms, was often unsuccessful and ended up as a mere exchange of information and reduction in uncertainty. As a result, more investment occurred and excess capacity increased through the 1960s (Imai, 1976; Miwa, 1988; Yamawaki, 1988).

---

[3] For classic cases of price discrimination, see Scherer and Ross (1990).

Another form of intervention implemented by the MITI in the 1950s and the 1960s was the introduction of a list-price system to coordinate prices among firms, particularly in the steel industry. Again, this policy did not result in the outcome the MITI expected. However, there was insufficient agreement among firms participating in the cartel to implement sanctions or penalties for firms that violated the agreement, and in a cartel in which sanctions are weak and threats to punish are not credible, there is a strong probability of competitive price discounts by participating firms. The reason that competitive price cutting arose from the late 1950s through the 1960s in the Japanese steel industry was that, as a result of competition in investment, there was substantial excess capacity in economic slowdowns. In industries such as steel, where fixed costs are a high proportion of total costs, a decrease in capacity utilization brings about a steep increase in unit fixed costs, which in turn induces price discounting.[4]

Japanese Exports in the 1970s and 1980s

Japanese Corporate Organization

The debate on the role of industrial policy in Japan's rapid growth raises a question of what the most significant impetus of industrial development was. Unfortunately, the empirical results presented in Chapters 3 and 4 are not particularly intuitive to provide insight on this question. They identify the key strategic areas in which Japanese firms had competitive advantages in comparison to their foreign rivals in the same industry, but the variables used do not reveal the specific source of such advantages. The existing literature in economics and management on Japanese firms and their management practices is useful to elaborate on this point. Aoki (1986, 1990) presents the most unified view of Japanese firms and attributes Japan's industrial performance to the ability of firms in certain industries to coordinate their operating activities flexibly and quickly in response to changing market conditions and to changes in the business environment. He suggests that horizontal coordination among operating units

---

[4]   See Green and Porter (1984) and Staiger and Wolak (1992) for a theoretical discussion on price wars and cyclical demand.

based on knowledge sharing, rather than skill specialization, is an important organizational characteristic of Japanese firms. The Japanese organization relies less on the one-way flow of instructions typically used in the vertical hierarchical structure of organization in Western companies. In the hierarchical structure planning and operation are hierarchically separated, and economies of specialization are emphasized. Prior planning is fixed for certain period of time and implemented by operating units at lower levels. Any unexpected event during the implementation period may be coped with by a priori devices such as buffer inventories, and new knowledge that emerges may be used only for the next round of planning (Aoki, 1990). To the contrary, the Japanese horizontal structure uses the sharing of onsite information to coordinate operating units. As new information becomes available to operating units during the implementation period, prior plans may be monitored in this structure. If market and technological environments are stable, or extremely volatile and uncertain, the hierarchical structure, he argues, may be superior. If environments are continually changing but not too drastically, however, the horizontal structure is superior. In this case, the information value created by learning and horizontal coordination at the operation level may more than compensate for the loss of efficiency due to sacrificing economies of specialization. The comparative advantage of these two organizational modes depends on the learning ability of personnel, the ease of communication within the organization, and economies of specialization (Aoki, 1986, 1990; Itoh, 1987).[5]

This theory is consistent with the development of Japanese firms in international markets. Beginning the 1960s and through the 1980s, the market and technological environments under which Japanese firms operated in industries such as machinery, electrical equipment, and automobiles were changing quickly but continuously. In such an environment, many Japanese firms developed their advantages through their organizational structure and performed well in the export markets. The Japanese corporate organization thus is effective in sophisticated assembly-type industries where consumers demand a wide variety of products; where

---

[5] For a comparative study based on questionnaire survey about American and Japanese management, see Kagono, Nonaka, Sakakibara, and Okumura (1985).

demands shift one variety to another quickly; where buyers demand swift delivery of ordered product; and where innovation is measured in terms of continuously improved quality (Abegglen and Stalk, 1985). However, their international competitiveness is relatively weak in certain industries such as multimedia, software, and microprocessors where market and technological environments are often extremely uncertain and volatile (Porter, Takeuchi, and Sakakibara, 2000).

Lean Production

The discussion above shows that the Japanese corporate structure is a source of Japan's competitive advantage in international markets in industries such as automobile manufacturing and electronic equipment. Their organizational capability to launch a variety of new products in response to quickly changing market demands to deliver their products swiftly without carrying large inventories is considered to be the key success factor in export markets. Although Aoki's model (1990) illustrates the organizational efficiency of this type of corporate structure and describes how information flows within the firm and how operating units are coordinated, the lean-production-system model played a central role in enhancement of operation efficiency in many Japanese corporations (Abegglen and Stalk, 1985; Womack, Jones, and Roos, 1990; Clark and Fujimoto, 1991; Fujimoto, 1999).

The origins of the now well-known lean production system go back to the late 1930s, but it was in the 1950s and the 1960s that Toyota made substantial progress in implementing the Toyota Production System. This system allowed Toyota to manufacture automobiles of many different kinds in small volumes with the same process. The core of this production system is the just-in-time (JIT) system, or the *kanban* system, in which the plant layout is designed to ensure a balanced work flow between the upstream work station and downstream work station with a minimum of work-in progress inventory. Thus, under this system production system, a factory produces what is needed when needed and no more (Monden, 1983).

Toyota has shown that JIT works at its best when several key components of the lean production system are in place in the corporate organization system. These components are total quality control (TQC), continuous improvement, close supplier relationship, and industrial engineering. In many Japanese corporations, workers assume responsibility for the quality of their own work and practice building quality into the process and not identifying quality by inspection. Workers are trained to improve quality by participating in problem-solving processes. As Aoki's model of Japanese organization suggests, at the core of this model are the learning capability of workers and continuous improvement through learning. In addition, coordinating the process of engineering and fabricating large number of parts in the JIT system was a key to the success of this system. All of the necessary parts must be of high quality and must come together at the right time. To this end, high quality parts and have Toyota established a network of suppliers and organized them into functional tiers. Their first-tier suppliers were responsible for working as an integral part of the product development team in developing a new product. Each first-tier supplier then formed a second tier of suppliers who were all manufacturing specialists and were assigned the job of manufacturing individual parts. Toyota frequently exchanged information, shared personnel, and had interlocking equity relationships with first-tier suppliers to provide incentives for improvements in efficiency and achieve a long-term relationship (Womack, Jones, and Roos, 1990; Fujimoto, 1999).[6]

Toyota continuously improved this system over the years, which many Japanese firms adapted by the late 1970s. According to Abbeglen and Stalk (1985), they doubled the productivity of their factory labor forces and almost doubled the productivity of the assets without requiring net capital investment.[7] With the lean production system, a firm can make a greater variety of products at lower cost and make the same variety of products at lower cost and higher quality. Audretsch and Yamawaki (1988) provide evidence to support this observation by examining the U.S.–Japan bilateral trade pattern for a cross section of 213 manufacturing industries in the late 1970s. Although the United States generally had the comparative advantage for industries that are R&D intensive, Japanese firms were able to offset this through their own efforts on improving the

[6] For a specific evidence of supplier networks as a source of competitive advantage in the automobile industry, see Dyer (1996). On the issue of relation-specific skills in subcontracting, see Asanuma (1989).
[7] See Abbeglen and Stalk (1985), Chapter 5. See also Lieberman (1989b).

quality of existing products and on cost-reducing process innovation for existing products.

Labor Practices

Although the empirical results presented in this book do not reveal any direct links to the human-resource policies implemented by Japanese corporations, human resources are the key to understanding how Japanese firms are organized and behave. The Japanese labor market is known for three features: (1) life-time employment, (2) seniority-based wages, and (3) enterprise unions. Whether or not these features are unique in Japan, has been discussed extensively in the existing literature (Koike, 1984, 1988; Shimada, 1983; Odagiri, 1992). More relevant to this book, however, is the question of how Japanese firms have developed and continuously improved their employees' skills. Lifetime employment and seniority-based wages were commonly used among large Japanese corporations in the 1950s through the 1980s. Although they are counterintuitive for Western corporations, incentive schemes for efficiency are in fact sustained in Japanese corporations through promotion tournaments that are determined by intensive long-term evaluations of employees. Koike (1984, 1988) suggests that most skills are learned by doing and that some of these skills are firm-specific or plant-specific. Firms have incentives to maintain life-time employment because it takes many years to educate workers and develop firm-specific skills in human reasources that are not easily and quickly replaced by a new hiring. Similarly, workers have incentives to stay in one company for many years because their firm-specific skills are not easily transferable to other firms. Thus, life-time employment with internal competition for promotion is conducive to efficient skill formation.

Another important feature of labor practices in Japan is that workers in large Japanese corporations have broader careers than their counterparts in U.S. companies. After examining chemical, steel, and machinery plants in Japan and the United States, Koike (1988) found that mobility of workers within a workshop and across workshops is more common in Japanese plants. As the worker moves from one job to another within the corporation by means of rotation, he experiences several jobs, acquires skills required to perform these jobs, and widens the breadth of his skills.

A prerequisite for implementing such job rotation is lifetime employment and long-term relationship between worker and management. Again, the underlying presumption is that it is less advantageous for the worker equipped with firm-specific skills to move to other companies for short-run gains. In Japanese corporations in the 1960s through the 1980s, this practice played an important role and contributed to enhancing efficiency. When a new technology is introduced, a new process is brought into production, and both are improved over time. The job-rotation system facilitated the exchange of information and communication between different operating units and departments within the firm and contributed to continuous improvements and learning (Imai and Komiya, 1989; Odagiri, 1992)

Japanese firms' emphasis on a set of human-resource policies, which led to efficient skill formation, together with the lean production system, were certainly the key drivers for their international competitive advantage. The essence of their advantage was continuous improvements through learning in the long-run. Continuing improvements and accumulation of experience by workers through long-term employment resulted in cost reductions through learning. The evidence that supports the effect of learning on export price was shown in Chapter 3 of this book.[8]

Research and Development

One of the findings in Chapter 2 was that the Japanese firms in industries such as steel (plates and sheets), construction machinery, metalworking machinery, radio and TV, cameras, telecommunication equipment, tape and video recorders, audio equipment, and photographic films, behaved as oligopolists in the international markets in the 1970s and early 1980s. One explanation of such behavior is their worldwide advantages in innovation and quality. Japanese producers in these industries were insulated from close substitutes and took advantage of the world demand conditions. Another finding from Chapter 5 of this book was that Japanese industries spending more in R&D in comparison to their U.S.

---

[8] For a discussion to link the internal labor system and the strategic goal of Japanese corporations, see Odagiri (1992).

counterparts are likely to have larger market shares in the U.S. market. These findings are intuitive as such, but some further discussion on the qualitative aspect of Japan's R&D capabilities will bring more insight to them.

Japanese firms' penchant to spend more on R&D in order to achieve a long-term growth has been described by many researchers (Rosenbloom and Abernathy, 1982; Abegglen and Stalk, 1985). During the 1950s, technology importation through various channels played a significant role in Japan's postwar technological progress. Rapidly growing markets for manufactured goods created a strong incentive and a high rate of return on investment for imported technology. Intensive competition in product markets pushed Japanese firms in many industries to invest in R&D in order not to be left behind (Odagri and Goto, 1996). Although technology importation was carried out mainly by the private sector, the government initially controlled technology importation based on the Foreign Exchange and Foreign Trade Control Law and the Foreign Investment Law, and the government allocated foreign currency to import technology. The importation of technology was subject to government approval especially before the major liberalization step was taken in 1968. By 1980, almost all technology importation became liberalized (Goto and Wakasugi, 1988).[9]

Although imported technology was a catalyst to raise the technology level of Japanese firms and industries in the 1950s and the early 1960s, technology importation alone cannot account for Japan's success in catching up to advanced industrial countries. High rates of return to investment in R&D,[10] intensive rivalry in product markets, entry of new firms into the existing industries and new industries,[11] the emergence of

---

[9] For a further discussion on the role of industrial policy and technology policy in industrial development, see Komiya, Okuno, and Suzumura (1988). From the late 1950s through the early 1990s, the government implemented several policies to encourage R&D activities by Japanese firms. One such policy was the development of subsidy programs through collaborative research among Japanese firms in certain industries. For a detailed account of such research associations, see Goto (1996). For empirical analysis of the effect of R&D consortia on R&D productivity, see Branstetter and Sakakibara (1998) and Sakakibara (1997).

[10] Goto and Suzuki (1989).

[11] According to Kawai and Urata (2002), of the 120 large firms that existed in the electrical industry in 1979, 54 firms were small- and medium-sized firms in 1955.

entrepreneurs,[12] and technological capabilities of Japanese firms to work with and improve imported technology were all the key factors underlying the successful development of Japan's R&D base (Odagiri, 1983; Odagiri and Goto, 1996).[13]

Between 1965 and 1980, Japanese R&D expenditures grew faster than those of any other major industrialized countries. In the early 1990s, Japan's R&D expenditures as a percentage of GNP were the highest among them. Contrary to this trend, Japanese expenditures on importing foreign technology grew less rapidly than those on total R&D expenditure, resulting in a gradual decline in the share of imported technology in total R&D expenditure in the 1970s through the early 1980s. The increasing importance of domestic R&D underlies its focus on applied research, engineering, and commercialization of new technology rather than on basic science (Tayler and Yamamura, 1990). Japanese firms' success in process innovation, quality improvement, and quick introduction of new products during the 1970s and the 1980s are all accounted for by their focus on these areas in R&D. It is, however, important to note that there were at least two factors that created an effective environment conducive to such performance: (1) the Japanese corporate structure that facilitates horizontal flow of communication and horizontal coordination among different departments within the firm (Aoki, 1990; Odagiri, 1992); (2) and the internal labor system in which the R&D personnel is rotated from the R&D department to other operating units and departments within the firm. These systems proved to be very effective in the process of new product development and engineering (Wakasugi, 1989; Odagiri, 1992; Odagiri and Goto, 1996).

Small Enterprises

The presence of a large number of small enterprises in Japanese manufacturing is well-documented. Although the idea that this phenomenon is unique in Japan has been examined in the past literature (Caves and Uekusa, 1976), more recent cross-country comparative research shows that the share of economic activity accounted for by small- and

[12] Hirschmeier and Yui (1975).
[13] For empirical evidence on imported technology on productivity, see Caves and Uekusa (1976). For its effect on trade performance, see Audretsch and Yamawaki (1988).

medium-sized enterprises (SMEs) in Japan is certainly much larger than it is in the United States, but it is comparable to some of the European countries such as Italy (Patrick and Rohlen, 1987; Audretsch, 2002). The share of Japan's SMEs in the total number of establishments in manufacturing was 99.4 percent in 1957 and remained the same in 1996. When the SMEs' share was measured by employment, its share was 73.5 percent in 1957, and it increased to 74.1 percent in 1996 (Kawai and Urata, 2002).[14]

It is also well-known that subcontracting is more prevalent among Japan's SMEs than elsewhere with more than 55 percent of SMEs engaging in some sort of subcontracting arrangements in the late 1980s. As discussed earlier in this section, the subcontracting system is widely used in Japanese industries such as automobile manufacturing, electrical equipment, and machinery. According to Uekusa (1987), the Japanese subcontracting system has several distinctive features: a high level of dependence by larger firms on subcontracting with SMEs; a cooperative and risk-sharing relationship between parents and subcontractors; a quick diffusion of technology among parents and subcontractors; and its crucial role in the development of lean production system (or *kanban* system) and consequently continuous improvements in quality.[15]

Another important feature related to this point is that SMEs are an integral part of regional clusters in Japan. The emergence of Japan's clusters is attributed to several factors such as historical circumstances, prior existence of large manufacturers in the region, prior existence of related and supporting industries in neighboring regions, transportation costs, and government policy. Japan's industrial clusters generate advantages by supporting large numbers of SMEs with specialized capabilities and skills and by organizing market structures that encourage interfirm linkages and facilitate the dissemination of knowledge among these SMEs. In addition, subcontracting arrangements in Japan often take place in regional clusters (Yamawaki, 2002b).

---

[14] SMEs are defined as firms with fewer than 299 employees. Among SMEs of different sizes, SMEs in the smallest group (one to four employees) declined in their number, while the larger SMEs continued to increase in their number. See tables 1 and 2 in Kawai and Urata (2002).

[15] For some specific issues of contracts in subcontracting, see Kawasaki and McMillan (1987).

The question of whether productivity levels differ between small and large enterprises within the same industry in Japan has been rigorously examined in past research. Productivity levels do seem to differ between different size classes in the industry when measured by value added per worker (Torii, 1992) and when measured by total factor productivity (TFP). Although small firms, on average, have lower productivity levels than larger firms within the industry, in some machinery sectors small plants even have achieved higher TFP growth rates and higher TFP levels (Urata and Kawai, 2002). Moreover, small enterprises may not be inefficient from the standpoint of technical efficiency. Addressing the question of whether the industry's production process is inefficient if it employs a larger amount of inputs than the minimum required to obtain the actual output, Torii (1992) shows that there is no evidence that large plants have a significantly larger advantage in technical efficiency than small plants in Japan. Finally, the subcontracting system supports Japan's advantage by enhancing TFP levels and TFP growth (Urata and Kawai, 2002) and by raising the efficiency frontier in Japan relative to the frontier in the United States (Torii and Caves, 1992).

Thus, the existence of SMEs and subcontracting arrangements within regional industrial clusters have been regarded an important element in Japanese manufacturing that have contributed to enhancing the international competitiveness in industries such as automobiles, electronics, and other machinery. In Chapter 5, we discuss that the statistical results shown by the negative effect of seller concentration on Japanese market share in the United States in the late 1970s can be interpreted as an evidence of the importance of Japan's SMEs in exporting.[16]

Foreign Direct Investment in the Late 1980s and 1990s

Corporate Groups
An important feature of the Japanese corporate model in the postwar era through the mid-1990s is the groupings of firms that are bound together

---

[16] Among the twenty-four industries in the sample used in Chapter 5, metalworking machinery, special industrial machinery, general machinery, pottery products, cotton fabrics, air conditioners, electrical equipment, and watches and clocks show relatively low levels of concentration measured by the largest four-firm concentration ratio.

by a variety of relationships.[17] One type of such corporate grouping is the financial *keiretsu* where member firms are based in different industries and tied together through reciprocal ownership relationships. It usually consists of a main bank with affiliated financial institutions who behave as the main supplier of funds. In the early 1990s, there were six major financial corporate groups: Mitsui, Mitsubishi, Sumitomo, Fuyo, Sanwa, and DKB (Daiichkangin).[18] Among these six groups, the first three were descendants of prewar *zaibatsu*. The main features of this type of corporate group were: (1) reciprocal shareholding; (2) interlocking directorates with member banks; (3) in-group loans through member financial institutions; (4) reciprocal business transactions with member firms; and (5) information exchange among member firms (Nakatani, 1984; Imai, 1989; Odagiri, 1992). Another type of corporate grouping is the vertical industrial *keiretsu* in which a large parent company forms a group with its affiliates and subsidiaries based on technological and transactional relationships.[19] Typical examples are the Hitachi group, NEC group, Matsushita group, Toyota group, and NEC group. Their organizational patterns differ markedly between individual groups. For example, the Toyota group is formed as a multilayer of subcontractors along the vertical chain of procurement-production activities, but the NEC group is formed based on regional manufacturing subsidiaries and hived-off business units (Imai, 1989; Odagiri, 1992).

The empirical analysis presented in this book does not directly examine the role of corporate groups in exports and foreign direct investment by Japanese firms. There are, however, several areas where the groupings of firms may have influenced the pattern of competition in exports and foreign direct investment.[20] The most specific influence of the vertical *keiretsu* membership on the pattern of Japanese direct investment is

---

[17] For detailed discussion, see, for example, Caves and Uekusa (1976), Nakatani (1984), Imai (1989), Sheard (1989), and Odagiri (1992).

[18] A number of mergers and alliances occurred during the late 1990s and the early 2000s changed this structure significantly.

[19] It is also called "independent corporate groups" (Imai, 1989).

[20] There is a large literature on the influence of *keiretsu* on imports in Japan and the issue of whether vertical *keiretsu* is exclusionary. See Fung (1991), Lawrence (1991), Saxonhouse (1993), Eaton and Tamura (1994), Ueda and Sasaki (1998), Qiu and Spencer (2001), and Head, Ries, and Spencer (2004).

observed in a complementary relationship between overseas production and home-country exports of parts and intermediate products. Exports to Europe by Japanese electronic firms that are members of the *keiretsu* firms are higher than the non-*keiretsu* firms if the leading *keiretsu* firm has invested there (Belderbos and Sleuwaegen, 1998), and exports of the *keiretsu* member increase as overseas investments of the *keiretsu* leader increase (Head and Ries, 2001).[21]

Another area in which a *keiretsu* membership played a role in FDI is the relationship between exports and FDI in distribution affiliates. The empirical result in Chapter 5 showed that Japanese FDI in distribution in the U.S. market promoted Japanese exports there. Although this result was obtained without taking into account the effect of *keiretsu* memberships on FDI in distribution, it may be affected by *keiretsu* memberships. If a member of a financial *keiretsu* exports, that firm may forgo investing in distribution in the destination market and instead use the service provided by a trading company in the *keiretsu*. In this case, the *keiretsu* member is likely to invest less in distribution in the export market (Sakakibara and Serwin, 2002).

Merger and Acquisition

One of the distinctive aspects of the massive FDI flow from Japan in the late-1980s was the extensive use of acquisitions by Japanese firms. As international rivalry in technology and R&D intensified among Japanese and foreign rivals, Japanese firms were more motivated to acquire local firms with technological capabilities and diversify into new businesses particularly in the United States. The Japanese firms who were at disadvantage in technology at home and lacked international experiences imitated rival firm's actions and acquired U.S. firms in the late 1980s. They followed the first-movers into the U.S. market because the first-movers' entries gave them a positive signal on the U.S. corporate market and because they felt strong competitive pressure from such moves.

---

[21] According to Hackett and Srinivasan (1998), Japanese multinational firms in the *keiretsu* system show stronger vertical relationships than those of firms in the United States. See also Horiuchi (1989). For a more general discussion of the potential role of various types of business networks on international trade, see Rauch (2001).

However, the Japanese firms that invested in new capacity were motivated differently. They were more focused, experienced, and owned stronger technological capabilities and skills. In addition, they invested in the United States not because rivals invested. Instead, their investment decisions were more independent from rivals' actions. As a consequence, their postentry performance was significantly different from those firms that entered the United States by acquiring local firms. The Japanese firms that entered the United States through acquisitions had a high likelihood of exit.

Although these findings from Chapters 6 and 9 are consistent, there are some puzzles that are unanswered in the statistical analysis. Japanese firms are known historically to prefer internal growth to external growth in their home market because they emphasize human resource policies and rely on the internal labor market to develop competitive advantage (Odagiri, 1992). And, they tend to focus more on acquiring financially distressed firms that need to be rescued more than foreign firms do in Japan.[22] Contrary to this pattern, Japanese firms actively sought foreign firms for acquisitions in the late 1980. A key to understanding this apparently asymmetric behavior of Japanese firms in the home and foreign markets is their need to source technological capabilities and other resources required for growth from foreign firms. Presumably, the changing business environment in the late 1980s – the emergence of global competitors, the emergence of new markets, the expansion of geographic scope of markets, motivated Japanese firms to go after foreign firms with technological advantage. And, when the Japanese yen appreciated against the U.S. dollar after 1985, the firm-specific assets of U.S. high-tech firms became more valuable to Japanese firms by generating returns in appreciated yen (Blonigen, 1997).

Imperfection in Capital Market and FDI

The second puzzle is the apparent lack of monitoring in the investment behavior of Japanese firms in the mid-1980s. Given its inherent inconsistency with their corporate system, pursuing growth through acquisitions may have exposed Japanese firms to high risk. What happened to the

---

[22] For some evidence on this pattern in Japan, see Fukao, Ito, and Kwon (2005).

main bank's monitoring activities? An answer to this question lies in the imperfection in Japan's capital market. Indeed, the existence of imperfection was the presumption required to explain the surge of Japanese FDI in the mid-1980s by the enhanced level of wealth experienced by Japanese firms. When the Japanese yen appreciated against the U.S. dollar, the purchasing power of corporate liquidity in the Japanese yen was enhanced over corporate assets denominated in the U.S. dollar (Froot and Stein, 1991). The impact of such wealth effects on foreign investment is significant when capital markets are imperfect. Given a premium for monitoring costs charged for external financing, Japanese firms with larger assets denominated in the appreciating yen experienced relative wealth gains and assigned a low opportunity cost to internally generated finds.[23]

One question that arises from the wealth effect on FDI, however, is the role of main banks and affiliated financial institutions in the Japanese corporate system.[24] The main bank system and its influence on corporate behavior and performance have been examined in the previous literature on market imperfection in capital and financial markets. By comparing investment functions of *keiretsu* members and nonmembers, Hoshi, Kashyap, and Sharfstein (1991) found that *keiretsu* membership and the main bank relationship helped member firms to overcome liquidity constraints by producing information. Although there is no existing research that examines the link between *keiretsu* membership under the main bank system and the surge of Japanese FDI in the late 1980s, their study gives an evidence of the imperfection in Japan's capital and financial market[25] and suggests a mechanism that could have led to the surge of Japanese FDI.

More recently, Fukao, Nishimura, Sui, and Tomiyama (2005) constructed an index that measures the extent of monitoring activities of

---

[23] In addition, the cost of capital measured by the accounting-earnings measure is lower than in the United States (Ando and Auerbach, 1988). This condition may have allowed Japanese firms to gain access to funds at a lower cost in Japan.

[24] For a description of the main bank system, see Horiuchi, Packer, and Fukuda (1988) and Sheard (1989).

[25] For evidence on the role of banks and the performance of borrowing firms, see Caves and Uekusa (1976), Nakatani (1984), Weinstein and Yafeh (1998), and Morck and Nakamura (1999).

Japanese banks and examined the effects of bank monitoring on the profitability of borrowing firms. They found that many banks significantly reduced their monitoring activities between 1981 and 1985, suggesting that this weakened governance contributed to the so-called bubble economy in the late 1980s. This finding is thus consistent with this book's conclusion about the exit of Japanese firms that entered the U.S. market through acquisitions.

11

Implications

To conclude this study, I offer some implications of my findings for policy and future research.

11.1. Conceptual Framework

The central aspect of the theoretical framework used in this study is the premise that most of the trade and foreign direct investment is in the industries that are characterized as oligopolies. The old assumption of pure competition is replaced by the assumption of imperfect competition and that domestic and foreign firms are oligopolies. Generally speaking, the empirical results of this book provide evidence to support the imperfect competition approach in international trade. It is, however, important to note that the pattern of competition differs from one industry to another and that the assumption of imperfect competition in international trade may not be relevant for some industries.

Another aspect of the international oligopoly approach is the introduction of the market structures of both home and foreign countries into the model. Assuming that there are two countries, A and B, and that the firms in industry X in both countries engage in international trade, the profit-maximizing levels of output for export and export prices for the firm in country A are determined by the elements of market structure and basic conditions in the home market as well as in the foreign market. This model, therefore, differs importantly from the international linkage model used in the early empirical literature in industrial organization that takes into account only the home country's market structure to explain the trade behavior and performance. The empirical analysis of this book provides some evidence that supports the hypothesis that the foreign country's market structure affects the home-country firm's trade performance. The statistical analysis in Chapter 3 finds that the profits on exports of Japanese firms increase within Japanese market structures as well as within U.S. market structures. Chapter 4 then confirms this finding and shows that the Japanese import share in the U.S. market increases with the competitive advantages of the Japanese industry relative to the U.S. advantages. Competitive advantages are measured here by a number of market-structure and cost-related variables.

Trade Patterns and Competitive Advantage

Traditional international economics explains trade flows simply on the basis of factor price differences and trade costs. Although this approach remains relevant for many industries, our empirical results strongly points out that for some industries the value-creating investments such as R&D, promotional activities, distribution, and plant capacity undertaken by both the domestic and foreign firms determine trade patterns.

The results in Chapters 4, 5, and 8 show that the share of imports in a particular country's market is likely to increase with the competitive advantage of exporting industries and is likely to decrease with the competitive advantage of the importing industries. The importance of this finding lies in that a firm's performance in the international market is determined by its behavior *relative* to that of its foreign counterpart. Although a firm may be positioned competitively and is therefore profitable in the domestic market, it may not be able to replicate the same performance in the international market when its foreign rivals possess more resources and capabilities that provide them with competitive advantages.

11.2. Foreign Market Entry and Oligopolistic Interactions

The foreign country's market structure influences the home exporter's price decision and hence its profitability. This finding suggests the existence of an obvious mechanism through which entry occurs. An oligopoly in the foreign market sets prices above marginal costs in industries where barriers to entry are high. The elevated prices attract new entries to the market. Home firms that have some competitive advantages are qualified to jump over the high entry barriers and earn positive profits in the foreign market. Indeed, high entry barriers may attract qualified foreign entrants rather than discourage them.

The home firm that can enter into the high-barrier industry in the foreign country may enjoy potentially large profits. The entrant, however, may face some challenges from the incumbents. The analysis in Chapter 8 shows that the incumbents in the entered industry may not respond to new entry initially but will eventually recognize the threat of new competition. The incumbent may become more competitive as the entrant's share increases and respond to entry strongly.

Although entrants are attracted to markets in which incumbents earn high profits, international entry itself is a competitive process with home firms matching the moves of their rivals into foreign markets. Our empirical analysis finds that herd-like behavior takes the form of followers choosing to enter markets by acquiring existing foreign firms rather than by building new facilities. Such entries by acquisition, however, subsequently turn out to have higher mortality rates. In other words, the firm that enters foreign markets independently with a strategy is more likely to survive than the firms that imitate a rival's actions.

11.3. Foreign Direct Investment and the Firm's Proprietary Assets

One of the classic questions researched in the field of international business is the role of the firm's proprietary assets in making foreign direct investment a profitable action. Recent evidence has shifted our perspective by indicating that firms sometimes invest abroad to access, rather than to exploit, such assets. The finding in Chapter 6 establishes a connection between the relative paucity of Japanese proprietary assets and the decision to enter foreign markets by the means of acquiring incumbent firms.

11.4. Evolution of International Competitiveness

This study describes the pattern of Japanese competition in the international market evolved over the 45-year period after World War II.

Japanese firms' international competitiveness evolved over time, which consequently changed the way in which they compete in international market. When Japanese firms resumed their exporting intensively after World War II, they were more likely the price-takers in the world market because of their relatively weak market position. As their competitiveness improved over time in Japan's capital-intensive and technology-intensive industries, Japanese industries started behaving as price-setters in the world market. As Japanese firms accumulated resources and capabilities to compete with foreign rivals through the 1980s, their strategic options widened from the sole option of exporting to several options that included foreign direct investments. When they entered into highly sophisticated segments in some of their comparatively competitive industries, they started to engage in oligopolistic rivalry in international markets. This suggests that the way in which firms compete in international markets is not necessarily unique to their countries of origin. It instead evolves over time and differs at different points in time.

11.5. Government Policy

One of the most well-known facts on the pattern of foreign direct investment is the persistent low level of inward foreign direct investment in Japan.[1] Although outward foreign investment and inward foreign investment are often reciprocal in advanced industrial countries such as the United States and Europe, the pattern observed in Japan is quite different. The empirical results in Chapter 7 suggest that Japan's institutions and business practices have not been associated with failures and exits by early foreign investors who actually were able to enter in Japan. If there is an entry barrier, however, it can keep out most foreign entrants without necessarily raising the exit rates of those who try. Our finding on the paucity of entry by U.S. and European firms into the Japanese market in response to Japanese entry into their home market suggests that foreign firms are indeed discouraged to enter into the Japanese market. In this perspective, therefore, recent policy initiatives taken by Japan's Ministry of Economy, Trade and Industry (METI) to encourage foreign direct investment

---

[1]   For a detailed discussion, see Chapter 7.

in Japan are welcome news. In 2003, the Japan Investment Council called for doubling inward foreign direct investment by 2008, which was subsequently endorsed by the Japanese government. As of May 2006, METI aimed to achieve this goal by making amendments to the Corporation Act and reforms to the taxation of corporate reorganization. In particular, through these policy measures, they expected direct investment in the form of M&A by foreign investors to increase in Japan. Whether this policy actually increases the level of direct investment in Japan or not is yet to be seen. The policy makers in Japan at least realized a need for reforms and reductions of entry barriers.

11.6. Future Research

A natural sequel to this study is the application of its approach to other international markets. The empirical findings and conclusions of this study were obtained mostly based on the data of Japanese firms in the United States. They can be tested for Japanese firms in different countries and for non-Japanese firms in different countries. For Japanese firms, a natural extension for this study is an analysis of their competitive behavior in the emerging markets in Asia. Do they adjust their prices in reaction to price changes made by their international rivals? Do they engage in a competitive process by matching the moves of their rivals to enter the Chinese markets? For non-Japanese firms, similar studies would be able to examine if their behavior in exports and direct investment is consistent with the imperfect competition approach. International comparison of export and investment behaviors of firms originating from different countries will provide an answer to the question if the pattern observed in this study is unique to Japanese firms or to specific industries.[2]

This study presented some attempts to examine market performance of FDI: exit of foreign firms in Japanese manufacturing (Chapter 7) and the consequence of concentrated entry (Chapter 9). Although these chapters produced, some interesting findings, the data used were far from ideal, thus restricted the use of more sophisticated econometric models. The use of microlevel panel data is expanding in the field of international

---

[2] For a review of the pattern of recent Japanese FDI in Asia, see Kimura (2006).

economics and it would make the tracing of entry and exit of particular firms feasible and by relating them to firm-specific characteristics and market structures. Recent empirical studies on Japanese FDI and other countries' FDI in Japan prove that such data are now accessible and can provide new insights to our understanding of the firm's performance in FDI. (See Fukao, Ito, and Kwon, 2005, for the effects of foreign entry by M&A on total factor productivity (TFP); Kimura and Kiyota, 2006a, 2006b, for the effect of different ownership types and TFP; and Sakakibara and Yamawaki, 2007, for the profitability of Japanese MNEs). It would be very interesting to see how a competitive process affects firm performance in international markets.

Another line of research that this study suggests is empirical examination of the effect of strategic interactions on the firm's location choice of various activities in different countries. This study examined the international activities most commonly engaged in by representative Japanese firms in the 1960s through the early 1990s. The stylized pattern was home centralization and exporting; FDI in distribution to support local sales of exported goods; vertical FDI in local production to procure intermediary goods; and horizontal FDI in local production to support and(or) substitute exports of final goods. Although this study did not examine the influence of strategic interactions between firms on their location choices of these activities, recent theories of horizontal FDI that assume imperfect competition between firms (Brainard, 1997; Markusen 2002) suggest that firms' choices on exporting and horizontal FDI differ among different firms. When we assume downward-sloping demand, fixed costs associated with FDI, trade costs, and Cournot behavior, the "market-crowding" effect occurs because more firms enter the foreign market through FDI to avoid trade costs and as a result depress the profits in the foreign market. Thus, the choice between FDI and exports would vary across different firms depending on differences in trade costs, plant-level fixed costs and scale economies, comparative production costs, market size, and the way in which these firms compete and interact in different markets (Head and Ries, 2002, 2004).

Moreover, a growing number of studies examine how differences in productivity across firms within the same industry influence their decisions to export (e.g., Bernard, Eaton, Jensen, and Kortum, 2003; Bernard and Jensen, 2004). Along this line of research, Helpman, Melitz, and Yeaple (2004) examine how productivity differences among firms in the same industry affects the choice between exporting and serving the local market by FDI. The firm heterogeneity hypothesis of FDI was tested for Japanese firms by Head and Ries (2003) and Kimura and Kiyota (2006a).

Although this economic literature of the relationship between the export-FDI choice and firm heterogeneity consider primarily the case of a single-product firm, Baldwin and Ottaviano (2001) examine how a multiproduct firm chooses between exporting and FDI. Head and Ries (2004) show that vertically integrated firms may engage in simultaneous exporting and FDI and that their modes may differ across firms depending on the differences in trade costs, plant-level scale economies, comparative advantage, and market sizes. The MNE's decision to choose between exporting and FDI, however, may be further complicated by its simultaneous use of horizontal and vertical FDI and by its decision to locate R&D and product development activities in different countries (Markusen, 2002; Yamawaki, 2004a).

These strands of literature clearly point out that the firm's choice between exporting and serving the local market through FDI is firm-specific and would be influenced by a competitive process with firms matching the moves of their rivals. The existing literature in the field of international business suggests that these questions are indeed relevant and that MNEs' geographic configurations of various activities are often strategically determined. For the multinational enterprise that is composed of a number of subsidiaries and operate under a network of subsidiaries with different characteristics (Ghoshal and Bartlett, 1990), the MNE's overall competitiveness would be determined by resources and capabilities developed at subsidiaries (Birkinshaw and Hood, 1998; Birkinshaw, Hood, and Jonsson, 1998) and its strategic focus on the scope of market (Ghemawat, 2005). New capabilities are often developed through establishment of R&D units in the subsidiary, suggesting the strategic importance of choosing locations of R&D activities as well as production facilities for the MNE (Gerybadze and Reger, 1999; Kuemmerle, 1999; Frost, Birkinshaw, and Ensign, 2002; Belderbos, 2003).

A broader empirical question suggested by this literature is: how do firms compete in choosing locations of various value-chain activities in different countries? Do they choose locations of various activities in reaction to the choices made by their rivals? Is this kind of matching behavior observed in emerging markets such as China, India, and Eastern Europe? To what extent is the firm's geographic configuration of various value-chain activities determined by competitive processes and strategic interactions? Or, is it determined primarily by the firm's organizational capability and assets as described in Chapter 10? One research design that is suitable for examination of strategic interactions between firms is *industry analysis* because time-series data on firm-specific factors are usually accessible for a cross section of firms in the same industry. Alternatively, access to micropanel data bases on FDI would make feasible the tracing of geographic configurations of particular firms and relating them to rivals' configurations over time. We would then be able to examine systematically the competitive process in choosing locations of economic activities among firms.

Appendixes

APPENDIX TO CHAPTER 1

The yearly value of exports used in Figure 1.2 and Table 1.5 is obtained from the Customs and Tariff Bureau, Ministry of Finance, Japan, *Nihon Gaikoku Boeki Nenpyo* [*Yearly Trade Statistics of Japan*]. Value of outward foreign direct investment used in Figures 1.2, 1.3, and 1.4 and Table 1.6 was obtained from the Ministry of Economy, Trade and Industry, Japan, *Wagakuni Kigyo no Kaigai Gigyo Katsudo* [*Business Activities Abroad by Japanese Corporations*] report, various years. The yearly statistics reported in this data source are based on the Ministry of Finance data. The value of the outward direct investment is the approval and notification base, and it is a gross figure.

The figures in Table 1.2, and the list of industries presented in Table 1.3 and Table 1.4, are all based on the OECD trade statistics. Audretsch, Sleuwaegen, and Yamawaki (1989, appendix A and appendix B) provide detailed accounts on these tables.

Figure 1.5 is based on figures for passenger cars, buses, and trucks. The statistics used in this exhibit were obtained from the Economic Research Division, JETRO. Mr. Dai Higashino at the Economic Research Division, JETRO Tokyo, and Mr. Minoru Hara at JETRO Los Angeles helped me greatly by providing these statistics and other information needed to prepare this chapter.

APPENDIX TO CHAPTER 2

Table A.2.1. *Definitions of variables used in Chapter 2*

Variable	Definition
XP	Average unit export price index (1970 = 100) in U.S. dollars. Total dollar volume of the industry's export sales to the world divided by the same export sales in quantities.
FP	Foreign average unit price index (1970 = 100) in U.S. dollars. This series is a trade-weighted average of price indices for competing foreign countries constructed in the same manner as XP.
DEMAND	Annual percentage deviation of the industry's domestic production in 1970 price from the time trend in total industry production in 1970 price.
ULC	Unit labor costs (1970 = 100). Total industry labor costs divided by total industry production in 1970 price.
UMC	Unit material costs (1970 = 100). Total industry material costs divided by total industry production in 1970 price.
SHARE	Share in the world export market. Total Japanese industry exports to the world divided by total world exports.
EXCH	Foreign exchange rate. Average Japanese yen price of U.S. dollars.

Table A.2.2. *Export price equations for Japanese manufacturing industries, 1970–1984 (dependent variable: XP)*

	Industry	Constant	FP	EXCH	DEMAND	SHARE	ULC	UMC	UC	Adj-R^2 / F	DW / ρ
1	Synthetic rubber	-3.437 (0.932)	1.549 (2.380)	0.363 (1.067)	0.397 (1.059)	0.087 (0.214)			-0.169 (0.372)	0.963 / 73.102	1.549
2	Synthetic fibers	0.034 (0.017)	0.928 (2.458)	0.176 (0.407)	0.285 (0.476)	0.182 (0.794)			0.235 (0.610)	0.909 / 29.086	1.940
3	Synthetic dyestuffs	6.184 (2.696)	0.195 (0.912)	-0.241 (0.779)	0.429 (1.434)	0.190 (0.805)	0.278 (0.721)	0.418 (1.646)		0.910 / 18.459	1.575 / 0.492
4	Paints and ink	5.409 (3.055)	0.318 (1.536)	0.158 (0.615)	0.460 (2.014)	-0.068 (0.476)	0.200 (1.133)	0.683 (3.248)		0.988 / 195.44	1.802
5	Soap and detergents	0.963 (0.828)	0.657 (3.812)	0.432 (2.144)	0.517 (3.854)	0.123 (0.857)			0.579 (3.808)	0.855 / 9.692	1.709 / 0.784
6	Fertilizers	-2.215 (0.969)	1.701 (3.637)		-0.210 (0.482)	0.147 (1.139)			-0.296 (0.751)	0.954 / 72.786	1.845
7	Plastic materials	0.391 (0.261)	0.808 (3.202)	0.606 (1.662)	0.415 (2.357)	-0.232 (1.003)			0.520 (2.333)	0.925 / 19.856	1.641 / 0.612
8	Paper and paperboard	4.798 (4.735)	0.126 (0.801)		1.066 (4.743)	0.420 (3.264)	0.064 (0.578)	0.752 (5.825)		0.995 / 572.73	1.947
9	Textile yarn	0.006 (0.004)	0.776 (2.812)	0.547 (1.902)	0.640 (2.776)	0.309 (2.016)			0.647 (2.399)	0.757 / 5.391	1.991 / 0.787
10	Cotton fabrics	5.502 (3.888)	0.428 (3.335)	0.271 (1.326)	0.794 (5.432)	-0.033 (0.287)	0.120 (0.222)	0.963 (2.057)		0.995 / 356.04	2.596 / -0.763
11	Cement	-1.575 (0.620)	0.814 (2.865)	0.538 (1.106)	0.851 (1.330)	0.114 (0.940)			0.289 (1.046)	0.833 / 8.287	1.549 / 0.461
12	Glassware	15.640 (3.579)	-1.431 (2.396)	0.799 (0.844)	0.027 (0.025)	-0.363 (1.017)			1.609 (2.799)	0.361 / 1.436	1.385 / 0.784

(continued)

209

Table A.2.2 (*Continued*)

Industry	Constant	FP	EXCH	DEMAND	SHARE	ULC	UMC	UC	Adj-R^2 / F	DW / ρ
13 Steel plates and sheets	2.503 (1.375)	0.600 (2.114)	0.587 (2.206)	0.413 (1.921)	-0.968 (3.174)			0.421 (1.655)	0.987 / 121.99	2.450 / -0.618
14 Steel bars	1.133 (0.407)	0.359 (1.096)	1.095 (2.136)	0.752 (1.965)	0.017 (0.097)	0.338 (1.337)	0.673 (2.049)		0.976 / 71.559	2.420 / -0.556
15 Boilers	-0.402 (0.267)	0.700 (4.738)		-0.054 (0.481)	0.340 (1.419)			0.061 (0.264)	0.853 / 21.246	2.379
16 Steam engines	-0.630 (0.482)	0.504 (3.752)		0.192 (1.706)	0.375 (1.759)			0.020 (0.122)	0.871 / 24.581	1.434
17 Tractors	-1.040 (0.400)	0.674 (2.274)	0.649 (3.560)	0.138 (0.540)	0.120 (1.558)	0.344 (1.268)	0.035 (0.358)		0.993 / 262.44	2.367 / -0.635
18 Construction machinery	2.691 (1.182)	0.338 (2.632)	0.151 (0.309)	0.265 (1.400)	0.408 (2.496)	0.444 (2.338)	0.127 (0.551)		0.970 / 76.360	1.742
19 Machine tools	3.853 (0.993)	0.404 (1.137)	0.474 (1.535)	0.203 (1.224)	-0.195 (1.110)	0.404 (1.651)	0.512 (3.256)		0.992 / 222.65	2.321 / -0.451
20 Metalworking machinery	-0.412 (0.119)	0.600 (3.992)	0.522 (0.849)	0.194 (1.040)	0.490 (2.519)			0.534 (2.783)	0.753 / 5.309	1.761 / 0.597
21 Pumps for liquids	-0.555 (0.276)	0.727 (3.991)	0.456 (1.266)	-0.134 (0.820)	0.195 (1.694)			0.375 (2.363)	0.966 / 80.684	1.655
22 Ball and roller bearings	3.739 (2.293)	0.168 (0.683)	0.181 (0.660)	0.152 (0.914)	-0.127 (0.529)			0.698 (2.291)	0.448 / 1.818	1.259 / 0.870
23 Radio and TV receivers	7.937 (4.719)	0.454 (2.670)		0.046 (0.759)	-0.859 (3.328)			0.705 (3.645)	0.878 / 20.883	1.443 / 0.452
24 Telephone equipment	-0.527 (0.249)	0.853 (2.829)	1.135 (1.946)	0.977 (2.688)	0.245 (1.897)			1.077 (1.812)	0.980 / 137.68	2.365

Table A.2.2 (Continued)

Industry		Constant	FP	EXCH	DEMAND	SHARE	ULC	UMC	UC	Adj-R² / F	DW / ρ
25	Electric circuit apparatus	7.143 (1.960)	0.199 (0.792)	0.358 (1.294)	0.211 (0.898)	0.121 (0.496)	1.112 (6.700)	0.085 (0.300)		0.997 / 586.28	1.823 / −0.711
26	Insulated wire and cable	7.507 (3.104)	−0.023 (0.075)	0.233 (0.524)	0.263 (0.788)	0.010 (0.056)	0.702 (2.589)	0.452 (2.241)		0.820 / 8.736	1.423 / 0.545
27	Passenger cars	4.272 (3.936)	0.195 (1.468)	0.327 (1.225)	−0.030 (0.306)	−0.005 (0.053)			0.986 (3.887)	0.663 / 3.611	1.226 / 0.906
28	Railway vehicles	−1.896 (0.511)	0.794 (1.939)	0.793 (0.871)	−0.163 (0.728)	0.340 (1.407)			0.602 (1.044)	0.964 / 42.101	2.098 / −0.380
29	Sewing machines	6.087 (2.664)	0.117 (0.185)	0.431 (0.769)	−0.002 (0.011)	−0.443 (0.824)			1.151 (2.676)	0.975 / 109.87	1.768
30	Semi conductors	−3.335 (2.490)	−0.141 (0.779)	0.635 (2.831)	0.043 (0.489)				0.932 (2.787)	0.502 / 3.019	1.055 / 0.821
31	Cameras	1.522 (1.702)	0.228 (3.121)	−0.086 (0.763)	0.203 (2.046)	−0.168 (2.065)	0.250 (2.443)	0.048 (0.448)		0.495 / 2.464	1.506 / 0.536
32	Integrated circuits	−1.011 (0.158)	0.676 (2.652)	0.529 (0.453)	0.406 (0.824)				2.579 (13.93)	0.983 / 115.72	2.356 / −0.572
33	Tape and video recorders	0.706 (0.952)		0.192 (1.751)	0.120 (1.511)	−0.464 (10.22)			0.019 (0.232)	0.961 / 86.201	1.797
34	Photographic films	−11.072 (6.036)	0.441 (2.813)	1.539 (6.117)	1.010 (3.742)	0.903 (6.688)			0.364 (1.962)	0.911 / 6.505	1.850 / −0.403

Notes: *t*-test statistics are in parentheses. All the variables are in logarithm. Unit costs are in terms of U.S. dollars from industries 1 through 29. From industries 30 through 34, unit costs and the dependent variable are in terms of the Japanese yen. Equations for industries 30 and 32 are estimated for 1976–1984.

211

Table A.2.3. *Names and industrial classification codes*

No.	Industry	SITC (Rev. 2)	SIC Japan
1	Synthetic rubber	233	2638
2	Synthetic fibers	266, 267	264
3	Synthetic dyestuffs	531, 532	2636
4	Paints and printing ink	533	2654, 2655
5	Soap and detergents	554	2652, 2656
6	Fertilizers	562	2611, 2612
7	Plastic materials	583	2637
8	Paper and paperboard	641	2421, 2422
9	Textile yarn	651	202
10	Cotton fabrics, woven	652	2041
11	Cement	6612	3021
12	Glassware	665	3014, 3015, 3016
13	Steel plates and sheets	674	311
14	Steel bars	6732	313
15	Boilers	711	3411
16	Steam engines and turbines	712	3412
17	Tractors	722	3432
18	Construction machinery	723	3431
19	Sewing machines	7243	3482
20	Machine tools	736	3441
21	Metalworking machinery	737	3442
22	Pumps for liquids	742	3471
23	Ball and roller bearings	7491	3494
24	Radio and TV receivers	761, 762	3543
25	Telephone equipment	7641	3541
26	Electric circuit apparatus	772	3513
27	Insulated wire and cable	7731	3251
28	Passenger motor vehicles	781	3611
29	Railway vehicles	791	3620
30	Semiconductors	7763	3572
31	Integrated circuits	7764	3573
32	Tape and video recorders	763	3544, 355914
33	Cameras	8811	3752
34	Photographic films	8822	2697

Notes: Industry names are based on the SITC system. Value of shipments to construct *DEMAND* is obtained by aggregating values of shipments at the constituting six-digit commodity level for industries 2041, 311, 313, 3544, 3611, 3752, and 2697. SITC 763 includes audio hi-fi equipment.

Table A.2.4. *Selection of competing foreign countries*

Group No.	Countries	SITC (Rev. 2) Industries
1	OECD Total	233
2	OECD Europe and US	266 + 267, 531 + 532
3	OECD Europe, US, and Canada	641, 674
4	OECD Europe	554, 651, 652, 711, 712, 723, 737, 742, 772, 791
5	E.C. Total	665, 722, 781
6	E.C. and US	583
7	E.C., US, and Canada	641
8	E.C., Sweden, and Switzerland	533, 736
9	France, West Germany, the Netherlands, and Switzerland	772
10	France, West Germany, UK, Italy, and Sweden	7731
11	Germany and Sweden	7491
12	OECD Europe and South Korea	761 + 762
13	OECD Europe (1970–1975), Spain, Greece, Turkey, and South Korea (1976–1984)	6612
14	West Germany	6732, 7243, 763, 7763, 8811, 8822
15	US, West Germany, and South Korea	7764

Notes: E.C. countries include Belgium, Luxemburg, the Netherlands, Denmark, France, West Germany, Ireland, Italy, and the UK. For 1970–1972, Denmark, Ireland, and the UK are also included whenever data are available. Japan is not included in OECD total.

Selection of Samples

The Japanese manufacturing industries used in the statistical analysis of this chapter were selected on the basis of the standard industry classification system (SIC) in Japan and the standard international trade classification system (SITC). Because the two systems are not perfectly matched, it was necessary to aggregate data for two or three Japanese industries and match the SITC industries, and vice versa. The basic level of industry classification used in this chapter is the three-digit SITC (Rev. 2) or the four-digit SIC in Japan. The SITC (Rev. 2) industries were compared to the SITC (Rev. 1) industries. This analysis provided a list of the thirty-four industries for which the necessary time-series and cross-sectional data are available. Table A2.3 presents the thirty-four industries in the sample.

Sources of Data

The annual export price index, *XP*, and the world price index, *FP*, were constructed from Organization for Economic Co-Operation and Development (OECD), *Trade by Commodities: Market Summaries, Exports.* However, data to construct *XP* for SITC industries 763, 7763, 7764, 8811, and 8822 were obtained from Bank of Japan, Research and Statistics Department, *Price Indexes Annual: Wholesale Price Indexes.* They are measured in terms of the Japanese yen. The observation period for industries 7763 and 7764 are for the 1976–1984 period. The missing values in the OECD statistics are filled in whenever possible from United Nations (UN), *International* Trade *Statistics Yearbook, Vol. I (Trade by Country)* and *Vol. II (Trade by Commodity).* The list of competing foreign countries was created on the basis of data availability and the significance of market contacts among Japanese exporting industries and foreign export industries. The list of foreign countries used to construct *FP* is given in Table A.2.4. Data to construct *FP* were also sourced from Statistisches Bundesamt, Wiesbaden, *Aussenhandel nach dem Internationalen Warenverzeichnis fuer den Aussenhandel (SITC-Rev. II).*

SHARE was constructed from the UN statistics. *ULC, UMC,* and *DEMAND* were constructed from the Ministry of International Trade and Industry (MITI), *Census of manufacturers: Report by Industries.* The unit price index to deflate value of shipment at the four-digit level was constructed from shipment volumes and quantities at the constituent six-digit commodity level and is obtained from the MITI, *Census of Manufacturers: Report by Commodities.* The total value of shipments at 1970 price was used for *DEMAND, ULC,* and *UMC.* Total domestic production was calculated by subtracting exports from total industry shipments. Exports are taken from the OECD and UN statistics. *EXCH* was obtained from the IMF Statistics Department, *International Financial Statistics Yearbook.*

APPENDIX TO CHAPTER 3

Table A.3.1. *Definitions of variables in the cross-sectional analysis*
of Section 3.3 (N = 34)

Variable	Definition
KO	Capital Intensity: Gross fixed assets divided by value of shipments, averaged over the 1970–1984 period.
RD	R&D Intensity: R&D expenditures divided by total sales, averaged over 1972, 1977, and 1982.
AD	Advertising Intensity: Purchased advertising divided by total output, 1975
EFT	Effective Rate of Tariff Protection, averaged over 1973 and 1975.
HI	Herfindahl index of producer concentration, 1977.
EXP	Export Share: Total exports divided by value of shipments, averaged over the 1970–1984 period.
SHARE	Share in World Export Market: Total Japanese exports divided by total world exports, averaged over the 1970–1984 period.
SUB	Subcontracting Intensity: Subcontracting payment divided by total sales for companies with more than 300 employees, 1976.
CONS	Consumer Goods: Dummy variable equal to one if the industry is selling primarily consumer goods.

Table A.3.2. *Definitions of variables used for the statistical analysis in Section 3.4*

Variable	Definition
CAP	Total industry crude steel production capacity.
CR4	Four-firm concentration ratio.
CU	Capacity utilization ratio: the ratio of total domestic crude steel production to total industry crude steel production capacity. $CU = DPROD/CAP$.
DP	Wholesale price index for steel products (1965 = 100).
DPROD	Production of steel products for the domestic market in terms of crude steel equivalent. The conversion rate is based on ECE, UN method.
XP	Average unit export price for steel products (1965 = 100).
EXP	Total exports of steel products in terms of crude steel equivalent.
FP	Foreign export price. $FP = [1 - (EXP/WEXP)] * GEP$.
GEP	Average unit price for German steel exports (1965 = 100).
GNP	Gross national product in real term (1965 = 100).
MP	Weighted index of materials prices (1965 = 100). The weights are: metalliferous ores and meal scrap, 0.6; petroleum, coal, and related products, 0.3; and electric power and gas, 0.1.
UMC	Unit material cost; total material cost divided by total industry production.
WEXP	World export of steel products in crude steel equivalent.
WPROD	Weighted index of industrial production (manufacturing, mining, electricity, and gas) for four regions. The weight for each region is average share on the Japanese steel exports. The weights are: East and South Asia (excluding Japan and China but including Iran), 0.417; North America, 0.380; Latin America, 0.112; and Europe (excluding the USSR, 0.091).

Sources of Data Used for the Statistical Analysis in Section 3.3

Cross-sectional data for *KO* were obtained from the MITI, *Census of Manufacturers: Report by Industries*. *AD* was constructed from the Administrative Management Agency, *1965–1970–1975 Link Input–Output Tables*, Data Report 1, 1980. *HI* at the four-digit level was constructed as a shipment-weighted average of constituent six-digit industries from A. Senoh (Ed.), *Gendai Nihon no Sangyo Shuuchu: 1971–1980* [*Industrial Concentration in Japan: 1971–1980*], Tokyo: Keizai Shinbun Sha, 1983. *EXP* and *SHARE* were constructed from the OECD and UN data described in the Appendix to Chapter 2. *SUB* was taken from M.

Uekusa (1982, p. 127, table 4.4). *EFT* data are the estimates by Y. Shouda (1982, p.11). *RD* was obtained from the Statistics Bureau, Management and Coordination Agency, *Report on the Survey of Research and Development*. *RD*, *SUB*, and *EFT* were available for only broadly defined industries, so I assigned the common value to each four-digit industry within the broadly defined industry.

Sources of Data Used in the Statistical Analysis in Section 3.4

CAP, *DPROD*, *XP*, *GNP*, *MP*, and *DP* were constructed from the Bank of Japan, Statistics Department, *Economic Statistics Annual*. *CR4* was obtained from Sumitomo Metal Industries Ltd., 1975, *Nihon no tekkogyo to tosha* [*The Japanese Steel Industry and Sumitomo Metal Industries*], Osaka: Sumitomo Metal Industries. *DPROD*, *EXP*, and the weights used for *WPROD* were obtained from the Iron and Steel Federation in Japan, *Statistical Year Book* and *Monthly Report of the Iron and Steel Statistics*. *GEP* was constructed from Wirtsschaftsvereinigung Eisen-und Stahlindustrie, *Statistisches Jahrbuch der Eisen-und Stahlindustrie*. *UMC* was constructed from the Ministry of International Trade and Industry, *Census of Manufacturers*. *WEXP* to construct *FP* was obtained from International Iron and Steel Institute, *World Steel in Figures*, 1978, Brussels: IISI. The index of industrial production to construct *WPROD* was obtained from United Nations, *Statistical Yearbook*.

Export price index, *XP*, and unit material costs, *UMC*, are in terms of the Japanese yen, and therefore the exchange rate is not included in the model specification. Foreign competitors' price index, *FP*, is a weighted index of average unit export price for Germany in terms of the Japanese yen. German export price was used because the German steel industry is comparable to its Japanese counterpart in terms of international competitiveness. The weight used for constructing *FP* is the share of foreign producers in the world market defined as [*1 − (EXP = WEXP)*]. In 1960, the Japanese share in the world market was 5.3 percent. However, it reached 14.7 percent in 1965, 17.2 percent in 1970, and 21.1 percent in 1975. By this construction, it is assumed that the German steel industry represents the group of foreign rivals with which the Japanese firms compete.

218 *Appendixes*

APPENDIX TO CHAPTER 4

Sources of Data

DS, *XS*, and *JADSL* were constructed from the Administrative Management Agency, *1965–1970–1975 Link Input–Output Tables*, Data Report 1, 1980. *JC4M* was constructed from the Economic Planning Agency, Economic Research Institute, *Sangyo soshiki bunseki datashu I* [*Data Base*

Table A.4.1. *Definitions of variables used in Chapter 4*

Variable	Definition
DS	Domestic share = 1 − export share (XS), Japan.
JADSL, USADSL	Purchased advertising divided by total output.
JC4M, USC4M	Four-firm producer concentration ratio divided by one plus the ratio of imports to total shipments.
JCDR, USCDR	Cost–Disadvantage Ratio: value added per worker in the smallest establishments accounting for half of shipments in the industry divided by value added per worker in the largest establishments accounting for the other half.
JGR	The change in industry shipments between 1967 and 1970 divided by shipments in 1967 and multiplied by 1/3.
JKSL	Gross book value of fixed assets divided by value of shipments.
JKREQ, USKREQ	The average shipments of the largest establishments accounting for 50% of industry shipments multiplied by the ratio of total assets to shipments in the industry if the cost–disadvantage ratio is less than 0.90; zero otherwise.
JMESCDR, USMESCDR	The average shipments of the largest establishments accounting for 50% of industry shipments divided by total industry shipments if the cost disadvantage ratio is less than 0.90; zero otherwise.
JPCM, USPCM	Price–Cost Margin: value added minus payroll divided by value of shipments, minus purchased advertising divided by total output.
USPCMFIT	Fitted value of U.S. price–cost margin estimated from an equation that determines USPCM by U.S. structural variables. See Yamawaki (1986).
XS	Export share: exports divided by total shipments, Japan.

Notes: (1) the prefixes *J* and *U* stand for Japan and United States, respectively.
(2) DS, *XS*, *JADSL*, *JKSL*, *JPCM* are constructed for 1970. *JC4M*, *JCDR*, *JKREQ*, and *JMESCDR*, are for 1968. All of the U.S. variables are constructed for 1967.
(3) The number of observations is 69.

for Industrial Organization Analysis I], 1976. When needed, *JC4M* was constructed as a shipment-weighted average of constituent product class concentration. *JGR, JKSL, JPCM, JKREQ, JCDR, JMESCDR* were constructed from the Ministry of International Trade and Industry, *Census of Manufacturers.*

USC4M was constructed from U.S. Bureau of the Census, *Census of Manufacturers,* 1967, vol. 1. The U.S. import share used to adjust concentration was obtained from U.S. International Trade Commission, Office of Economic Research, *The U.S. International Trade Commission's Industrial Characteristics and Trade Performance Databank,* 1975. *USCDR, USKREQ,* and *USMESCDR* were constructed from, U.S. Bureau of Census, *Census of Manufacturers.* And *USADSL* was constructed from U.S. Bureau of Economic Analysis, *Input–Output Structure of the U.S. Economy:* 1967, 1974.

APPENDIX TO CHAPTER 5

Notes to the Theoretical Model

To obtain equilibrium solutions, the following conditions are imposed:

$$\Pi_{dd} = \partial^2 \Pi / \partial D^2 < 0,$$
$$\Pi^*_{ff} = \partial^2 \Pi^* / \partial D^{*2} < 0,$$
$$\Pi_{df} = \partial^2 \Pi / \partial D \partial D^* < 0,$$
$$\Pi^*_{fd} = \partial^2 \Pi^* / \partial D^* \partial D < 0,$$
$$J = \Pi_{dd}\Pi^*_{ff} - \Pi_{df}\Pi^*_{fd} > 0.$$

The last condition means that the effects of output on marginal profits exceed the cross effects.

The partial effects of a change in the predetermined variables are obtained by totally differentiating the first-order conditions, and by using the conditions above to obtain:

$\partial D/\partial t > 0, \partial D/\partial g > 0, \partial D/\partial W < 0, \partial D/\partial W^* > 0, \partial D/\partial K > 0, \partial D/\partial K^* < 0, \partial D/\partial Z > 0, \partial D/\partial Z^* < 0, \partial D/\partial A_d > 0, \partial D/\partial A^*_d < 0, \partial D^*/\partial t < 0, \partial D^*/\partial g < 0, \partial D^*/\partial W > 0, \partial D^*/\partial W^* < 0, \partial D^*/\partial K < 0, \partial D^*/\partial K^* > 0, \partial D^*/\partial Z < 0, \partial D^*/\partial Z^* > 0, \partial D^*/\partial A_d < 0, \partial D^*/\partial A^*_d > 0.$

These partial effects on the equilibrium level of output are realized through shifts in the reaction functions. The partial effect on the equilibrium level of import share, $m(y)$, of a predetermined variable y_i is

$$\partial m/\partial y_i = \{D(\partial D^*/\partial y_i)[(1 - 1/e_{ff}) + \eta_{df}] - D^*(\partial D/\partial y_i)$$
$$\times [(1 - 1/e_{dd}) + \eta_{fd}]\}/(P_d D + P_d^* D^*)^2,$$

where

$$e_{ff} = -(\partial D^*/\partial P_d^*)(P_d^*/D^*),$$
$$e_{dd} = -(\partial D/\partial P_d)(P_d/D),$$
$$\eta_{df} = -(\partial P_d/\partial D^*)(D^*/P_d),$$
$$\eta_{fd} = -(\partial P_d^*/\partial D)(D/P_d^*).$$

The domestic and foreign firms always operate where $e_{dd} > 1$ and $e_{ff} > 1$, so that the terms in both square brackets in the equation above are positive, yielding conditions (5.14) and (5.15) in the text.

Table A.5.1. *Definitions of variables used for the statistical analysis in Section 5.3*

Abbreviated Name	Variable
USMJ	Japanese imports in U.S./(U.S. total shipments – U.S. total exports + U.S. total imports), 1977.
USMNONJ	Non-Japanese imports in U.S./(U.S. total shipments – U.S. total exports + U.S. total imports), 1977.
DISTANCE	Mile radius within which 80% of industry shipments were made, 1963.
USNTB	U.S. nontariff barrier index, 1970.
USNOT	U.S. nominal rate of tariff protection, 1970.
CONSD	Dummy variable equal to one if the industry sells primarily consumer goods, zero if producer goods.
AD	Purchased advertising/total output, 1967 for US and 1970 for Japan.
RD	R&D expenditure/total sales, averaged for 1968, 1972, and 1976.
KGROW	Change in gross fixed assets (in 1972 price) 1972–1977/gross fixed assets 1972.
SGROW	Change in shipments 1967–1977/shipments 1967.
CR4	Four-firm producer concentration ratio, 1967 for US and 1968 for Japan.
ULC	(Wages paid/number of production workers)*(total employment/value added), 1975.

Notes: The number of observations is 24.

Table A.5.2. *Definitions of variables used in the statistical analysis in Section 5.4*

Abbreviated Name	Variable
DIST	Total employment in U.S. distribution subsidiaries more than 50% owned by Japanese manufacturing companies, 1986
EXP	Total Japanese exports to U.S. markets, 1986
USEMP	Total industry employment, US, 1984
JKL	Gross fixed assets/total industry employment, Japan, 1984
TRN	Mile radius within which 80% of industry shipments were made, U.S., 1963
USRDS	Cost of company R&D/sales, U.S., 1977
USGR	Change in shipments 1976–1984/shipments 1976, U.S.
CONSD	Dummy variable equal to one if the industry is judged to sell primarily consumer nonconvenience goods.

Notes: The number of observations is 44.

Sources of Data Used for the Statistical Analysis in Section 5.3

JAD was constructed from the Administrative Management Agency, *1965–1970–1975 Link Input–Output Tables,* Data Report 1, 1980. *JCR4* was constructed from the Economic Planning Agency, Economic Research Institute, *Sangyo shoshiki buseki datashu I [Database for industrial organization analysis],* 1976. For some industries, it is a shipment-weighted average of constituent product class concentration. *JKGROW, JSGROW,* and *JULC* were constructed from the Ministry of International Trade and Industry, *Census of manufacturers.* The 1977 gross fixed assets to construct *JKGROW* were deflated by the GNP deflator for nonresidential durable equipment estimated by the Bank of Japan. *JRD* was taken from the Bureau of Statistics, Office of the Prime Minister, *Report on the Survey of Research and Development in Japan.* The data are available for only twenty-four broadly defined industries. It is assumed that the value for each was common for each of the forty-two industries included within it.

The 1977 *USIMPJ* was obtained from the U.S. Bureau of Census, *U.S. Imports: Consumption and General SIC-based Products by World Areas,* Report FT 210/Annual 1977. *USNOT* and *USNTB* were obtained from the U.S. International Trade Commission, Office of Economic Research, *The U.S. International Trade Commission's Industrial Characteristics and Trade Performance Databank,* 1975. *USNTB* is an index based on fifteen nontariff barriers in 1970, described in U.S. Tariff Commission, *Trade Barriers,* Report to the Committee on Finance of the United States Senate, Part 4, Washington, DC, 1974. *USCR4, USULC, USKGROW,* and *USSGROW* were constructed from U.S. Bureau of the Census, *Census of Manufacturers,* Vol. 1. The 1977 gross fixed assets to construct *USKGROW* were deflated by the GNP implicit deflator for nonresidential producers' durable equipment. *USCR4* at the four-digit U.S. SIC level was aggregated to the level used in Chapter 5 using shipments as weights. *USAD* was constructed from the U.S. Bureau of Economic Analysis, *Input-Output Structure of the U.S. Economy: 1967,* 1974. *USRD* was taken from National Science Foundation, *Research and Development in Industry,* Washington, DC. It is based on two-digit SIC data with values repeated at the three-digit level as in the case of Japanese R&D variable. *DISTANCE* was obtained from Weiss (1972) and is a weighted average of the four-digit shipping radius.

Sources of Data Used in the Statistical Analysis in Section 5.4

DIST was constructed from Toyokeizai, *kaigai shishutsu kigyo soran: 1988* [*Directory of Japanese Corporations Abroad*], Tokyo: Toyokeizaishinposha, 1988. The number of employees in the U.S. distribution subsidiaries of Japanese manufacturing corporations was aggregated to the industry level to obtain this variable. A U.S. subsidiary is defined as a subsidiary more than 50-percent owned by these manufacturing companies.

EXP was obtained from Japan External Trade Organization, *White Paper on International Trade, Japan,* Tokyo: JETRO. *JKL* was constructed from the Japan, Ministry of International Trade and Industry, *Census of Manufacturers: Report by Industries.*

USRDS was constructed from U.S. Federal Trade Commission, *Statistical Report: Annual Line of Business Report 1977.* (The *FTC* industry was converted by using the table in appendix E in the volume.) *USEMP* and *USGR* were constructed from U.S. Bureau of Census, *Census of Manufacturers.* The 80 percent shipping radius, *TRN,* was obtained from Weiss (1972, appendix) and is a weighted average of the four-digit shipping radius. *CONSD* was constructed based on Porter (1976, table 6.1, pp. 139–140).

APPENDIX TO CHAPTER 6

Table A.6.1. *Definitions of variables used in Section 6.3*

Variables defined at the subsidiary level:

DIV	Dummy variable equal to one if the subsidiary's principal two-digit industry is different from the parent's principal two-digit industry, zero otherwise. (US:0.210, 0.408; Europe: 0.096, 0.296.)
EMODE	Dummy variable equal to one if the subsidiary is established by acquisition, zero if it is established by green-field investment. (US: 0.283, 0.451; Europe: 0.310, 0.464.)
EXPRNC	Number of countries in which the parent firm has subsidiaries prior to the establishment of the subsidiary. (US: 10.181, 8.195; Europe: 12.736, 9.268.)
US	Dummy variable equal to one if the subsidiary's source country is the United States. (Full sample: 0.653, 0.476.)

Variables defined at the industry level:

RTA	An index of revealed technological advantage. The index is defined as $RTA_{ijt} = (P_{ijt}/\Sigma_j P_{ijt}) / (\Sigma_i P_{ijt} \Sigma_i \Sigma_j P_{ijt})$ where P_{ijt} is the number of patents granted in the United States in industry i to residents of country j in period t. This variable is constructed for the Japanese industry at the three-digit level to which the parent's product is classified. It is the average over the 7-year period, 1980–1986. (US: 1.189, 0.443; Europe: 1.332, 0.464.)
GROW	Rate of growth of industry shipments at the three-digit industry in which the subsidiary is established. The U.S variable is constructed for the census years, 1982 and 1987, while the European variable is for the period of 1981–1988. (US: 0.349, 0.327; Europe: 0.804, 0.457.)
SCALE	Employment in the subsidiary divided by total employment of the entered industry (in percentage). In the regression analysis, *SCALE* is estimated as an instrumental variable. The instrumental variable was obtained by regressing *SCALE* on a set of exogenous variables such as capital intensity, R&D intensity, industry growth, concentration and parent size. (US: 0.501, 1.886; Europe; 0.284, 0.786.)

Time-dependent variables

YENUSD *YENDM* *YENGBP*	Average annual nominal exchange rate expressed in units of the Japanese yen per unit of the U.S. dollar (*YENUSD*), the German mark (*YENDM*), and the British pound (*YENGBP*).

Numbers reported in parentheses are (mean, standard deviation) for the U.S. sample ($N = 371$), the European sample ($N = 198$), and the full sample ($N = 371$) used for the estimation in Tables 6.3 and 6.4.

Sources of Data

The data on the subsidiary were obtained from Toyo keizai, *kaigai shin-shutsu kigyo soran* [*Directory of Japanese Firms Investing Abroad*], Tokyo: Toyo keizai shinposha, various years. *EXPRNC* and *EMODE* were constructed from this data source. The data on the parent firm were obtained from Nihon keizai shinbunsha, *nikkei kaisha joho*, Tokyo: Nihon keizai shinbunsha. The data at the subsidiary level were matched with the data at the parent level to construct *DIV*.

RTA was constructed from the patent data published by U.S. Patent and Trademark Office, *Patenting Trends in the United States: 1963–1986*, Washington, DC: U.S. Patent and Trademark Office, 1987. *RTA* is defined at the three-digit level of industry classification to which the subsidiary's primary product is classified and is measured as an average of annual figures over the period of 1980–1986. *GROW* for the U.S. industry was constructed from the U.S. Bureau of the Census, *Census of Manufacturers*. *GROW* for the European industry is constructed from Statistical Office of the European Communities, *Structure and Activity of Industry*. These variables were defined for the subsidiary's industry at the three-digit level of industry classification.

SCALE was constructed for the subsidiary's primary industry defined at the three-digit level of industry classification for each region. Because of the unavailability of data for several European countries, the European industry is represented by Germany, France, the United Kingdom, and Italy. This procedure presumably overestimates the subsidiary's share in the European market. Because data on the initial scale of entry were unavailable, this variable was constructed for 1990. Because more than 90 percent of Japanese entries in the U.S. sample and more than 80 percent in the European sample took place after 1985, measurement error, if any, caused by this procedure is expected to be minimal.

YENUSD, YENDM, and *YENGBP* were obtained from the IMF Statistics Department, *International Financial Statistic Yearbook*.

Table A.6.2. *Definitions of variables used in Section 6.4*

Variables	
AQECI	The total number of entries by acquisition that took place during the 5- and 3-consecutive years *prior* to the establishment of the subsidiary, divided by the total of all entries that were established by acquisition during the 1980–1990 period. These indexes are constructed from the data on Japanese entrants to the United States in the same three-digit industry to which the subsidiary is classified.
GFECI	The total number of entries by green-field investments that took place during the 5- and 3-consecutive years *prior* to the establishment of the subsidiary, divided by the total of all subsidiaries that were established by green-field investments during the 1980–1990 period. These indexes are constructed from the data on Japanese entrants to the United States in the same three-digit industry to which the subsidiary is classified.
CR8	Eight-firm producer concentration ratio.
GROUP	Dummy variable equal to one if the subsidiary is identified as supplier within a vertical assembler–supplier corporate group.

Sources of Data

The data on the subsidiary were obtained from Toyo keizai, *kaigai shin-shutsu kigyo soran* [*Directory of Japanese firms investing abroad*], Tokyo: Toyo keizai shinposha, various years. *GFECI*, *AQECI*, and *GROUP* were all constructed from this data source. All these variables were defined at the subsidiary level. The data on the parent firm was obtained from Nihon keizai shinbunsha, *nikkei kaisha joho*, Tokyo: Nihon keizai shinbunsha. *CR8* was obtained from Ministry of International Trade and Industry, *Heisei 7 nen kigyokatsudo kihonchosa hokokusho* [1995 benchmark survey of *corporate activity*]: *sogo tokeihyo*, vol. 1. *CR8* was constructed for 1991. The definitions of all other variables used here are the same as those in Chapter 6.

APPENDIX TO CHAPTER 7

Table A.7.1. *Definitions of variables used in Section 7.2*

JFDIinUS	Number counts of Japanese entries into the U.S. manufacturing industry.
JFDIinEU	Number counts of Japanese entries into the European manufacturing industry.
EUFDIinJ	Number counts of European entries into the Japanese manufacturing industry.
USFDIinJ	Number counts of U.S. entries into the Japanese manufacturing industry.

All these variables are defined at the three-digit SIC in Japan and measured annually between 1980 and 1990. To make the data comparable between Japanese entries and U.S. and European entries, the industries where Japanese entries in the U.S. and European markets are observed are identified and used as units of observations. Although the U.S. and European firms entered in the Japanese industries where no Japanese entry to U.S. and European markets are recorded, these industries are not included in the statistical analysis. This treatment of data created some missing data for the U.S. and European samples. Japanese entry equations are estimated for 1980–1990, and the U.S. and European data are estimated for 1982–1990.

The data source for Japanese entries in the U.S. and European markets is the same as the source used in the analysis of Chapter 6. The data source for U.S. and European entries in Japan is described in Sources of Data in this appendix.

Table A.7.2. *Definitions of variables used in Section 7.3*

Variables defined at the subsidiary level:

EXIT — Dummy variable equal to one if the subsidiary exited, and zero otherwise (0.146, 0.354).

SUBSIZE — Employment of the subsidiary (in logarithm) (4.079, 1.362).

PARSIZE — Employment of the subsidiary's parent (in logarithm) (9.273, 2.153).

KEIRETSU — Dummy variable equal to one if the subsidiary is joint venture with a Japanese company that belongs to the presidents' club of the leading six horizontal *keiretsu*. The six horizontal *keiretsu* (or *kigyo shudan*) members are Mitsui, Mitsubishi, Sumitomo, Fuyo, Sanwa, and, DKB (0.203, 0.403).

JV — Dummy variable equal to one if the subsidiary is joint venture with a Japanese company that is not the member of the six horizontal *keiretsu* (0.467, 0.500).

VIDIST — Dummy variable equal to one if the MNE has a distribution subsidiary or forms a joint venture with agreement to sell its product directly to the Japanese partner, and zero otherwise (0.199, 0.400).

NOPLANT — Dummy variable equal to one if the subsidiary does not maintain own manufacturing facility in Japan, and zero otherwise. (0.390, 0.489).

EXPORT — Share of the subsidiary's total sales accounted for by its exports (in percentage) (9.773, 17.916).

IMPORT — Share of the subsidiary's total procurement accounted for by imports (in percentage) (38.082, 38.234).

Variables defined at industry level:

ADSL — Ratio of advertising expenditure to the value of shipments. (0.011, 0.010).

RDSL — Ratio of R&D expenditure to the value of shipments (0.035, 0.023).

HI — The Herfindahl index of seller concentration. (0.054, 0.039).

DISTSIZE — Size of Japanese independent wholesalers relative to U.S. wholesalers in the industry, defined as Japanese sales per wholesale establishments as percentage of U.S. establishments (69.661, 21.931).

WAGEDIF — Difference in average salary per employee between foreign firms (w_f) and Japanese firms (w_d) in the industry, defined as $(w_f - w_d)/w_d$. (0.179, 0.214).

Numbers reported in parentheses are (Mean, Standard Deviation) for the full sample ($N = 246$) used to estimate Probit models reported in Table 7.2.

Sources of Data

The information on subsidiaries was obtained from Toyo Keizai (Ed.), *Gaishikei kigyo soran* [*Foreign Affiliated Companies in Japan: A Comprehensive Directory*], Tokyo: Toyo Keizai Shinposha, various years. This survey has been published annually since 1986. *EXIT, EXPORT, IMPORT, NOPLANT, PARSIZE, SUBSIZE*, and *VIDIST* were all constructed from this data source. These variables were constructed for 1994 if the subsidiary survived and for the last year before exit otherwise. *KEIRETSU* and *JV* were constructed based on information provided in Toyo Keizai (Ed.), *Kigyo keiretsu soran* [*Directory of Corporate Keiretsu*], Tokyo: Toyo Keizai Shinposha.

Among the industry-specific variables, *ADSL, RDSL*, and *HI* were constructed from The Ministry of International Trade and Industry (MITI), *Heisei 7nen kigyokatsudo kihonchosa hokokusho* [*1995 benchmark survey of corporate activity*]: *sogo tokeihyo*, vol. 1, (Tokyo: MITI). *WAGEDIF* was estimated from data provided in appendix table 1 of Nakamura, Fukao, and Shibuya (1995). These industry variables were constructed for 1991 for which the data were available. The level of aggregation is at the three-digit level defined by the Japanese industry classification system. The subsidiary's primary product is classified to this three-digit industry classification. *DISTSIZE* was constructed from the MITI, *Census of Retail and Wholesale Trade* (Tokyo: MITI).

APPENDIX TO CHAPTER 8

Table A.8.1. *Definitions of variables used in Chapter 8*

Market Share	Market share, defined as unit sales divided by total unit sales of Audi, BMW, Mercedes-Benz, Jaguar, Lexus, Cadillac, and Lincoln. Unit sales of convertibles and SUV are not included.
Entry	Market share of Lexus, defined as Lexus's unit sales divided by total unit sales of Audi, BMW, Mercedes-Benz, Jaguar, Lexus, Cadillac, and Lincoln. Unit sales of convertibles and SUV are not included.
Exchange Rate	Annual average nominal exchange rate expressed in units of the source country's currency per unit of U.S. dollars (in logarithm).
Wage	Annual average hourly earnings in terms of the source country's currency (in logarithm).
Tax	Dummy variable equal to one for the 1991–1997 period, and zero for the 1986–1990 period.
New Model	Dummy variable equal to one if a new model is introduced, and zero otherwise.
Time	Time trend.
Price	Annual dealer list price for a basic model in the model class in terms of U.S. dollars (in logarithm).

Sources of Data

Exchange Rate and *Wage* were obtained from the IMF Statistics Department, *International Financial Statistics Yearbook*. *Entry*, *Market Share*, *Price*, and *New Model* were all constructed from the data published in *Automotive News* and *Ward's Automotive Yearbook*.

Price is constructed for the following models: Audi, 5000-series(A6; BMW, 3-series (325/328), 5-series (525/528), and 7-series (735/740); Mercedes-Benz, 190(C-class (C-280), E-class (300/320), and S-class (420); Jaguar, XJ-6(XJ-40/XJ8, and Vanden Plus; Cadillac, DeVille, and SeVille; Lincoln, MKVII/VIII, Town Car, and Continental; Lexus, ES, GS (after 1993), and LS.

APPENDIX TO CHAPTER 9

Table A.9.1. *Definitions of variables used in Chapter 9*

Variables defined at the subsidiary level:

EMODE	Dummy variable equal to one if the subsidiary is established by acquisition; zero if it is established by green-field investment (0.301, 0.459).
AQECI	The total number of entries by acquisition that took place during the 5 consecutive years *prior* to the establishment of the subsidiary, divided by the total of all entries that were established by acquisition during the 1980–1990 period. These indexes are constructed from the data on Japanese entrants to the United States in the same three-digit industry to which the subsidiary is classified (0.128, 0.167).
DIV	Dummy variable equal to one if the subsidiary's principal two-digit industry is different from the parent's principal two-digit industry; zero otherwise (0.222, 0.416).
ECI	The total number of entries that took place during the 5 consecutive years *prior* to the establishment of the subsidiary, divided by the total of all subsidiaries that were established during the 1980–1990 period. These indexes are constructed from the data on Japanese entrants to the United States in the same three-digit industry to which the subsidiary is classified (0.215, 0.138).
GFECI	The total number of entries by green-field investments that took place during the 5 consecutive years *prior* to the establishment of the subsidiary, divided by the total of all subsidiaries that were established during the 1980–1990 period. These indexes are constructed from the data on Japanese entrants to the United States in the same three-digit industry to which the subsidiary is classified (0.226, 0.178).
EXIT	Dummy variable equal to one if the subsidiary exits from the U.S. market in the 1990–2000 period, and zero otherwise (0.146, 0.353).
EXPRNC	Number of countries in which the parent firm has subsidiaries prior to the establishment of the subsidiary in logarithm (1.947, 0.937).
PSIZE	Employment size of the Japanese parent in logarithm (8.521, 1.304).
SCALE	Employment size in the subsidiary divided by total employment of the entered industry. In the regression analysis of Table 9.2, *SCALE* is estimated as an instrumental variable. The instrumental variable was obtained by regressing *SCALE* on a set of exogenous variables such as capital intensity, R&D intensity, industry growth, and seller concentration (0.523, 1.207).

Variables defined at the industry level:

KL	Gross fixed assets divided by total industry employment (12.606, 6.562).
RDSL	R&D expenditure divided by industry shipments (0.040, 0.062).

Table A.9.1. *(Continued)*

RTA	An index of revealed technological advantage. The index is defined as $RTA_{ijt} = (P_{ijt}/\Sigma_j P_{ijt}) / (\Sigma_i P_{ijt} \Sigma_i \Sigma_j P_{ijt})$, where P_{ijt} is the number of patents granted in the United States in industry i to residents of country j in period t. This variable is constructed for the Japanese industry at the three-digit level to which the parent's product is classified. It is the average over the 7-year period, 1980–1986 (1.178, 0.437).
GROW	Rate of growth of shipments between the census years, 1982 and 1987, in the U.S. three-digit industry in which the subsidiary is classified (0.353, 0.328).
GROWP	Rate of growth of shipments between 1987 and 1996, in the U.S. three-digit industry in which the subsidiary is classified (0.693, 0.397).

Time-dependent variable defined at the time of entry

YENUSD	Average annual nominal exchange rate expressed in units of the Japanese yen per unit of the U.S. dollar (152.01, 29.01).

Numbers reported in parentheses are (mean, standard deviation) for the sample ($N = 316$).

Sources of Data

The data on the subsidiary was obtained from Toyo keizai, *kaigai shinshutsu kigyo soran* [*Directory of Japanese firms investing abroad*], Tokyo: Toyo keizai shinposha, various years. *GFECI, AQECI, ECI, EXRNC, SCALE, EMODE, PSIZE* were all constructed from this data source. All these variables are defined at the subsidiary-level. The data on the parent firm was obtained from Nihon keizai shinbunsha, *nikkei kaisha joho*, Tokyo: Nihon keizai shinbunsha. The data at the subsidiary level was matched with the data at the parent level to construct *DIV*. The subsidiary's industry in the U.S. market was defined at the three-digit level to construct *SCALE*.

The industry variables defined for the Japanese industry, *KL* and *RDSL*, were all constructed from Ministry of International Trade and Industry, *Heisei 7-nen kigyokatsudo kihonchosa hokokusho* [*1995 benchmark survey of corporate activity*]: *sogo tokeihyo*, vol. 1, Tokyo: The Ministry of International Trade and Industry. These industry variables were constructed for 1991 for which data were available. This data source was used instead of other government sources because this new data set published R&D

expenditures and seller concentration at the three-digit level. However, the first observation year available from this data source is 1991. The level of aggregation is at the three-digit level defined by the Japanese industry classification system.

RTA was constructed from the patent data published by U.S. Patent and Trademark Office, *Patenting Trends in the United States: 1963–1986,* Washington, DC: U.S. Patent and Trademark Office, 1987. *RTA,* here, is defined as the three-digit level of industry classification to which the subsidiary's primary product is classified and measured as an average of annual figures over the period of 1980–1986. *GROW* and *GROWP* were constructed from U.S. Bureau of the Census, *Census of Manufacturers.* They were defined for the subsidiary's industry at the three-digit level of industry classification. *YENUSD* was obtained from the IMF Statistics Department, *International Financial Statistics Yearbook.*

References

Abegglen, J. C., and G. Stalk, Jr. 1985. *Kaisha: The Japanese Corporation*. New York: Basic Books.

Administrative Management Agency. Japan. 1980. *1965–1970–1975 Link Input–Output Tables*, Data Report 1. Tokyo: Administrative and Management Agency.

Altomonte, C., and E. Pennings. 2003. "Oligopolistic Reaction to Foreign Investment in Discrete Choice Panel Data Models," Universita Bocconi, IGIER Working Paper No. 243.

Andersson, T., and T. Fredriksson. 2000. "Distinction between Intermediate and Finished Products in Intra-Firm Trade," *International Journal of Industrial Organization, 18*(5), 773–792.

Ando, A., and A. Auerbach. 1988. "The Cost of Capital in the United States and Japan: A Comparison," *Journal of the Japanese and International Economies, 2,* 134–158.

Aoki, M. 1984. "Shareholders' Non-Unanimity on Investment Financing: Banks vs. Individual Investors," in M. Aoki (Ed.), *The Economic Analysis of the Japanese Firm.* Amsterdam: North-Holland, 193–224.

Aoki, M. 1986. "Horizontal vs. Vertical Information Structure of the Firm," *American Economic Review, 76,* 971–983.

Aoki, M. 1987. "The Japanese Firm in Transition," in K. Yamamura and Y. Yasuba (Eds.), *The Political Economy of Japan: Volume 1. The Domestic Transformation.* Palo Alto, CA: Stanford University Press, 263–288.

Aoki, M. 1990. "Toward an Economic Model of the Japanese Firm," *Journal of Economic Literature, 28,* 1–27.

Artus, J. R. 1970. "The Short-Run Effects of Domestic Demand Pressure on British Export Performance," *IMF Staff Papers, 17*(July), 247–275.

Asaba, S., and M. B. Lieberman. 1997. "Market Share Instability and Size Similarity: Some Evidence of Behavioral Similarity among Japanese Firms," John E. Anderson Graduate School of Management at UCLA, Working paper.

Asaba, S., and M. B. Lieberman. 1999. "Why Do Firms Behave Similarly? A Study of New Product Introduction in the Japanese Soft-Drink Industry," *Academy of Management Proceedings,* 1999 BPS: M1–M6.

Asaba, S., and H. Yamawaki. 2005. "Changes in the Determinants of Profits: A Study of Foreign Subsidiaries in the Japanese Manufacturing Industries in the 1980s and 1990s," in T. Roehl and A. Bird (Eds.), *Japanese Firms in Transition: Responding to the Globalization Challenge, Advances in International Management, 17,* 289–324.

Asanuma, B. 1989. "Manufacture–Supplier Relationships in Japan and the Concept of Relation-Specific Skill," *Journal of the Japanese and International Economies, 3,* 1–30.

Audretsch, D. B. 1995. *Innovation and Industry Evolution.* Cambridge, MA: MIT Press.

Audretsch, D. B. 2002. "The Dynamic Role of Small Firms: Evidence from the US," *Small Business Economics, 18,* 13–40.

Audretsch, D. B., and H. Yamawaki. 1988. "R&D Rivalry, Industrial Policy, and U.S.-Japanese Trade," *Review of Economics and Statistics, 70,* 438–447.

Audretsch, D. B., L. Sleuwaegen, and H. Yamawaki. 1989. "The Dynamics of Export Competition," in D. B. Audretsch, L. Sleuwaegen, and H. Yamawaki (Eds.), *The Convergence of International and Domestic Markets.* Amsterdam: North-Holland, 211–248.

Bain, J. S. 1956. *Barriers to New Competition: Their Characters and Consequences in Manufacturing Industries.* Cambridge, MA: Harvard University Press.

Balassa, B., and M. Noland. 1989. "The Changing Comparative Advantage of Japan and the United States," *Journal of the Japanese and International Economies, 3,* 174–188.

Baldwin, J. R. 1995. *The Dynamics of Industrial Competition: A North American Perspective.* Cambridge, UK: Cambridge University Press.

Baldwin, R. E. 1988. "Hysteresis in Import Prices: The Beachhead Effect," *American Economic Review, 78*(September), 773–785.

Baldwin, R. E., and P. R. Krugman. 1988a. "Market Access and International Competition: A Simulation Study of 16K Random Access Memories," in R. C. Feenstra (Ed.), *Empirical Methods for International Trade.* Cambridge, MA: MIT Press, 171–197.

Baldwin, R. E., and P. R. Krugman. 1988b. "Industrial Policy and International Competition in Wide-Bodied Jet Aircraft," in R. E. Baldwin (Ed.), *Trade Policy and Empirical Analysis.* Chicago: University of Chicago Press, 45–71.

Baldwin, R. E., and G. I. P. Ottaviano. 2001. "Multiproduct Multinationals and Reciprocal FDI Dumping," *Journal of International Economics, 54,* 429–448.

Ball, R. J., J. R. Eaton, and M. D. Steuer. 1966. "The Relationship between United Kingdom Export Performance in Manufacturers and the Internal Pressure of Demand," *Economic Journal, 76*(September), 501–518.

Banerjee, A. V. 1992. "A Simple Model of Herd Behavior," *Quarterly Journal of Economics, 107,* 797–817.

Barkema, H. G., J. H. J. Bell, and J. Pennings. 1996. "Foreign Entry, Cultural Barriers, and Learning," *Strategic Management Journal, 17*(2), 151–166.

Belderbos, R. 1997a. *Japanese Electronic Multinationals and Strategic Trade Policies.* Oxford: Oxford University Press.

Belderbos, R. 1997b. "Antidumping and Tariff Jumping: Japanese Firms' FDI in the European Union and the United States," *Weltwirtschaftliches Archiv, 133,* 419–457.

Belderbos, R. 2003. "Entry Mode, Organizational Learning, and R&D in Foreign Affiliates: Evidence from Japanese Firms," *Strategic Management Journal, 24*, 235–259.

Belderbos, R., and L. Sleuwaegen. 1996. "Japanese Firms and the Decision to Invest Abroad: Business Groups and Regional Core Networks," *Review of Economics and Statistics, 78*, 221–231.

Belderbos, R., and L. Sleuwaegen. 1998. "Tariff Jumping DFI and Export Substitution: Japanese Electronics Firms in Europe," *International Journal of Industrial Organization, 16*, 601–638.

Bergsten, F. C., T. Horst, and T. H. Moran. 1978. *American Multinationals and American Interests.* Washington, DC: Brookings Institution.

Bernard, J. R., J. Eaton, J. B. Jensen, and S. Kortum. 2003. "Plants and Productivity in International Trade," *American Economic Review, 93*, 1268–1290.

Bernard, J. R., and J. B. Jensen. 2004. "Why Some Firms Export?" *Review of Economics and Statistics, 86*, 561–569.

Biggadike, E. R. 1979. *Corporate Diversification: Entry, Strategy, and Performance.* Cambridge, MA: Harvard University Press.

Bikhchandani, S., D. Hirshleifer, and I. Welch. 1992. "A Theory of Fads, Fashion, Custom, and Cultural Change as Informational Cascades," *Journal of Political Economy, 100*, 992–1026.

Birkinshaw, J., and N. Hood. 1998. "Multinational Subsidiary Evolution: Capability and Charter Change in Foreign-Owned Subsidiary Companies," *Academy of Management Review, 23*, 773–795.

Birkinshaw, J., N. Hood, and S. Jonsson. 1998. "Building Firm-Specific Advantages in Multinational Corporations: The Role of Subsidiary Initiative," *Strategic Management Journal, 19*, 221–241.

Blonigen, B. A. 1997. "Firm-Specific Assets and the Link between Exchange Rates and Foreign Direct Investment," *American Economic Review, 87*(June), 447–465.

Blonigen, B. A. 2001. "In Search of Substitution between Foreign Production and Boyan, J. Exports," *Journal of International Economics, 53*, 81–104.

Brainard, S. L. 1993. "A Simple Theory of Multinational Corporations and Trade, with a Trade-Off between Proximity and Concentration," NBER Working Paper No. 4269.

Boyan, J. Brainard, S. L. 1997. "An Empirical Assessment of the Proximity-Concentration Trade-Off between Multinational Sales and Trade," *American Economic Review, 87*, 520–544.

Brandenburger, A., and B. Polak. 1996. "When Managers Cover Their Posteriors: Making the Decisions the Market Wants to See," *Rand Journal of Economics, 27*, 523–541.

Brander, J. A. 1981. "Intra-Industry Trade in Identical Commodities," *Journal of International Economics, 11*(February), 1–14.

Brander, J. A., and P. R. Krugman. 1983. "A Reciprocal Dumping Model of International Trade," *Journal of International Economics, 15*(November), 313–321.

Brander, J., and B. Spencer. 1984. "Tariff Protection and Imperfect Competition," in H. Kierzkowski (Ed.), *Monopolistic Competition and International Trade.* Oxford: Clarendon Press, 194–206.

Branstetter, L., and M. Sakakibara. 1998. "Japanese Research Consortia: A Microeconometric Analysis of Industrial Policy," *Journal of Industrial Economics, 46,* 207–233.

Bunch, D., and R. Smiley. 1992. "Who Deters Entry? Evidence on the Use of Strategic Entry Deterrents," *Review of Economics and Statistics, 74,* 509–521.

Cabral, L. M. B. 1995. "Conjectural Variations as a Reduced Form," *Economic Letters, 49,* 397–402.

Cantwell, J. 1989. *Technological Innovations in Multinational Corporations.* London: Basil Blackwell.

Casson, M. and Associates. 1986. *Multinationals and World Trade: Vertical Integration and the Division of Labor in World Industries.* London: Allen & Unwin.

Caves, R. E. 1971. "International Corporations: The Industrial Economics of Foreign Investment," *Economica, 38*(February), 176–193.

Caves, R. E. 1974. "International Trade, International Investment, and Imperfect Markets," Special Papers in International Economics, No. 10, November, International Finance Section, Department of Economics, Princeton University.

Caves, R. E. 1989. "International Differences in Industrial Organization," in R. Schmalensee and R. Willig (Eds.), *Handbook of Industrial Organization* (Vol. 2). Amsterdam: North-Holland, 1225–1252.

Caves, R. E. 1991. "Corporate Mergers in International Economic Integration," in A. Giovannini and C. Mayer (Eds.), *European Financial Integration.* Cambridge, UK: Cambridge University Press, 136–171.

Caves, R. E. 1993. "Japanese Investment in the United States: Lessons for the Economic Analysis of Foreign Investment," *World Economy, 16*(May), 279–300.

Caves, R. E. 1996. *Multinational Enterprise and Economic Analysis* (2nd ed.). Cambridge, UK: Cambridge University Press.

Caves, R. E. 1998. "Industrial Organization and New Findings on the Mobility and Turnover of Firms," *Journal of Economic Literature, 36*(December), 1947–1982.

Caves, R. E., J. Khalizadeh-Shirazi, and M. E. Porter. 1975. "Scale Economies in Statistical Analysis of Market Power," *Review of Economics and Statistics, 57,* 130–140.

Caves, R. E., and Mehra, S. K. 1986. "Entry of Foreign Multinationals into U.S. Manufacturing Industries," in M. E. Porter (Ed.), *Competition in Global Industries.* Boston: Harvard Business School Press, 449–482.

Caves, R. E., and M. E. Porter. 1976. "Barriers to Exit," in R. T. Masson and P. D. Qualls (Eds.), *Essays on Industrial Organization in Honor of Joe S. Bain.* Cambridge, MA: Ballinger, 39–70.

Caves, R. E., and M. E. Porter. 1977. "From Entry Barriers to Mobility Barriers: Conjectural Decisions and Contrived Deterrence to New Competition," *Quarterly Journal of Economics, 81,* 243–261.

Caves, R. E., M. E. Porter, and A. M. Spence, with J. T. Scott. 1980. *Competition in the Open Economy: A Model Applied to Canada.* Cambridge, MA: Harvard University Press.

Caves, R. E., and T. Pugel. 1980. "Intraindustry Differences in Conduct and Performance: Viable Strategies in U.S. Manufacturing Industries," *Monograph Series in Finance and Economics*, 1980, No. 2, Salomon Brothers Center for the Study of Financial Institutions, New York University.

Caves, R. E., and P. J. Williamson. 1985. "What is Product Differentiation, Really?" *Journal of Industrial Economics*, *34*(December), 113–131.

Caves, R. E., and M. Uekusa. 1976. *Industrial Organization in Japan.* Washington, DC: Brookings Institution.

Chang, S.-J. 1995. "International Expansion Strategy of Japanese Firms: Capability Building through Sequential Entry," *Academy of Management Journal*, *38*, 383–407.

Clark, D. P. "On the Relative Importance of International Transport Charges as a Barrier to Trade," *Quarterly Review of Economics and Business*, *21*, 127–135.

Clark, K. B., and T. Fujimoto. 1991. *Product Development Performance: Strategy, Organization and Management in the World Auto Industry.* Boston: Harvard Business School Press.

Coase, R. H. 1971. "The Nature of the Firm," *Economica*, *4*(November), 386–405.

Collis, D. J. 1991. "A Resource-Based Analysis of Global Competition: The Case of the Bearing Industry," *Strategic Management Journal*, *12*, 49–68.

Comanor, W. S., and T. A. Wilson. 1974. *Advertising and Market Power.* Cambridge, MA: Harvard University Press.

Cool, K., and I. Dierickx. 1993. "Rivalry, Strategic Groups and Firm Profitability," *Strategic Management Journal*, *14*, 47–59.

Cowling, K., and M. Waterson. 1976. "Price–Cost Margins and Market Structure," *Economica*, *43*, 267–274.

Cubbin, J., and S. Domberger. 1988. "Advertising and Post-Entry Oligopoly Behavior," *Journal of Industrial Economics*, *37*, 123–140.

Customs and Tariff Bureau, Ministry of Finance, Japan, *Nihon Gaikoku Boeki Nenpyo [Yearly Trade Statistics of Japan].* Various years.

Davies, S. W., and A. J. McGuinness. 1982. "Dumping at Less than Marginal Cost," *Journal of International Economics*, *12*(February), 169–182.

Deardorff, A. V. 1984. "Testing Trade Theories and Predicting Trade Flows," in R. W. Jones and P. B. Kenen (Eds.), *Handbook of International Economics* (Vol. 1). Amsterdam: North-Holland, 467–517.

Dixit, A. 1980. "The Role of Investment in Entry Deterrence," *Economic Journal*, *90*, 95–106.

Dockner, E. J. 1992. "A Dynamic Theory of Conjectural Variations," *Journal of Industrial Economics*, *40*, 377–395.

Dornbusch, R. 1987. "Exchange Rates and Prices," *American Economic Review*, *77*(March), 93–106.

Drake, T. A., and Caves, R. E. 1992. "Changing Determinants of Japan's Foreign Direct Investment in the United States," *Journal of the Japanese and International Economies*, *6*, 228–246.

Dubin, M. 1976. *Foreign Acquisitions and the Growth of the Multinational Firm*. Graduate School of Business Administration, Harvard University, D.B.A. dissertation.

Dunlevy, J. A. 1980. "A Test of the Capacity Pressure Hypothesis within a Simultaneous Equations Model of Export Performance," *Review of Economics and Statistics*, 62(February), 131–135.

Dunne, T., M. J. Roberts, and L. Samuelson. 1988. "Patterns of Firm Entry and Exit to U.S. Manufacturing Industries," *Rand Journal of Economics*, 19(Winter), 495–513.

Dunning, J. H. 1977. "Trade, Location of Economic Activity, and the MNE: A Search for an Eclectic Approach," in B. Ohlin, P.-O. Hesselborn, and P. M. Wijkman (Eds.), *The International Allocation of Economic Activity: Proceedings of a Nobel Symposium Held at Stockholm*. London: Macmillan, 395–418.

Dunning, J. H. 1986. *Japanese Participation in British Industry*. London: Croom Helm.

Dunning, J. H. 1996. "Explaining Foreign Direct Investment in Japan: Some Theoretical Insights," in M. Yoshitomi and E. M. Graham (Eds.), *Foreign Direct Investment in Japan*. Cheltenham: Edward Elgar, 8–63.

Dyer, J. H. 1996. "Specialized Supplier Networks as a Source of Competitive Advantage: Evidence from the Auto Industry," *Strategic Management Journal*, 17, 271–291.

Eads, G. C., and K. Yamamura. 1987. "The Future of Industrial Policy," in K. Yamamura and Y. Yasuba (Eds.), *The Political Economy of Japan: Volume 1. The Domestic Transformation*. Palo Alto, CA: Stanford University Press.

Eaton, J., and A. Tamura. 1994. "Bilateralism and Regionalism in Japanese and U.S. Trade and Direct Foreign Investment Patterns," *Journal of the Japanese and International Economics*, 8(December), 478–510.

Eichengreen, B. J. 1982. "The Simple Analytics of Dumping," Harvard Institute of Economic Research, Discussion Paper 943 (December).

Eichengreen, B. J., and H. van der Ven. 1984. "U.S. Antidumping Policies: The Case of Steel," in Robert E. Baldwin and A. O. Krueger (Eds.), *The Structure and Evolution of Recent U.S. Trade Policy*. Chicago: University of Chicago Press, 67–110.

Encarnation, D. J. 1987. "Cross-Investment: A Second Front of Economic Rivalry," *California Management Review*, 29, 20–48.

Encarnation, D. 1992. *Rivals Beyond Trade: America versus Japan in Global Competition*. Ithaca: Cornell University Press.

Encarnation, D., and M. Mason. 1990. "Neither MITI nor America: The Political Economy of Capital Liberalization in Japan," *International Organization*, 44(1), 25–54.

Erdilek, A. (Ed.). 1985. *Multinational as Mutual Invaders: Intra-Industry Direct Foreign Investment*. London: Croom Helm.

Ethier, W. J. 1982. "Dumping," *Journal of Political Economy*, 90(June), 487–509.

Evans, D. S. 1987. "The Relationship Between Firm Growth, Size, and Age: Evidence for 100 Manufacturing Industries," *Journal of Industrial Economics*, 35(June), 567–581.

Feenstra, R. C. 1989. "Symmetric Pass-Through of Tariffs and Exchange Rates Under Imperfect Competition: An Empirical Test," *Journal of International Economics*, 27, 25–45.

Fiegenbaum, A., and H. Thomas. 1990. "Strategic Groups and Performance: The U.S. Insurance Industry, 1974–84," *Strategic Management Journal, 11*, 197–215.

Flowers, E. B. 1976. "Oligopolistic Reactions in European and Canadian Direct Investment in the United States," *Journal of International Business Studies, 7*(Fall/Winter), 43–55.

Franko, L. G. 1976. *The European Multinationals: A Renewed Challenge to American and British Big Business.* Stamford, CT: Greylock.

Franko, L. G. 1983. *The Threat of Japanese Multinationals – How the West Can Respond.* Norwich: IRM.

Froot, K. A. 1991. "Japanese Foreign Direct Investment," NBER Working Paper, Series No. 3737.

Froot, K. A., and J. C. Stein. 1991. "Exchange Rates and Foreign Direct Investment: An Imperfect Capital Markets Approach," *Quarterly Journal of Economics, 106,* 1191–1217.

Frost, T. S., J. M. Birkinshaw, and P. Ensign. 2002. "Centers of Excellence in Multinational Corporations," *Strategic Management Journal, 23*, 997–1018.

Fujimoto, T. 1999. *The Evolution of a Manufacturing System at Toyota.* New York: Oxford University Press.

Fujita, M., P. Krugman, and A. J. Venables. 1999. *The Spatial Economy: Cities, Regions, and International Trade.* Cambridge, MA: MIT Press.

Fukao, K., and T. Amano. 2004. *Tainichi Chokusetsu Toshi to Nihon Keizai [Foreign Direct Investment and the Japanese Economy].* Tokyo: Nikkei Shinbun-Sha.

Fukao, K., K. Ito, and H. U. Kwon. 2005. "Do Out-In M & As Bring Higher TFP to Japan?: An Empirical Analysis Based on Micro-data on Japanese Manufacturing Firms," *Journal of the Japanese and International Economies, 19,* 272–301.

Fukao, K., K. G. Nishimura, Q.-Y. Sui, and M. Tomiyama. 2005. "Japanese Banks' Monitoring Activities and the Performance of Borrower Firms: 1981–1996," *International Economics and Economic Policy, 2,* 337–362.

Fung, K. C. 1991. "Characteristics of Japanese Industrial Groups and Their Potential Impact on US-Japan Trade," in R. Baldwin (Ed.), *Empirical Studies of Commercial Policy.* Chicago: University of Chicago Press, 137–168.

Gaskins, Jr., D. W. 1971. "Dynamic Limit Pricing: Optimal Pricing under Threat of Entry," *Journal of Economic Theory, 3,* 306–322.

Geroski, P. A. 1995. "What Do We Know about Entry?" *International Journal of Industrial Organization, 13*(December), 421–440.

Geroski, P. A., and J. Schwalbach. 1991. *Entry and Market Contestability, An International Comparison.* Oxford: Basil Blackwell.

Gerybadze, A., and G. Reger. 1999. "Globalization of R&D: Recent Changes in Management of Innovation in Transnational Corporation," *Research Policy, 28,* 251–274.

Ghemawat, P. 1984. "Capacity Expansion in the Titanium Dioxide Industry," *Journal of Industrial Economics, 33*(December), 145–163.

Ghemawat, P. 2005. "Regional Strategies for Global Leadership," *Harvard Business Review, 83,* 98–109.

Ghoshal, S., and C. Bartlett. 1990. "The Multinational Corporation as an Interorganizational Network," *Academy of Management Review, 15*, 603–625.

Gilbert, R. J., and Newbery, D. M. 1992. "Alternative Entry Paths: The Build or Buy Decision," *Journal of Economics and Management Strategy, 1*(Spring), 129–150.

Girma, S., D. Greenaway, and K. Wakelin. 2002. "Does Antidumping Stimulate FDI? Evidence from Japanese Firms in the UK," *Weltwirtschaftliches Archiv, 138*, 414–436.

Goldberg, P. K., and M. M. Knetter. 1997. "Goods Prices and Exchange Rates: What Have We Learned?" *Journal of Economic Literature, 35*, 1243–1272.

Gorecki, P. K. 1976. "The Determinants of Entry by Domestic and Foreign Enterprises in Canadian Manufacturing Industries: Some Comments and Empirical Evidence," *Review of Economics and Statistics, 58*, 485–488.

Goto, A. 1996. "Cooperative Research in Japanese Manufacturing Industries: Innovation in R&D System," in A. Goto and H. Odagiri (Eds.), *Innovation in Japan: Empirical Studies in the National and Corporate Activities.* Oxford: Oxford University Press, 256–274.

Goto, A., and K. Suzuki. 1989. "R&D Capital, Rate of Return on R&D Investment and Spillover of R&D in Japanese Manufacturing Industries," *Review of Economics and Statistics, 71*, 555–564.

Goto, A., and R. Wakasugi. 1988. "Technology Policy," in R. Komiya, M. Okuno, and K. Suzumura (Eds.), *Industrial Policy of Japan.* Tokyo: University of Tokyo Press, 183–204.

Graham, E. M. 1978. "Transatlantic Investment by Multinational Firms: A Rivalistic Phenomenon?" *Journal of Post Keynesian Economics, 1*, 82–99.

Graham, E. M. 1996. "What Can the Theory of Foreign Direct Investment Tell Us about the Low Level of Foreign Firm Participation in the Economy of Japan?" in M. Yoshitomi and E. M. Graham (Eds.), *Foreign Direct Investment in Japan.* Cheltenham: Edward Elgar, 64–93.

Graham, E. M., and P. R. Krugman. 1989. *Foreign Direct Investment in the United States.* Washington, DC: Institute for International Economics.

Green, E. J., and R. H. Porter. 1984. "Noncooperative Collusion under Imperfect Price Information," *Econometrica, 52*, 87–100.

Gron, A., and D. L. Swenson. 1996. "Incomplete Exchange-Rate Pass-Through and Imperfect Competition: The Effect of Local Production," *American Economic Review, 86*, 71–76.

Gruenspecht, H. K. 1988. "Dumping and Dynamic Competition," *Journal of International Economics, 25*, 225–248.

Hackett, S. C., and K. Srinivasan. 1998. "Do Suppliers Switching Costs Differ across Japanese and U.S. Multinational Firms?" *Japan and the World Economy, 10*, 13–32.

Harberler, G. 1937. *The Theory of International Trade with Its Application to Commercial Policy.* New York: Macmillan.

Harrigan, J., and R. Vanjani. 2003. "Is Japan's Trade (Still) Different?" *Journal of the Japanese and International Economies, 17*, 507–519.

Haskel, J., and P. Scaramozzino. 1997. "Do Other Firms Matter in Oligopolies?" *Journal of Industrial Economics, 45*, 27–45.

Hazledine, T. 1980. "Testing Two Models of Pricing and Protection with Canada/United States Data," *Journal of Industrial Economics*, 29(December), 145–154.

Head, K., and T. Mayer. 2004. "Market Potential and the Location of Japanese Investment in the European Union," *Review of Economics and Statistics*, 86, 959–972.

Head, K., T. Mayer, and J. Ries. 2002. "Revisiting Oligopolistic Reaction: Are FDI Decisions Strategic Complements?" *Journal of Economics and Management Strategy*, 11, 453–472.

Head, K., and J. Ries. 2001. "Overseas Investment and Firm Exports," *Review of International Economics*, 9, 108–122.

Head, K., and J. Ries. 2003. "Heterogeneity and the FDI versus Export Decision of Japanese Manufacturers," *Journal of the Japanese and International Economies*, 17, 448–467.

Head, K., and J. Ries. 2004. "Exporting and FDI as Alternative Strategies," *Oxford Review of Economic Policy*, 20, 409–423.

Head, K., Ries, J., and B. Spencer. 2004. "Vertical Networks and US Auto Parts Exports: Is Japan Different?" *Journal of Economics and Management Strategy*, 13, 37–67.

Head, K., J. Ries, and D. Swenson. 1995. "Agglomeration Benefits and Location Choice: Evidence from Japanese Manufacturing Investments in the United States," *Journal of International Economics*, 38, 223–247.

Heitger, B., and J. Stehn. 1990. "Japanese Direct Investments in the E.C.: Response to the Internal Market 1993?" *Journal of Common Market Studies*, 29, 1–15.

Helpman, E. 1984. "A Simple Theory of International Trade with Multinational Corporations," *Journal of Political Economy*, 92, 451–471.

Helpman, E., and P. R. Krugman. 1985. *Market Structure and Foreign Trade: Increasing Returns, Imperfect Competition, and the International Economy*. Cambridge, MA: MIT Press.

Helpman, E., M. J. Melitz, and S. R. Yeaple. 2004. "Export Versus FDI with Heterogeneous Firms," *American Economic Review*, 94, 300–316.

Hennart, J.-F., and Y. R. Park. 1994. "Location, Governance, and Strategic Determinants of Japanese Manufacturing Investments in the United States," *Strategic Management Journal*, 15, 419–436.

Hennart, J.-F., and Park, Y.-R. 1993. "Greenfield vs. Acquisition: The Strategy of Japanese Investors in the United States," *Management Science*, 39(September), 1054–1070.

Hirschmeier, J., and T. Yui. 1975. *The Development of Japanese Business, 1600–1973*. Cambridge, MA: Harvard University Press.

Horaguchi, H. 1995. "tainichi chokusetsu toshi: keiretsu wa sogaiyouin ka? [*Foreign Direct Investment in Japan: Is Keiretsu a Structural Impediment?*] in M. Uekusa (Ed.), *nihon no sangyo soshiki [Industrial Organization in Japan]*. Tokyo: Yuhikaku, 265–286.

Horiuchi, A., F. Packer, and S. Fukuda. 1988. "What Role Has the 'Main Bank' Played in Japan?" *Journal of the Japanese and International Economies*, 2, 159–180.

Horiuchi, T. 1989. "The Flexibility of Japan's Small and Medium-Sized Firms and Their Foreign Direct Investment," in K. Yamamura (Ed.), *Japanese Investment in the United States: Should We Be Concerned?* Seattle: University of Washington Press, 151–181.

Horst, T. 1972. "The Industrial Composition of U.S. Exports and Subsidiary Sales to the Canadian Market," *American Economic Review*, 62, 37–45.

Horstmann, I., and J. Markusen. 1987. "Strategic Investment and the Development of Multinationals," *International Economic Review*, 28, 109–121.

Hoshi, T., A. Kashyap, and D. Scharfstein. 1991. "Corporate Structure, Liquidity, and Investment: Evidence from Japanese Industrial Groups," *Quarterly Journal of Economics*, 106, 33–60.

Hufbauer, G. C. 1970. "The Impact of National Characteristics and Technology on the Commodity Composition of Trade in Manufactured Goods," in R. Vernon (Ed.), *The Technology Factor in International Trade*. New York: National Bureau of Economic Research, 145–231.

Huveneers, C. 1981. "Price Formation and the Scope for Oligopolistic Conduct in a Small Open Economy," *Recherches Economiques de Louvain*, 47(September), 209–242.

Hymer, S. H. 1960/1976. *The International Operations of National Firms: A Study of Direct Foreign Investment*. Cambridge, MA: MIT Press.

Imai, K. 1976. *Gendai Sangyo Soshiki [Modern Industrial Organization]*. Tokyo: Iwanami Shoten.

Imai, K. 1989. "Kigyo Group [Corporate Groups]," in K. Imai and R. Komiya (Eds.), *Nihon no Kigyo [The Japanese Corporation]*. Tokyo: Tokyo Daigaku Shuppankai, 131–162.

Imai, K., I. Nonaka, and H. Takeuchi. 1985. "Managing the Product Development Process: How Japanese Companies Learn and Unlearn," in K. Clark, R. H. Hayes, and C. Lorenz (Eds.), *The Uneasy Alliance Managing the Productivity-Technology Dilemma*. Boston: Harvard Business School Press, 337–375.

Imai, K., and R. Komiya. 1989. "Nihon Kigyo no Tokucho," in K. Imai and R. Komiya (Eds.), *Nihon no Kigyo [The Japanese Corporation]*. Tokyo: Tokyo Daigaku Shuppankai, 3–26.

Ito, T. 1992. *The Japanese Economy*. Cambridge, MA: MIT Press.

Ito, T., and M. Maruyama. 1991. "Is the Japanese Distribution System Really Inefficient?" in P. Krugman (Ed.), *Trade with Japan: Has the Door Opened Wider?* Chicago: University of Chicago Press, 149–174.

Itoh, H. 1987. "Information Processing Capacities of the Firm," *Journal of the Japanese and International Economies*, 1, 299–326.

Jacquemin, A., and P. Buigues. 1991. "Foreign Direct Investments and Exports in the Common Market: Theoretical, Empirical, and Policy Issues," Center for European Policy Studies, Bruxelles, Working Documents 20/10/91.

Johnson, C. 1982. *MITI and the Japanese Miracle: The Growth of Industrial Policy, 1925–1975*. Palo Alto, CA: Stanford University Press.

Jovanovic, Boyan. 1982. "Selection and the Evolution of Industry," *Econometrica*, 50(May), 649–670.

Kagono, T., I. Nonaka, K. Sakakibara, and A. Okumura. 1985. *Strategic vs. Evolutionary Management: A U.S.-Japan Comparison of Strategy and Organization*. Amsterdam: North-Holland.

Kaplan, S. N., and M. S. Weisbach. 1992. "The Success of Acquisitions: Evidence from Divestitures," *Journal of Finance*, 47, 107–138.

Kawai, H., and S. Urata. 2002. "Entry of Small and Medium Enterprises and Economic Dynamism in Japan," *Small Business Economics, 18*, 41–51.

Kawasaki, S., and J. McMillan. 1987. "The Design of Contracts: Evidence from Japanese Subcontracting," *Journal of the Japanese and International Economies, 1*, 327–349.

Kennedy, R. E. 2002. "Strategy Fads and Competitive Convergence: An Empirical Test for Herd Behavior in Prime-Time Television Programming," *Journal of Industrial Economics, 50*, 57–84.

Kester, W. C. 1991. *Japanese Takeovers: The Global Market for Corporate Control.* Boston: Harvard Business School Press.

Khalizadeh-Shirazi, J. 1974. "Market Structure and Price-Cost Margins in United Kingdom Manufacturing Industries," *Review of Economics and Statistics, 56*(February), 67–76.

Kimura, F., 2006. "International Production and Distribution Networks in Asia: 18 Facts, Mechanics, and Policy Implication," *Asian Economic Policy Review, 1*, 326–344.

Kimura, F., and T. Fujii 2003. "Globalizing Activities and Rate of Survival: Panel Data Analysis on Japanese Firms," *Journal of the Japanese and International Economies, 17*, 538–560.

Kimura, F., and K. Kiyota. 2006a. "Exports, FDI, and Productivity: Dynamic Evidence from Japanese Firms," *Weltwirtschaftliches Archiv, 142*, 695–719.

Kimura, F., and K. Kiyota. 2007. "Foreign-Owned versus Domestically-Owned Firms: Economic Performance in Japan," *Review of Development Economics, 11*, 31–48.

Kindleberger, C. P. 1969. *American Business Abroad: Six Lectures on Direct Investment.* New Haven: Yale University Press.

Kiyota, K., and S. Urata. 2005. "The Role of Multinational Firms in International Trade: The Case of Japan," Research Institute of Economy, Trade, and Industry (RIETI), Discussion Paper 05-E-012.

Knetter, M. M. 1989. "Price Discrimination by U.S. and German Exporters," *American Economic Review, 79*, 198–210.

Knetter, M. M. 1993. "International Comparisons of Pricing-to-Market Behavior," *American Economic Review, 83*, 473–486.

Knickerbocker, F. T. 1973. *Oligopolistic Reaction and Multinational Enterprise.* Boston: Division of Research, Graduate School of Business Administration, Harvard University.

Kogut, B. 1989. "The Stability of Joint Ventures: Reciprocity and Competitive Rivalry," *Journal of Industrial Economics, 38*(December), 183–198.

Kogut, B. 1996. "Commentary," in M. Yoshitomi and E. M. Graham (Eds.), *Foreign Direct Investment in Japan.* Cheltenham: Edward Elgar.

Kogut, B., and S.-J. Chang. 1996. "Platform Investments and Volatile Exchange Rates: Direct Investment in the U.S. by Japanese Electronic Companies," *Review of Economics and Statistics, 78*, 221–231.

Kogut, B., and S.-J. Chang. 1991. "Technological Capabilities and Japanese Foreign Direct Investment in the United States," *Review of Economics and Statistics, 73*, 400–413.

Kogut, B., and Singh, H. 1988. "The Effect of National Culture on the Choice of Entry Mode," *Journal of International Business Studies, 19*(Fall), 411–432.

Koike, K. 1984. "Skill Formation Systems in the U.S. and Japan: A Comparative Study," in M. Aoki (Ed.), *The Economic Analysis of the Japanese Firm.* Amsterdam: North-Holland, 47–75.

Koike, K. 1988. *Understanding Industrial Relations in Modern Japan.* London: Macmillan Press.

Kojima, K. 1978. *Direct Foreign Investment: A Japanese Model of Multinational Business Operations.* New York: Praeger.

Komiya, R. 1987. "Japanese Firms, Chinese Firms: Problems for Economic Reform in China, Part II," *Journal of the Japanese and International Economics, 1,* 229–247.

Komiya, R. 1988. "Introduction," in R. Komiya, M. Okuno, and K. Suzumura (Eds.), *Industrial Policy of Japan.* San Diego: Academic Press, 1–24.

Komiya, R., and M. Itoh. 1988. "Japan's International Trade and Trade Policy, 1955–1984," in T. Inoguchi and D. I. Okimoto (Eds.), *The Political Economy of Japan, Volume 2. The Changing International Context.* Palo Alto, CA: Stanford University Press, 173–225.

Komiya, R., M. Okuno, and K. Suzumura. 1988. *Industrial Policy of Japan.* San Diego: Academic Press.

Kosai, Y. 1988. "The Reconstruction Period," in R. Komiya, M. Okuno, and K. Suzumura (Eds.), *Industrial Policy of Japan.* San Diego: Academic Press, 25–48.

Kravis, I. B., and R. E. Lipsey. 1982. "Prices and Market Shares in the International Machinery Trade," *Review of Economics and Statistics, 64*(February), 110–116.

Kravis, I. B., and R. E. Lipsey. 1971. *Price Competitiveness in World Trade.* New York: National Bureau of Economic Research.

Kreps, D. M., and R. Wilson. 1982. "Reputation and Imperfect Information," *Journal of Economic Theory, 27,* 253–279.

Kreps, D. M., and J. Scheinkman. 1983. "Quality Precommitment and Bertrand Competition Yield Cournot Outcomes," *Rand Journal of Economics, 14,* 326–337.

Krugman, P. R. 1983. "The New Theories of International Trade and the Multinational Enterprise," in D. B. Audretsch and C. Kindleberger (Eds.), *The Multinational Corporation in the 1980s.* Cambridge, MA: MIT Press, 57–73.

Krugman, P. R. 1984. "Import Protection as Export Promotion: International Competition in the Presence of Oligopoly and Economies of Scale," in H. Kierzkowski (Ed.), *Monopolistic Competition and International Trade.* Oxford: Clarendon Press, 180–193.

Krugman, P. R. 1989. "Industrial Organization and International Trade," in R. Schmalensee and R. Willig (Eds.), *Handbook of Industrial Organization* (Vol. 2). Amsterdam: North-Holland, 1179–1223.

Kuemmerle, W. 1999. "The Drivers of Foreign Direct Investment into Research and Development: An Empirical Investigation," *Journal of International Business Studies, 30,* 1–24.

Kujawa, D. 1986. *Japanese Multinationals in the United States: Case Studies.* New York: Praeger.

Lapham, B., and R. Ware. 1994. "Markov Puppy Dogs and Related Animals," *International Journal of Industrial Organization*, *12*, 569–593.

Lawrence, R. 1991. "Efficient or Exclusionist?: The Import Behavior of Japanese Corporate Groups," *Brookings Papers of Economic Activity*, *1*, 311–331.

Lawrence, R. 1993. "Japan's Low Levels of Inward Investment: The Role of Inhibitions on Acquisitions," in K. A. Froot (Ed.), *Foreign Direct Investment*. Chicago: University of Chicago Press, 85–107.

Leamer, E. E. 1984. *Sources of International Comparative Advantage: Theory and Evidence*. Cambridge, MA: MIT Press.

Lee, T.-J., and R. E. Caves. 1998. "Uncertain Outcomes of Foreign Investment: Determinants of the Dispersion of Profits after Large Acquisitions," *Journal of International Business Studies*, *29*(3), 563–583.

Lichtenberg, F. R., and D. Siegel. 1987. "Productivity and Changes in Ownership of Manufacturing Plants," *Brooking Papers on Economic Activity: Special Issues on Microeconomics*, *3*, 643–673.

Lieberman, M. B. 1984. "The Learning Curve and Pricing in the Chemical Processing Industries," *Rand Journal of Economics*, *15*(Summer), 213–228.

Lieberman, M. B. 1987a. "Excess Capacity as a Barrier to Entry: An Empirical Appraisal," *Journal of Industrial Economics*, 35, 365–378.

Lieberman, M. B. 1987b. "Post Entry Investment and Market Structure in the Chemical Processing Industries," *Rand Journal of Economics*, *18*, 533–549.

Lieberman, M. B. 1989a. "The Learning Curve, Technological Barriers to Entry, and Competitive Survival in the Chemical Processing Industries," *Strategic Management Journal*, *10*, 431–447.

Lieberman, M. B. 1989b. "Learning, Productivity and US-Japan Industrial 'Competitiveness,'" in K. Ferdows (Ed.), *Managing International Manufacturing*. Amsterdam: North-Holland, 215–238.

Lincoln, E. J. 1984. *Japan's Industrial Policies*. Washington, DC: Japan Economic Institution of America.

Lyons, B. 1981. "Industrial Behavior, the Technology of Demand, and the Pattern of International Trade between Identical Countries," *Recherches Economique de Louvain*, *47*, 243–258.

Mann, C. L. 1986. "Prices, Profit Margins, and Exchange Rates," *Federal Reserve Bulletin*, *72*(June), 366–379.

Mann, C. L. 1990. "Determinants of Japanese Direct Investment in U.S. Manufacturing Industries," Federal Reserve Board, Washington, DC, mimeo.

Markusen, J. R. 2002. *Multinational Firms and the Theory of International Trade*. Cambridge, MA: MIT Press.

Markusen, J. R., and A. J. Venables. 1996. "The Increased Importance of Multinationals in North American Economic Relationships: A Convergence Hypothesis," in M. W. Canzoneri, W. J. Ethier, and V. Grilli (Eds.), *The New Transatlantic Economy*. London: Cambridge University Press, 169–189.

Martin, S. 2001. *Advanced Industrial Economics* (2nd ed.). Oxford: Blackwell.

Marvel, H. P. 1980. "Foreign Trade and Domestic Competition," *Economic Inquiry*, *18*(January), 103–122.

Mason, M. 1992. *American Multinationals and Japan: The Political Economy of Capital Controls, 1899–1980.* Cambridge, MA: Harvard University Press.

Masson, R. T., and J. Shaanan. 1982. "Stochastic-Dynamic Limit Pricing: An Empirical Test," *Review of Economics and Statistics, 64,* 413–422.

Masson, R. T., and J. Shaanan. 1986. "Excess Capacity and Limit Pricing: An Empirical Test," *Economica, 53,* 365–378.

Masson, R. T., and J. Shaanan. 1987. "Optimal Oligopoly Pricing and the Threat of Entry: Canadian Evidence," *International Journal of Industrial Organization, 5,* 323–329.

Mata, J., and P. Portugal. 1994. "Life Duration of New Firms," *Journal of Industrial Economics, 27,* 227–246.

Mata, J., and P. Portugal. 1997. "The Survival of New Foreign and Domestic Firms," Banco de Portugal, mimeo.

McCulloch, R. 1988. "International Competition in Services," in M. Feldstein (Ed.), *The United States in the World Economy.* Chicago: University of Chicago Press, 367–406.

Micossi, S., and G. Viesti. 1991. "Japanese Direct Manufacturing Investment in Europe," in L. A. Winters and A. Venables (Eds.), *European Integration: Trade and Theory.* Cambridge, UK: Cambridge University Press, 200–231.

Milgrom, P., and J. Roberts. 1982. "Predation, Reputation and Entry Deterrence," *Journal of Economic Theory, 27,* 280–312.

Ministry of Economy, Trade and Industry. Japan. *Wagakuni Kigyo no Kaigai Gigyo Katsudo [Business Activities Abroad by Japanese Corporations].* Tokyo: METI. Various years.

Ministry of International Trade and Industry. Japan. 1995. *Heisei 7-nen kigyokatsudo kihonchosa hokokusho [1995 benchmark survey of corporate activity]: sogo tokeihyo,* vol. 1, Tokyo: The Ministry of International Trade and Industry.

Ministry of International Trade and Industry. Japan. *Census of Manufacturers.* Tokyo: MITI.

Mitchell, W., J. M. Shaver, and B. Yeung. 1994. "Foreign Entrant Survival and Foreign Market Share: Canadian Companies' Experience in the United States Medical Sector Markets," *Strategic Management Journal, 15*(September), 555–567.

Miwa, Y. 1988. "Coordination Within Industry: Output, Price, and Investment," in R. Komiya, M. Okuno, and K. Suzumura (Eds.), *Industrial Policy in Japan.* San Diego: Academic Press, 475–496.

Modigliani, F. 1958. "New Developments on the Oligopoly Front," *Journal of Political Economy, 66,* 215–232.

Monden, Y. 1983. *Toyota Production System.* Atlanta: Industrial Engineering and Management Press.

Morck, R., and M. Nakamura. 1999. "Banks and Corporate Control in Japan," *Journal of Finance, 54,* 319–339.

Motta, M. 1994. "International Trade and Investments in a Vertically Differentiated Industry," *International Journal of Industrial Organization, 12,* 179–196.

Nakamura, T. 1995. *The Postwar Japanese Economy: Its Development and Structure, 1937–1994* (2nd ed.). Tokyo: University of Tokyo Press.

Nakamura, Y., K. Fukao, and M. Shibuya. 1995. "tainichi chokusetsu toshi [Inward Foreign Direct Investment in Japan]," Research Institute of International Trade and Industry, Ministry of International Trade and Industry, Discussion paper # 95-DOJ-63.

Nakatani, I. 1984. "The Economic Role of Financial Corporate Grouping," in M. Aoki (Ed.), *The Economic Analysis of the Japanese Firm*. Amsterdam: Elsvier, 227–327.

Nishimura, K. G., T. Nakajima, and K. Kiyota. 2005. "Does the Natural Selection Mechanism Still Work in Severe Recessions? – Examination of the Japanese Economy in the 1990s," *Journal of Economic Behavior and Organization*, 58, 53–78.

Norman, G., and J. H. Dunning. 1984. "Intra-Industry Foreign Direct Investment: Its Rationales and Trade Effects," *Weltwirtschaftliches Archiv*, 120, 522–539.

Odagiri, H. 1983. "R&D Expenditures, Royalty Payments and Sales Growth in Japanese Manufacturing Corporations," *Journal of Industrial Economics*, 32, 62–71.

Odagiri, H. 1992. *Growth Through Competition, Competition Through Growth: Strategic Management and the Economy in Japan*. Oxford: Oxford University Press.

Odagiri, H., and A. Goto. 1996. *Technology and Industrial Development in Japan*. Oxford: Oxford University Press.

Odagiri, H., and H. Yamawaki. 1986. "A Study of Company Profit-Rate Time Series: Japan and the United States," *International Journal of Industrial Organization*, 4, 1–23.

Organization for Economic Co-Operation and Development (OECD), *Trade by Commodities: Market Summaries, Exports*. Paris: OECD. Various years.

Okimoto, D. I., and G. R. Saxonhouse. 1987. "Technology and the Future of the Economy," in K. Yamamura and Y. Yasuba (Eds.), *The Political Economy of Japan. Volume 1. The Domestic Transformation*. Palo Alto, CA: Stanford University Press.

Orr, D. 1974. "The Determinants of Entry: A Study of the Canadian Manufacturing Industries," *Review of Economics and Statistics*, 56, 58–66.

Ozawa, T. 1979. *Multinationalism, Japanese Style: The Political Economy of Outward Dependency*. Princeton: Princeton University Press.

Paprzycki, R., and K. Fukao. 2005. "The Extent and History of Foreign Direct Investment in Japan," Institute of Economic Research, Hitotsubashi University, Discussion Paper Series No. 84.

Patrick, H., and H. Rosovsky. 1976. "Japan's Economic Performance: An Overview," in H. Patrick and H. Rosovsky (Eds.), *Asia's New Giant: How the Japanese Economy Works*. Washington, DC: Brookings Institution.

Patrick, H., and T. P. Rohlen. 1987. "Small-Scale Family Enterprises," in K. Yamamura and Y. Yasuba (Eds.), *The Political Economy of Japan. Volume 1. The Domestic Transformation*. Palo Alto, CA: Stanford University Press.

Pennic, T. E. 1956. "The Influence of Distribution Costs and Direct Investments on British Exports to Canada," *Oxford Economics Papers*, 8, 229–244.

Peteraf, M. A. 1993. "The Cornerstones of Competitive Advantage: A Resource-Based View," *Strategic Management Journal*, 14, 179–192.

Petri, P. A. 1991. "Market Structure, Comparative Advantage, and Japanese Trade under the Strong Yen," in P. Krugman (Ed.), *Trade with Japan: Has the Door Opened Wider?* Chicago: University of Chicago Press.

Porter, M. E. 1976. *Interbrand Choice, Strategy, and Bilateral Market Power.* Cambridge, MA: Harvard University Press.

Porter, M. 1979. "The Structure within Industries and Companies' Performance," *Review of Economics and Statistics, 61,* 214–227.

Porter, M. E. 1980. *Competitive Strategy: Techniques for Analyzing Industries and Competitors.* New York: Free Press.

Porter, M. E. 1990. *The Competitive Advantage of Nations.* London: Macmillan.

Porter, M. E., H. Takeuchi, and M. Sakakibara. 2000. *Can Japan Compete?* London: Macmillan.

Pugel, T. A. 1978. *International Market Linkages and U.S. Manufacturing: Prices, Profits, and Patterns.* Cambridge, MA: Ballinger.

Pugel, T. A. 1980. "Foreign Trade and U.S. Market Performance," *Journal of Industrial Economics, 29*(December), 119–129.

Pugel, T. A., E. S. Kragas, and Y. Kimura. 1996. "Further Evidence on Japanese Direct Investment in U.S. Manufacturing," *Review of Economics and Statistics, 78,* 208–213.

Qiu, L. D, and B. Spencer. 2002. "Keiretsu and Relationship-Specific Investments: Implications for Market-Opening Policy," *Journal of International Economics, 58,* 49–79.

Rauch, J. E. 2001. "Business and Social Networks in International Trade," *Journal of Economic Literature, 39,* 1177–1203.

Ravenscraft, D., and F. M. Scherer. 1987. *Mergers, Selloffs, and Economic Efficiency.* Washington, DC: Brookings Institution.

Robinson, J. R. 1933. *The Economics of Imperfect Competition.* London: Macmillan.

Rosenbloom, R. S., and W. J. Abernathy. 1982. "The Climate for Innovation in Industry: The Role of Management Attitudes and Practices in Consumer Electronics," *Research Policy, 11,* 209–225.

Sabourian, H. 1992. "Rational Conjectural Equilibrium and Repeated Games," in P. Dasgupta, D. Gale, O. Hart, and E. Maskin (Eds.), *Economic Analysis of Markets and Games: Essays in Honor of Frank Hahn.* Cambridge, MA: MIT Press, 228–257.

Sakakibara, M. 1997. "Evaluating Government-Sponsored R&D Consortia in Japan: Who Benefits and How?" *Research Policy, 26,* 447–473.

Sakakibara, M., and M. E. Porter. 2001. "Competing at Home to Win Abroad: Evidence from Japanese Industry," *Review of Economics and Statistics, 83,* 310–321.

Sakakibara, M., and K. Serwin. 2000. "U.S. Distribution Entry Strategy of Japanese Manufacturing Firms: The Role of Keiretsu," *Journal of the Japanese and International Economies, 14,* 43–72.

Sakakibara, M., and H. Yamawaki. 2007. "What Determines the Profitability of Foreign Direct Investment?: A Subsidiary-Level Analysis of Japanese Multinationals," *Managerial and Decision Economics, 28,* forthcoming.

Salinger, M. A. 1984. "Tobin's *q,* Unionization, and the Concentration-Profits Relationships," *RAND Journal of Economics, 15,* 159–170.

Saxonhouse, G. R. 1976. "Estimated Parameters as Dependent Variables," *American Economic Review*, 66(March), 178–183.

Saxonhouse, G. R. 1979. "Industrial Restructuring in Japan," *Journal of Japanese Studies*, 5, 273–300.

Saxonhouse, G. R. 1983. "The Micro-and Macroeconomics of Foreign Sales to Japan," in W. R. Cline (Ed.), *Trade Policy in the 1980s*. Cambridge, MA: MIT Press, 259–304.

Saxonhouse, G. R. 1993. "What Does Japanese Trade Structure Tell Us about Japanese Trade Policy?" *Journal of Economic Perspectives*, 7, 21–43.

Scharfstein, D. S., and J. C. Stein. 1990. "Herd Behavior and Investment," *American Economic Review*, 80, 465–479.

Scherer, F. M., and D. Ross. 1990. *Industrial Market Structure and Economic Performance* (3rd ed.). Boston: Houghton Mifflin.

Senoh A. (Ed.) 1983. *Gendai Nihon no Sangyo Shuuchu: 1971–1980 [Industrial Concentration in Japan: 1971–1980]*, Tokyo: Keizai Shinbun Sha.

Shapiro, C. 1989. "Theories of Oligopoly Behavior," in R. Schmalensee and R. D. Willig (Eds.), *Handbook of Industrial Organization* (Vol. I). Amsterdam: North-Holland, 329–414.

Shapiro, D. M. 1983. "Entry, Exit, and Theory of the Multinational Corporation," in C. P. Kindleberger and D. B. Audretsch (Eds.), *The Multinational Corporation in the 1980s*. Cambridge, MA: MIT Press, 103–122.

Sheard, P. 1989. "The Main Bank System and Corporate Monitoring and Control in Japan," *Journal of Economic Behavior and Organization*, 11, 399–422.

Shimada, H. 1983. "Japanese Industrial Relations – A New General Model?" in T. Shirai (Ed.), *Contemporary Industrial Relations in Japan*. Madison: University of Wisconsin Press, 3–27.

Singh, S., M. Utton, and M. Waterson. 1997. "Strategic Behavior of Incumbent Firms in the UK," *International Journal of Industrial Organization*, 16, 227–251.

Smiley, R. 1988. "Empirical Evidence on Strategic Entry Deterrence," *International Journal of Industrial Organization*, 6, 167–180.

Spence, A. M. 1977. "Entry, Capacity, Investment and Oligopolistic Pricing," *Bell Journal of Economics*, 8, 534–544.

Spence, A. M. 1981. "The Learning Curve and Competition," *Bell Journal of Economics*, 12(Spring), 49–70.

Spencer, B. J., and J. A. Brander. 1983. "International R&D Rivalry and Industrial Strategy," *Review of Economic Studies*, 30(October), 707–722.

Staiger, R. W., and F. A. Wolak. 1992. "Collusive Pricing with Capacity Constraints in the Presence of Demand Uncertainty," *Rand Journal of Economics*, 23, 203–220.

Sumitomo Metal Industries Ltd. 1975. *Nihon no tekkogyo to tosha [The Japanese Steel Industry and Simutomo Metal Industries]*, Osaka: Sumitomo Metal Industries.

Sylos-Labini, P. 1962. *Oligopoly and Technical Progress*. Cambridge, MA: Harvard University Press.

Takacs, W. E. 1982. "Cyclical Dumping of Steel Products: Comments," *Journal of International Economics*, 12(May), 381–383.

Tarr, D. G. 1982. "Cyclical Dumping of Steel Products: Another Look," *Journal of International Economics*, 12(May), 377–379.

Tarr, D. G. 1979. "Cyclical Dumping: The Case of Steel Products," *Journal of International Economics*, 9(February), 57–63.

Taylor, S., and K. Yamamura. 1990. "Japan's Technological Capabilities and Its Future: Overview and Assessments," in G. Heiduk and K. Yamamura (Eds.), *Technological Competition and Interdependence: The Search for Policy in the United States, West Germany, and Japan*. Seattle: University of Washington Press, 25–63.

Teece, D. J., G. Pisano, and A. Shuen. 1997. "Dynamic Capabilities and Strategic Management," *Strategic Management Journal*, 18, 509–533.

Thomas, L. A. 1999. "Incumbent Firms' Response to Entry: Price, Advertising, and New Product Introduction," *International Journal of Industrial Organization*, 17, 527–555.

Torii, A. 1992. "'Dual Structure' and Differences of Efficiency between Japanese Large and Small Enterprises," in R. E. Caves, *Industrial Efficiency of Six Nations*. Cambridge, MA: MIT Press, 385–424.

Torii, A., and R. E. Caves. 1992. "Technical Efficiency in Japanese and U.S. Manufacturing Industries," in R. E. Caves, *Industrial Efficiency of Six Nations*. Cambridge, MA: MIT Press, 425–458.

Toyo Keizai. *Gaishikei kigyo soran. [Foreign Affiliated Companies in Japan: A Comprehensive Directory]*. Tokyo: Toyo Keizai Shinposha.

Toyo Keizai. *Kaigai shishutsu kigyo soran [Directory of Japanese Corporations Abroad]*. Tokyo: Toyo Keizai Shinposha.

Tsurumi, Y. 1976. *The Japanese Are Coming: A Multinational Interaction of Firms and Politics*. Cambridge, MA: Ballinger.

Tsuruta, T. 1988. "The Rapid Growth Era," in R. Komiya, M. Okuno, and K. Suzumura (Eds.), *Industrial Policy of Japan*. San Diego: Academic Press, 49–87.

Ueda, K., and Y. Nagataki-Sasaki. 1998. "The Import Behavior of Japanese Coporate Groups: Evidence from Micro-Survey Data," *Japan and the World Economy*, 10, 1–11.

Uekusa, M. 1982. *Sangyo Soshikiron [Industrial Organization]*. Tokyo: Chikuma Shobo.

Uekusa, M. 1987. "Industrial Organization: The 1970s to the Present," in K. Yamamura and Y. Yasuba (Eds.), *The Political Economy of Japan. Volume 1. The Domestic Transformation*. Palo Alto, CA: Stanford University Press, 469–515.

United Nations (UN). *International Trade Statistics Yearbook, Vol. I (Trade by Country)* and *Vol. II (Trade by Commodity)*. New York: U.N.

Urata, S. 1983. "Factor Inputs and Japanese Manufacturing Trade Structure," *Review of Economics and Statistics*, 65, 678–684.

Urata, S., and H. Kawai. 2002. "Technological Progress by Small and Medium Enterprises in Japan," *Small Business Economics*, 18, 53–67.

U.S. Bureau of Economic Analysis. *Input–Output Structure of the U.S. Economy*. Washington, DC, U.S. Department of Commerce.

U.S. Bureau of Economic Analysis. *Survey of Current Business*. Washington, DC: U.S. Department of Commerce.

U.S. Bureau of the Census. *Census of Manufacturers.* Washington, DC.: U.S. Bureau of Census.

U.S. Patent and Trademark Office. 1987. *Patenting Trends in the United States: 1963–1986,* Washington, DC.: U.S. Patent and Trademark Office.

U.S. International Trade Commission. Office of Economic Research. 1975. *The U.S. International Trade Commission's Industrial Characteristics and Trade Performance Databank.* Washington, DC: U.S. International Trade Commission.

Van den Bulcke, D., J. J. Boddewyn, B. Martens, and P. Klemmer. 1980. *Investment and Divestment Policies of Multinational Corporations in Europe.* New York: Praeger.

Vernon, R. 1977. *Storm Over the Multinationals: The Real Issues.* Cambridge, MA: Harvard University Press.

Viner, J. 1923. *Dumping: A Problem in International Trade.* Chicago: University of Chicago Press.

Wagner, J. 1994. "Small-Firm Entry in Manufacturing Industries," *Small Business Economics,* 5, 211–214.

Wakasugi, R. 1989. "Kenkyu Kaihatsu no Soshiki to Kodo [Organization and Behavior in R&D]," in K. Imai and R. Komiya (Eds.), *Nihon no Kigyo [The Japanese Corporation].* Tokyo: Tokyo Daigaku Shuppankai, 189–214.

Wakasugi, R. 1996. "Why Foreign Firms' Entry Has Been Low in Japan: An Empirical Examination," in M. Yoshitomi and E. M. Graham (Eds.), *Foreign Direct Investment in Japan.* Cheltenham: Edward Elgar, 111–135.

Ward's Automotive Yearbook. Detroit: Ward's.

Wares, W. A. 1977. *The Theory of Dumping and American Commercial Policy.* Lexington, MA: Lexington Books.

Weinstein, D. 1996. "Structural Impediments to Investment in Japan: What Have We Learned over the Last 450 Years?" in M. Yoshitomi and E. M. Graham (Eds.), *Foreign Direct Investment in Japan.* Cheltenham: Edward Elgar, 136–172.

Weinstein, D., and Y. Yafeh. 1995. "Japan's Corporate Groups: Collusive or Competitive? An Empirical Investigation of *Keiretsu* Behavior," *Journal of Industrial Economics,* 18(December) 359–376.

Weiss, L. W. 1972. "The Geographic Size of Markets in Manufacturing," *Review of Economics and Statistics,* 54, 245–257.

Wilkins, M. 1974. *The Maturing of Multinational Enterprise: American Business Abroad from 1914 to 1970.* Cambridge, MA: Harvard University Press.

Wilkins, M. 1990. "Japanese Multinationals in the United States: Continuity and Change, 1879–1990," *Business History Review,* 64, 585–629.

Williamson, P. J., and H. Yamawaki. 1991. "Distribution: Japan's Hidden Advantage," *Business Strategy Review,* 2, 85–105.

Womack, J. P., D. T. Jones, and D. Roos. 1991. *The Machine that Changed the World: The Story of Lean Production.* New York: HarperCollins.

Yamawaki, H. 1984. "Market Structure, Capacity Expansion, and Pricing: A Model Applied to the Japanese Iron and Steel Industry," *International Journal of Industrial Organization,* 2, 29–62.

Yamawaki, H. 1985. "Dominant Firm Pricing and Fringe Expansion: The Case of the U.S. Iron and Steel Industry, 1907–1930," *Review of Economic and Statistics, 67*, 429–437.

Yamawaki, H. 1986. "Exports, Foreign Market Structure and Profitability in Japanese U.S. Manufacturing," *Review of Economics and Statistics, 68*(November), 618–627.

Yamawaki, H. 1988. "The Steel Industry," in R. Komiya, M. Okuno, and K. Suzumura (Eds.), *Industrial Policy of Japan*. San Diego: Academic Press, 281–305.

Yamawaki, H. 1989. "A Comparative Analysis of Intertemporal Behavior of Profits: Japan and the United States," *Journal of Industrial Economics, 37*, 389–409.

Yamawaki, H. 1991a. "Exports and Foreign Distributional Activities: Evidence on Japanese Firms in the United States," *Review of Economics and Statistics, 73*, 294–300.

Yamawaki, H. 1991b. "The Effects of Business Conditions on Net Entry: Evidence from Japan," in P. A. Geroski and J. Schwalbach (Eds.), *Entry and Market Contestability: An International Comparison*. Oxford: Basil Blackwell, 168–186.

Yamawaki, H. 1993. "Location Decisions of Japanese Multinational Firms in European Manufacturing Industries," in K. Hughes (Ed.), *European Competitiveness*. Cambridge, UK: Cambridge University Press, 11–28.

Yamawaki, H. 1994. "Patterns of Entry by Japanese Multinationals into the U.S. and European Manufacturing Industries," in D. Encarnation and M. Mason (Eds.), *Does Ownership Matter?: Japanese Multinationals in Europe*. Oxford: Oxford University Press, 91–121.

Yamawaki, H. 1997. "Exit of Japanese Multinationals in U.S. and European Manufacturing Industries," in P. J. Buckley and J.-L. Mucchielli (Eds.), *Multinational Firms and International Relocation*. Cheltenham: Edward Elgar, 220–237.

Yamawaki, H. 2002a. "Price Reactions to New Competition: A Study of U.S. Luxury Car Market, 1986–1997," *International Journal of Industrial Organization, 20*, 19–39.

Yamawaki, H. 2002b. "The Evolution and Structure of Industrial Clusters in Japan," *Small Business Economics, 18*, 121–140.

Yamawaki, H. 2004a. "The Determinants of Geographic Configuration of Value-Chain Activities: Foreign Multinational Enterprises in Japanese Manufacturing," *International Economics and Economic Policy, 1*, 195–214.

Yamawaki, H. 2004b. "Who Survives in Japan? An Empirical Analysis of European and U.S. Multinational Firms in Japanese Manufacturing Industries," *Journal of Industry, Competition, and Trade, 4*, 135–153.

Yamawaki, H. 2006. "The Location of American and Japanese Multinationals in Europe," *International Economics and Economic Policy, 3*, 157–173.

Yamawaki, H., and D. B. Audretsch. 1988. "Import Share under International Oligopoly with Differentiated Products: Japanese Imports in U.S. Manufacturing," *Review of Economics and Statistics, 70*, 569–579.

Yamawaki, H., L. Barbarito, and J.-M. Thiran. 1998. "U.S. and Japanese Multinationals in European Manufacturing: Location Patterns and Host Region/Country Characteristics," in K. Fukasaku, F. Kimura, and S. Urata (Eds.), *Asia and Europe: Beyond Competing Regionalism*. Brighton: Sussex Academic Press.

Yip, G. S. 1982. *Barriers to Entry: A Corporate-Strategy Perspective.* Lexington, MA: D.C. Heath.

Yntema, T. O. 1928. "The Influence of Dumping on Monopoly Price," *Journal of Political Economy, 36,* 686–698.

Yonekura, S., and S. McKinney. 2005. "Innovative Multinational Forms: Japan as a Case Study," in A. D. Chandler, Jr. and B. Mazlish (Eds.), *Leviathans: Multinational Corporations and the New Global History.* Cambridge, UK: Cambridge University Press.

Yoshida, M. 1987. *Japanese Direct Manufacturing Investment in the United States.* New York: Praeger.

Yoshino, M. Y., and T. B. Lifson. 1988. *The Invisible Link Japan's Sogo Shosha and the Organization of Trade.* Cambridge, MA: MIT Press.

Yu, C.-M. J., and K. Ito. 1988. "Oligopolistic Reaction and Foreign Direct Investment: The Case of the U.S. Tire and Textiles Industries," *Journal of International Business Studies, 19,* 449–460.

Zejan, M. C. 1990. "New Ventures or Acquisition: The Choice of Swedish Multinational Enterprises," *Journal of Industrial Economics, 38*(March), 349–355.

Zwiebel, J. 1995. "Corporate Conservatism and Relative Compensation," *Journal of Political Economy, 103,* 1–25.

Zysman, J., and L. Tyson. 1983. *American Industry in International Competition.* Ithaca, NY: Cornell University Press.

Author Index

255

Subject Index

For EU product safety concerns, contact us at Calle de José Abascal, 56–1°,
28003 Madrid, Spain or eugpsr@cambridge.org.

www.ingramcontent.com/pod-product-compliance
Ingram Content Group UK Ltd.
Pitfield, Milton Keynes, MK11 3LW, UK
UKHW042316180425
457623UK00005B/27